The Franklin Conspiracy

*Dedicated to my mother, my father,
and my brother, D.K.,
whose writing is my inspiration*

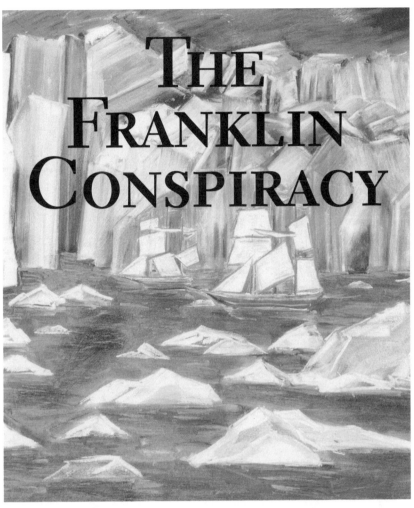

THE FRANKLIN CONSPIRACY

Cover-up, Betrayal, and the Astonishing
Secret Behind the Lost Arctic Expedition

Jeffrey Blair Latta

Foreword by John Robert Colombo

A HOUNSLOW BOOK
A MEMBER OF THE DUNDURN GROUP
TORONTO · OXFORD

Publisher: Anthony Hawke
Editor: Gene Shannon
Design: Jennifer Scott
Printer: University of Toronto Press

Canadian Cataloguing in Publication Data

Latta, Jeffrey Blair
    The Franklin conspiracy: cover-up, betrayal, and the astonishing secret behind the lost Arctic expedition

Includes bibliographical references.
ISBN 0-88882-234-0

1. Franklin, John, Sir, 1786–1847. 2. Northwest Passage – Discovery and exploration. 3. Arctic regiions – Discovery and exploration – British. I. Title.

FC3961.3.L37 2001   917.19'5041'092   C2001-930645-8   G660.L37 2001

1   2   3   4   5   05   04   03   02   01

THE CANADA COUNCIL | LE CONSEIL DES ARTS
FOR THE ARTS | DU CANADA
SINCE 1957 | DEPUIS 1957

Canada

ONTARIO ARTS COUNCIL
CONSEIL DES ARTS DE L'ONTARIO

We acknowledge the support of the *Canada Council for the Arts* and the *Ontario Arts Council* for our publishing program. We also acknowledge the financial support of the *Government of Canada* through the *Book Publishing Industry Development Program, The Association for the Export of Canadian Books*, and the *Government of Ontario* through the *Ontario Book Publishers Tax Credit* program.

Dundurn Press
8 Market Street
Suite 200
Toronto, Ontario, Canada
M5E 1M6

Dundurn Press
73 Lime Walk
Headington, Oxford,
England
OX3 7AD

Dundurn Press
2250 Military Road
Tonawanda NY
U.S.A. 14150

Acknowledgements

I would like to give special thanks to John Robert Colombo. His assistance and encouragement went far beyond anything I dreamed of. I will have to take a bullet for him someday. Thanks also to Tony Hawke. His enthusiasm and confidence saw me through a lot of nail chewing. Without their help, this book would still be languishing in the back of a drawer. Finally, thanks to my mother and my brother who patiently read over the manuscript, suggested ways to make it better, and kept telling me to quit stalling and submit it already.

Table of Contents

FOREWORD
Can Such Things Be?

John Robert Colombo

Strange is a good word to describe the mail and the e-mail that I receive.

Indeed, I sometimes think that I receive more strange — even weird — letters than anyone else in the country. People who send these letters do so in response to the books that I have published and continue to write on a variety of subjects — quotations, fantastic literature, native studies, research and reference questions about obscure Canadiana, anthologies, poetry, literary translations, UFOs, ghosts, hauntings, and mysteries!

That last word, "mysteries," came to my mind on June 19, 2000, when the following e-mail appeared on my computer screen:

Dear John Robert Colombo,

I am writing to you hoping for advice and perhaps hoping you might be interested in writing the foreword for a non-fiction book I have written about the Lost Franklin Expedition called *The Shaman Light: The Terrifying Truth Behind the Lost Franklin Expedition*. As you know, many books have already been written on this topic, but I think I can say without fear of contradiction that this is the very first to take this peculiar route to a solution.

The letter came out of the blue and it caught my attention. The fate of the Franklin Expedition was an interest of mine. I had read books about the ill-fated expedition which vanished in the wastes of the Arctic, but I had never written anything about it. I assumed that it was merely a matter of time before the remains of the *Erebus* and the *Terror*, Franklin's twin vessels, would be discovered preserved in the polar permafrost. The subject was of considerable interest but hardly of compelling concern. Yet I found myself momentarily wondering, What did happen to Sir John Franklin, his men, and his vessels?

I had read some of the best-selling books that had described the expedition — Farley Mowat's *The Polar Passion* and Pierre Berton's *The Arctic Grail*, not to mention Gwendolyn MacEwen's powerful long poem *Erebus and Terror* and Donald C. Woodman's study of the oral traditions of the Inuit concerning Franklin's fate — but the only reference to Sir John Franklin that made its way into my book *Mysterious Canada* concerned his chance encounter at Fort Chipewyan in April 1827 with a "Manlike Woman," an Indian shaman who professed to have supernatural powers and knowledge of the future. So I knew that Franklin was interested in the mysterious world of prophecy. But what was behind his disappearance? Perhaps it had something to do with "the Shaman Light," whatever that was.

To find out, I scrolled down the computer's screen and read further:

> As you know, it is a mystery without equal. In 1845, two British Royal Navy ships, *Erebus* and *Terror*, under the command of Sir John Franklin, entered the Arctic in search of a Northwest Passage to China. Neither ship returned. After a fifteen-year search, evidence of unparalleled disaster was uncovered on King William Island, but to this day no one knows what happened, how those 129 men met their deaths. The Inuit said only that a "year of horror" came to their land.

I found myself becoming increasingly interested in what the author was saying. Here was a great story, and my correspondent (whoever he was) wrote well. I read on:

> So much seems inexplicable. There was evidence of cannibalism — and yet the men still had food. Inuit witnesses claimed the

men died "of a sickness" — but could not identify this sickness. The body of a giant was found, by the Inuit, aboard one of the ships just before it sank — but was the "giant" a ship's figurehead, as historians have supposed, or something stranger? How could Franklin have failed to leave even a single record to mark his progress, when he had carried 200 message cylinders for this precise purpose? Were the records found and "suppressed" by the Royal Navy searchers, as one civilian searcher claimed? How is it that, in fifteen years, the Royal Navy managed to comb every single Arctic island except the right one?

I took a pause from scrolling. The author had done his research and was asking the right questions, questions about the "giant" and the "message cylinders." But when he used the words "suppressed" and "claimed," I rubbed my nose. I could detect a whiff of conspiracy theory in the air. It has the smell of sulphur.

Stranger still, years before, explorer Thomas Simpson had visited lonely King William Island, then, on his return, applied for permission to go back. Before he could, he was murdered, according to his brother, for the "secret of the Northwest Passage" kept in his papers. What was this "secret"?

There it was. The suggestion that there was a "secret" that had been long-suppressed.

Was there evidence of a conspiracy? Had my correspondent stumbled onto some information that had eluded the grasp of a legion of historians and journalists? The account continued and supplied an answer to these questions:

The Shaman Light: The Terrifying Truth Behind the Lost Franklin Expedition is a carefully researched answer to that question. It is an attempt to explain the seemingly inexplicable by following one simple rule: No answer would be rejected so long as it fit the known facts. The result is a frightening saga of conspiracy, cover-up, and an unbelievable secret which spelled the deaths of 129 men. At the heart of *The Shaman Light* are two completely original premises: first, that the Franklin expedition was dispatched, not to find a Northwest Passage, but to make a scientific study of a previously discovered, but secret, phenomenon; and, second, when the expedition didn't return, the Royal Navy did everything in its power to keep the lost expedition from being found. Strangest of all is the secret itself — what the Inuit called the "shaman light." The result is a complex and disturbing tale to rival Roswell and the JFK conspiracy theory combined.

So there was a conspiracy, at least in the mind of my correspondent. At this point the sole conspiracy I was prepared to recognize was the conspiring of the author to get my attention. Because I was vaguely annoyed, I remained wary. The e-mail alluded to the supposed landing of flying saucers at Roswell, N.M., and to all those cabal-like theories surrounding the assassination of U.S. President John F. Kennedy. Was the fate of the Franklin Expedition destined to join such tangled theories of intrigue and coverup? It seemed unlikely.

It is my contention that the Franklin expedition could be Canada's answer to Roswell. It is a fantastic, nightmarishly frightening story, labyrinthine in its complexity, involving duplicity and corruption, heroism and bravery, and the unknown.

My correspondent was saying, Yes, I have found evidence of a full-fledged, polar conspiracy. Yet evidence is not proof, so I felt it would be hard to convince me or any other reader that a conspiracy and coverup existed. But my immediate question was, Why is the correspondent sending this letter to me? The answer to that question came next:

My hope was to submit this manuscript to Hounslow Press, since they are the main market for this sort of thing in Canada. As Canada's "Mr. Mystery," and since you have had extensive dealings with them, I thought you might be able to help me. Might you be willing to read the complete manuscript, perhaps with an eye towards writing a foreword?

So ... my correspondent wanted to whet my appetite so that I would use my contacts in the world of books to help him find a publishing house for his manuscript. (The correspondent was not the first would-be writer to try this tactic.) I read further:

> I will send two follow-up e-mails: one with the Table of Contents and the Prologue; and another with the Epilogue. The manuscript is completed and has been extensively researched (and of course includes a bibliography).
>
> Any suggestions you might make or advice you might give would be very, very appreciated.
>
> Kind regards,
> Jeffrey Blair Latta

Now I knew the name of my correspondent. It meant nothing at all to me.

I e-mailed back that I was interested in seeing the additional material, but I withheld the fact that I was quite interested in reading it. I knew that when it arrived I would read it without delay. Jeffrey Blair Latta had whetted my appetite with the promise of the Table of Contents, the Prologue, and the Epilogue. So Mr. Latta's e-mail strategy had worked.

The material arrived and I scanned the Table of Contents and then turned my attention to the Prologue and the Epilogue. (These texts appear elsewhere in the present volume, which has been retitled *The Franklin Conspiracy: Cover-up, Betrayal, and the Astonishing Secret Behind the Lost Arctic Expedition,* so I am not reprinting them in this Foreword.) There is another reason why I am not reprinting them and that is so the reader will have the pleasure of encountering them in the proper sequence. Do not read these sections now. Read the sections and chapters in the order the author wishes you to read them. This advice applies particularly to the last chapters of the book, especially to the Epilogue, where the plot thickens! Allow the author the leisure to develop his thesis in his own good time. Permit him to take you, the reader, by surprise. He does offer a denouement to the mystery of the Franklin Expedition and a suggestion as to the fate of its 129 missing men and vessels.) But back to these words of Mr. Latta's that also appeared on my screen:

If you are willing to read what I have sent, I would very much appreciate any advice you might be able to give me. If you are interested in reading the complete manuscript, I would be even more pleased to send it to you as an e-mail attachment or as a printed manuscript. The Lost Franklin Expedition is more than a historical curiosity. When looked at from this new perspective, it becomes a truly epic tale, a conspiracy to rival the John F. Kennedy conspiracy, and a supernatural saga to rival Roswell or the Bermuda Triangle. Indeed, it is the great Canadian mystery, and once you read this book (if you read this book) you may never again be able to think of it as history. You will think of it as legend.

Strong words indeed! To the list of conspiracies had now been added the mysterious Bermuda Triangle. Critics have battered and beaten the life out of this "triangle of death" in the North Atlantic Ocean, yet it continues to fascinate readers of books about the mysterious and viewers of television programs on the unexplained. But to my knowledge no one had suggested that the Arctic itself had such a sinister reputation ... until now, that is.

Naturally I requested that Mr. Latta send me the full text in hardcopy form because I hate trying to read a bookful of words on a computer screen. The manuscript of 336 pages arrived within a week and I devoted three enjoyable evenings to reading the text and wondering about the book's thesis and about the background of its author.

I did not have to wonder long about the author's background because he appended a biographical note to the manuscript. I am reproducing it here:

Though I started university majoring in Physics, I ended up graduating in Film Studies (the medalist for that year) at Queen's University and I am primarily a freelance screenwriter (much to the chagrin of my physicist uncle!) One screenplay, "Forgive Me Father," has recently premiered in Indianapolis, co-starring Charles Napier. My popular science articles have appeared in several Canadian newspapers including the *Ottawa Citizen*, the *Winnipeg Free Press* and the *Kingston Whig-Standard*. My science-fiction one-act play, "Haemo," won several awards at the Sears Drama Festival and was subsequently performed by various theatre troupes in Eastern Ontario. My science-fiction short story, "The Blood is the Life," won Judges' Choice in the *Toronto Star* Short Story Competition. My ghostship ballad, "The Legend of Murray's Light," won second prize in the *Kingston Whig-Standard's* Great Canadian Poetry Competition and was subsequently taught in a local school. My short non-fiction film, "Martian Canals," about the Rideau Canal, won third prize in the Canada 125 Competition. And I once had a letter printed in *Nature*, the prestigious science journal. On aphids, yet! Finally, I edit a "fanzine" on the Internet called Pulp and Dagger Fiction Webzine which publishes old fashion pulp-style serials. My brother is D.K. Latta, who manages "The Great Canadian Guide to the Movies (and TV)," the largest collection of reviews of Canadian films on the Internet.

Then he added:

The Shaman Light is the result of many years of research and a continuing obsession with the Lost Franklin Expedition. I am presently employed completing another screenplay, and am working on a rock opera about the War of 1812.

A rock opera about the War of 1812? Wonders never cease!

After reading the manuscript, I sent an e-mail to Blair (as he prefers to be known) expressing my enthusiasm for his work. I wrote that I found the text to be highly readable. I commented favourably on the amount of research that he had undertaken, and on the skill that had gone into setting forth his findings in their historical context. I found, as well, that the author cared about the missing men. I realized, finally, that I too cared about their fate.

At the same time, because I am a long-time book editor, I offered a few suggestions about streamlining the work, notably anticipating the reactions of readers and addressing some of these in the Prologue. I added that he could make these and other changes if he wanted, but that in the meantime I would forward the manuscript to my friend Tony Hawke, publisher of Hounslow Press, part of the

Dundurn Group. I would recommend whole-heartedly that the work be published — and soon. This, of course, is what Mr. Latta had intended right from the start. He replied:

> Most definitely I would be more than pleased and honoured for you to foreword my "The Shaman Light" manuscript to Hounslow Press. I would also like to thank you for your quick response, and for your kind and encouraging words about my manuscript. I tried hard to prepare it as fully as possible — although my maps may have left something to be desired!). I would be pleased to hear your criticisms, particularly regarding the Prologue. Could you please let me know when you have forwarded it? Incidentally, I use my middle name, Blair. Again, thanks very much.

Tony Hawke loves reading books about mysteries and he enjoys adding them to the Hounslow list. So within a week or two of sending him the manuscript, I was quite pleased — but not really surprised — to hear from Tony on the phone (he does not yet use e-mail on a regular basis) that he was really enjoying reading the manuscript and that all things being equal he would show it to the other editors at Dundurn and to the publisher J. Kirk Howard. It took some months for everyone to be heard from, but they agreed with Tony's assessment of the work's interest (and saleability). Tony carried the ball from there. Both Tony and Blair (whom I have yet to meet) wanted me to add a Foreword to the book. At first I demurred; then I agreed.

I must state that I miss the old title, *The Shaman Light*, but I have to admit that the present title, *The Franklin Conspiracy*, is much more commercial than the author's working one. As I read the work in proof, I found myself recalling the question asked by Professor Van Helsing in the stage version of Bram Stoker's novel *Dracula*. After the curtain falls on the third act, the old vampire-slayer steps between the curtains and faces the audience and asks, "Can such things be?"

Indeed, can there be such things as are described in this book? Blair has asked such intriguing questions and provided such stupendous answers about the fate of the Franklin Expedition that I have the feeling that when the ruins of the *Erebus* and the *Terror* are discovered in the Arctic wastes, people will remember this book ... and begin to worry!

John Robert Colombo is nationally known as "the Master Gatherer" and "Canada's Mr. Mystery" for his books about Canada. Among them are *Ghost Stories of Canada* (Hounslow) and *Colombo's Famous Lasting Words* (Douglas & McIntyre).

And much of Madness, and more of Sin,
And Horror the soul of the plot.
        Edgar Allan Poe,
        The Conqueror Worm

PROLOGUE

The Vanishing Ships

Will you, won't you, will you, won't you,
Will you join the dance?
Lewis Carroll,
Alice's Adventures in Wonderland

It always begins the same way.

No matter who tells the tale, no matter the reason for the telling, it always begins the same. It begins with four ships meeting amongst the towering, sapphire-and-ivory icebergs of Baffin Bay, west of Greenland, east of Canada. The smaller two of the four were whaling vessels, the *Prince of Wales* and the *Enterprise*. They had come upon the two larger vessels purely by chance, stopping out of courtesy and because, in the lonely icy wastes of the Arctic whaling grounds, human contact was treasured above all else. To Captain Dannett, master of the *Prince of Wales*, the initial sight of the larger ships must have made him wonder if his eyes were playing tricks on him, as was so common in those waters where ghost ships were frequently seen hanging in the air and mysterious mountains might be sighted one trip, but be gone the next.

Both of the great ships were black as coal, but with yellow along the weather works above the water line. Each sported three masts, barquerigged and painted white. The shape of their hulls was like no other craft, their sides thick and fortified with wood and their prows strengthened by solid bulwarks of sheet iron, giving them the look of two black bricks with their forward edges rounded just enough to suit their purpose. Clearly they were not built for speed. They were built for ice. They were built to take all that Nature could deliver. They were built to succeed.

If their black hulls and iron-shod prows were not reason enough to give Captain Dannett pause, the names painted on their sterns must surely have been. The one was named *Erebus*; in Greek mythology, this was the darkest part of Hades, the underworld. Those who had named her could never have imagined how appropriate that name would come to be in later years, though never so appropriate as her sister's. This one, the smaller of the two, was christened *Terror*.

Captain Dannett found the *Erebus* and *Terror* secured to an iceberg, atop which their crews had constructed a temporary observatory. Having successfully managed the one month voyage from England, they were merely waiting for favourable weather before commencing their journey of discovery into the unknown waters of Arctic Canada, in search of the final link in the chain which would complete the fabled Northwest Passage. In the meantime, Captain Dannett invited their expedition's commanding officer, Sir John Franklin, along with some of his officers, to join him aboard the *Prince of Wales*.

Dannett must surely have known who Franklin was. Franklin was a living legend. Honours had been bestowed upon him countless times for his exploratory expeditions into the North. He had attempted to reach the Orient by ship, travelling east over the Norwegian island of Spitsbergen (as opposed to westward over Canada as he now intended). He had trekked overland to the northern rim of mainland Canada, not once but twice, suffering from cold and starvation, and returning with tales of unspeakable hardship. Now, in his twilight years, he had become a giant among explorers. Others of his calling had honoured him by bestowing his name on innumerable land features as they pushed further and further into the chill, forbidding reaches of the Arctic.

To the people of the time it must have seemed that they were seeing history in the making, as if the great voyages of exploration into the North would carry the names of their explorers down through the ages, just as, in a later time, people would speak of a "Space Age" and imagine that their astronaut heroes would live on in legend forever. Such names as John Ross and Edward Parry, James Clark Ross and George Back, Peter Dease and Thomas Simpson seemed imperishable and eternal. Thus, when Captain Dannett invited Franklin aboard his whaler in July of 1845, he could not have known that it was Franklin alone, of all his contemporaries, who would pass into legend. And that it would not be for what the great explorer had already accomplished, but rather for what was yet to come.

As the changing winds forced the *Prince of Wales* and the *Enterprise* too soon to part company with the naval expedition, Captain Dannett would have caught one last glimpse of the two black-and-yellow vessels secured to their iceberg before losing sight of them in the bluewhite haze. He had no way of knowing that no one would ever see either the *Erebus* or the *Terror* again.

This is how it always begins...

There are many details to the Franklin tale that have attained the status of myth. They are the little things that, whether true or not, serve to add that extra touch of mystery to a story that is mysterious enough in its own right. There is the story of how Franklin's wife, Jane Franklin, embroidered him a flag to take on his final voyage into the North, as was traditional. Ill with influenza, Franklin fell asleep on the couch. His wife placed the Union Jack across his legs, thinking he might be cold. When Franklin awoke to discover what she had done, he grew pale with horror. The Union Jack, after all, was what they draped over a corpse.

Then there was the story told of a dove seen to alight on the mast of one of the ships as they cast off from a dock near Gravesend. A good omen. A sign of success.

Such details are recounted because they serve to add a dash of the supernatural. They add to the magic, chillingly prophetic and darkly ironic.

In the final analysis, details are all we have. For all the books written on the subject, for all the reconstructions of the Franklin tragedy offered by the many experts, there are no witnesses to tell us what happened. There were Inuit who saw *something*, but what exactly, we cannot be sure. Often their testimony was second-hand and distorted by imperfect translation, overly zealous interrogators, and the passage of time itself. Still, we are left with details, but no overview. No big picture.

In another context, we would call these details "clues". Clues that present tantalizing, *infuriatingly* tantalizing, hints of a larger truth. Clues that, if only we could look at them in just the right manner and under just the right light, might combine and coalesce to reveal the final answer to the Franklin tragedy. I say "the final answer", but in truth there can be no final answer in the way that a murder mystery climaxes with the revelation of the true identity of the murderer. In this case, the final answer is a final story that explains all the facts, answers all the questions, and incorporates all the details into a satisfying whole. In science it would be called a "model". For our purposes, we shall call it a "story".

Over the years, this story has been presented in many different guises — tragedy, disaster, black comedy, mystery, morality tale. Here, I propose to enter into a far stranger, far darker realm, a country hitherto unexplored. In writing this book, I began with one simple purpose — to seek answers to questions that have proven unanswerable for a century-and-a-half. To do this, I made myself a promise at the outset. I promised myself that no solution, no matter how bizarre, would be rejected, so long as it fit the known facts. As we shall see, at times this was a difficult promise to keep. When those facts led me into a maze of deception and conspiracy, I hesitated. Like some Arctic explorer suddenly faced with dangerously thin ice, I nearly turned back. But, remembering my promise, I trudged grimly on, determined to follow the trail of clues, no matter where it might lead. Then, as the terrain grew steadily darker, the landscape alien and unexpected, as it became clear that the conspiracy was only the beginning, was positively mundane compared to what came after — I nearly faltered again. But still I kept on, step by step, detail by detail, until the terrifying end...

PART I
The Secret

'Tis the sunset of life gives me mystical lore,
And coming events cast their shadows before.
Thomas Campbell,
Lockiel's Warning

CHAPTER ONE

Prelude to Disaster

> The Pobble who has no toes
> Had once as many as we;
> When they said, "Some day you may lose
> them all"; –
> He replied, – "Fish fiddle de-dee!"
> Edward Lear,
> *The Pobble Who Has No Toes*

THE NORTHWEST PASSAGE

We will begin with a hypothesis. It is a very strange hypothesis but a fundamental one to our story. Therefore, we must lead into it gradually.

Ostensibly, the purpose of the Franklin expedition was to discover the Northwest Passage. This passage had been sought for hundreds of years dating back to Columbus' famed voyage in 1492. Contrary to myth, no one in Columbus' day thought the world was flat. They did, however, think it was about three times larger than Columbus believed it to be. And they were right. Both he and his crew would have perished at sea, their fate unknown, had they not run up against an unexpected land barrier and "discovered" the New World.

While Columbus was pleased with his discovery, to those who came after him North and South America meant only one thing — a very large obstacle on the way to the Spice lands of the East. For a time, ships probed every inlet and bay along the east coasts of both continents, confident that anything so large had to be bisected somewhere. But the search was in vain and gradually the searchers were forced to increasingly move their attentions south and north. Although a passage at the southern tip of South America was found by Magellan and often used, it was hardly convenient to seagoing nations situated in the northern hemisphere. Thus the "Quest for the Northwest Passage" began in earnest.

In 1610, when Henry Hudson sailed through the Hudson Strait and down into Hudson Bay, he thought he had reached the Pacific Ocean. As things turned out, the fact that he was wrong was really the least of his problems. His crew mutinied, setting him adrift and leaving him to die; then, through an incredible feat of navigation by Hudson's former mate Robert Bylot, they made it back to England, where they were tried for murder and acquitted. More importantly, they returned with the news that a titanic bay had been discovered in the north. Columbus wasn't the only one confused by distances, and the theory quickly developed that there must be a strait connecting the west shore of Hudson Bay with the Pacific Ocean, most likely at the Gulf of California. They called this the Strait of Anian and it was to occupy searchers fruitlessly for many years to come.

Six years later, William Baffin (acting as pilot for the same Robert Bylot who had set Hudson adrift) took a stab at the Northwest Passage further north and discovered Baffin Bay. Furthermore, by following the coast of the bay, Baffin discovered three possible straits, any one of which had the potential to serve as the fabled Passage to the Orient. After a time, however, interest in the search for the Passage waned. Decades passed, then a century, then two, and even Baffin's discovery gradually faded from memory until people began to wonder whether Baffin Bay really existed at all.

WHAT DID JOHN ROSS SEE?

Finally, two hundred years later, in another age, England took up the cudgel once again. Following the end of the war with Napoleon, the English Navy found itself burdened by too many soldiers and ships and nothing to do with them. In essence, the resumption of the quest for the Northwest Passage was a gargantuan makework project.

The first to take up the challenge was John Ross, a fairly standoffish member of His Majesty's Royal Navy who believed it was not befitting for officers to mingle with the crew even when trapped for years in the frozen wastes of the high Arctic. In 1818, he sailed from England with two ships, the *Isabella* and the *Alexander*. Ross had two goals in mind: the foremost being the traversing of the fabled Northwest Passage, the secondary being to either prove or disprove the existence of Baffin Bay [see map 1].

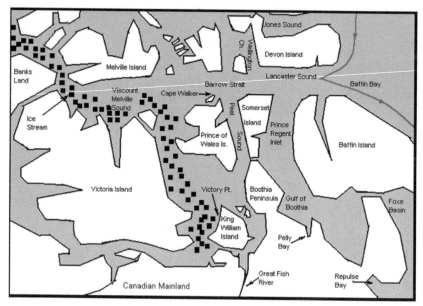

Map 1
John Ross' First Expedition, 1818

Since Baffin Bay did exist, Ross quickly found it. He sailed to the northern shores of the bay, then down the western coast where he redis-covered one of the straits which Baffin had reported two centuries ear-lier and which Ross now named Lancaster Sound. This strait was clear-ly headed in the right direction, so Ross decided to follow it in hopes it would lead him to the Pacific. With the slower *Alexander* trailing far behind, Ross had only followed Lancaster Sound a mere thirty miles when a thick fog closed in forcing him to stop. What happened next remains a tantalizing mystery to the present day.

After a short time, the officer on duty called Ross from his cabin with news that the fog was beginning to lift. On deck, Ross scrutinized the drifting veils to the west, seeking to determine what might lie ahead. Then, for just a matter of minutes, the fog parted and allowed him a glimpse of ... something. Something that caused him to abrupt-ly break off his journey, turn around and rush back out of Lancaster Sound "as if some mischief was behind him".[1] The amazed Edward Parry, commander of the *Alexander*, could only turn around reluctant-ly and follow his fast departing leader back to England.

Ross' explanation for his sudden loss of heart was that he had spot-ted a mountain range blocking Lancaster Sound, a range that he named the Croker Mountains after the First Secretary of the Admiralty. No one else apparently saw this mysterious mountain range, and many doubted it even existed — Parry among them. And, as events would later prove, it did not exist. Ross later described the scene this way: "At three I went on deck; it completely cleared for ten minutes, when I distinctly saw the land round the bottom of the bay, forming a chain of mountains connected with those which extended along the north and south side."[2] To further explain his inexplicable flight, Ross claimed to have also spotted ice blocking their path — ice that was also not seen by anyone else.

But even if Ross believed he had sighted a mountain range blocking Lancaster Sound (or ice), that does not explain why he returned to England. The expedition had planned to winter in the Arctic. They were not pressed for time. There were certainly other bays to explore; after all, no European had visited this place since Baffin's time. Every inlet discovered, every cove charted, would be theirs to name, their contribution to the maps of the future.

As the excellent Canadian historian Pierre Berton wondered in *The Arctic Grail*, "But why the haste? Why this sudden scramble to get home?" Ross' actions placed him in the Admiralty's black books for life, and alienated him from the explorers who would follow in his footsteps. Eventually he would return to the Arctic, but not under the aegis of the Royal Navy.

What did Ross see for those few minutes as the fog thinned to the west? What did he think he saw? A mountain range? What could have caused him to return home, destroying his career and separating him from his peers? Thus, twenty-six years before Franklin's fateful voyage, we encounter the first question in the mystery.

What did Ross see?

Edward Parry's miracle voyage

After Ross, Edward Parry, having been forced to retreat once, set out to prove he was made of sterner stuff than his former leader. Parry, devoutly religious, was far less standoffish than Ross, making life for his crews in the Arctic much more bearable than under Ross. He was to command no less than three separate expeditions into the Arctic, the first being the most successful, the last the most disastrous.

In a single season, the next year, Parry very nearly succeeded in crossing the entire Arctic from east to west by taking a straight line course down Lancaster Sound, through Barrow Strait and into Viscount Melville Sound [see map 2]. His luck was incredible. The

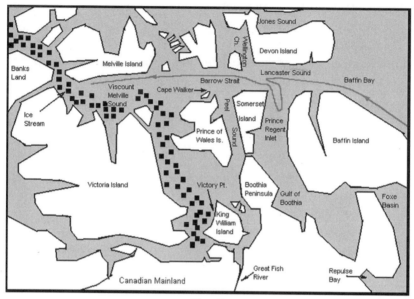

Map 2
Edward Parry's First Expedition, 1819–1820

weather turned warmer than it would ever be again for any other expedition in this period. The ice fields parted before him, the route to the Orient stretched like the Thames. Only briefly in Lancaster Sound was he halted by ice. Immediately he turned south down Prince Regent Inlet where he coasted Somerset Island before again running into ice and returning to Lancaster Sound. Finally finding a path through the ice to the west, Parry continued on to Viscount Melville Sound, eventually crossing 110 degrees Longitude, thus allowing him to claim the five thousand pound reward that the government had set.

But then, on the very brink of completing the Passage (and the twenty thousand pound prize that came with *that* feat), Parry ran up against a vast river of ice stretching across his path. Unable to find a way through the ice, he wintered near Melville Island and tried again in the spring. But all his efforts were in vain. The ice was impenetrable.

What Parry did not realize was that this river of ice originated in the permanent ice fields of the Beaufort Sea far to the northwest, where titanic mountains of ice fifty feet thick were formed. Only later would it be understood that this ice river flows south and east, through Viscount Melville Sound, then abruptly abuts up against Prince of Wales Island and is forced south down McClintock Strait and past King William Island.

But for Parry there was no alternative. Defeated on the very brink of success, he turned back and sailed home.

THE LOSS OF THE FURY

The next year, Parry set out again on his second voyage, this time to attempt a completely different route. Eschewing Baffin Bay altogether, instead he followed Henry Hudson's old route, passing through Hudson Strait farther south, then turning north into Foxe Basin. The attempt was unsuccessful and again he was thwarted by ice.

Parry's third attempt took him over familiar ground as he passed through Lancaster Sound, then turned south down Prince Regent Inlet as he had briefly done when temporarily blocked by ice in 1819 [see map 3]. This time, however, the results were far more disastrous. Icebergs crushed one of his ships, the *Fury*, against the coast of

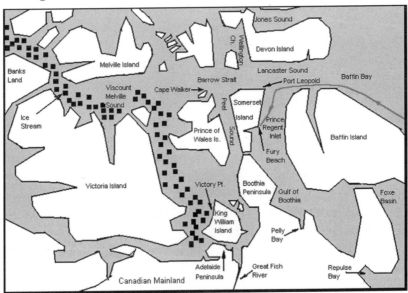

Map 3
Edward Parry's Third Expedition, 1824–1825

Somerset Island, forcing him to abandon it and its provisions on Fury Beach. With his entire expedition desperately crowded aboard his other ship, the *Hecla*, they barely made it out alive.

The *Fury* was the first ship lost in the modern search for the Passage. The loss of a ship was the ultimate failing in the eyes of the Admiralty. But, though a court martial was convened against Henry Hoppner, the *Fury*'s commander, he was nonetheless acquitted. Parry and his officers were praised for their efforts. Where John Ross had been ostracized for turning back, Parry was praised for losing a ship.

JOHN ROSS TRIES AGAIN

After Parry's failed third attempt, the government cancelled the twenty-thousand-pound reward for the first ship to traverse the Passage and actively dissuaded others from embarking on the quest. But now John Ross wanted another crack at it. As official channels would not support him (indeed, they cancelled the reward precisely to discourage him), he was forced to seek private backing for his expedition and he found a patron in Felix Booth, a distillery king and sheriff of London. Aboard an eighty-five ton steam packet, the *Victory*, Ross followed the exact same route that Parry had taken on his third voyage.

The *Victory* sailed through Lancaster Sound, then south into Prince Regent Inlet where the expedition wintered on the east shore of Somerset Island and the Boothia Peninsula [see map 4]. For four years, the longest any expedition had yet remained in these waters, Ross was forced to winter on this coast, having chosen a harbour that was too shallow. Thus for three winters he remained trapped, unable to sail clear even when the ice broke up each spring. Finally, Ross had no choice but to abandon the *Victory* and travel north by foot up the coast to the provisions and small boats abandoned by Parry at Fury Beach. Reaching these, he and his crew attempted to sail out of Prince Regent Inlet in hopes they might be picked up by whalers in Baffin Bay. But they were turned back by ice and forced to spend a fourth winter at Fury Beach, this time without even a ship to keep them warm. In the spring they finally made their escape and were indeed picked up by a ship in Baffin Bay. Thus, in the search for the Northwest Passage, two ships had so far been lost, both on the same coast.

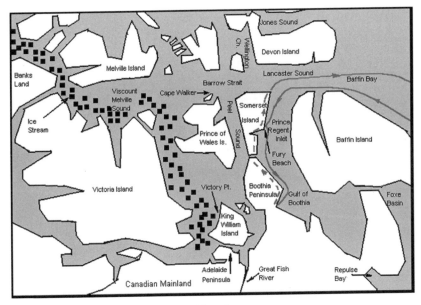

Map 4
John Ross' Second Expedition, 1829–1833

THE FRANKLIN EXPEDITION

This is how things stood when the Franklin expedition was organized. The government had decided it didn't want anyone else going in search of the Passage. John Ross had gone anyway and nearly perished. Now, after all this, the Admiralty reversed itself with a vengeance.

It organized a final voyage and it organized it well. More money was spent on preparing the Franklin expedition than had been lavished on any previous expedition. The *Erebus* and *Terror* were better built and better prepared than any previous ships. The crew of 134 men (reduced to 129 at the last minute) was larger than any crew that had sailed before in search of the Passage. For the first time, the Navy would employ ships capable of self-propulsion in the Arctic. A massive railway locomotive was installed in the hold of each ship, capable of turning a specially adapted screw propeller in the event of an emergency. *Terror's* engine could supply twenty horsepower; *Erebus'* could offer twenty-five. The ship's living spaces would be heated by hot water pumped through pipes throughout the ships. Desalinators were built into the galley stoves. All that modern science could offer was to be employed in this one final push into the unknown.

Which then begs the question: why?

The Admiralty had earlier decided the search for the Passage simply wasn't worth the expense. Now it was prepared to spend more than ever. After so many centuries, it was finally understood that the Passage, assuming it really did exist, would never be useable for merchant ships. That ancient dream, to discover a western route to the East, had already died in the harsh light of cold hard geographical reality. The ice was simply too unpredictable. The summer season in the high Arctic was simply too short. Even if the *Erebus* and *Terror* were able to batter their way through, there were no ships capable of following in their tracks. Their very invincibility proved the commercial irrelevance of their mission.

It has become a truism that the Passage grew to be an end in itself; that it was a matter of national honour that the British finish what they had started before any other nation beat them to it. And for many it was. But there were much more economical ways to complete the Passage. Expeditions dispatched overland had already accomplished more than all the sea voyages combined. Franklin's two treks through the Barren Grounds of Canada had mapped the western leg of the Passage along the roof of the continent. Peter Warren Dease and Thomas Simpson had extended Franklin's Passage along the continent into the east as far as King William Island until only a tiny stretch remained — somewhere north of King William Island was where the final strait had to lie, if it lay anywhere. One more overland trip would have determined once and for all whether a Passage existed. A dozen men, a few small boats, a single, simple trip — the result would have been the same. The Northwest Passage would have been completed by the British. National honour would have been satisfied.

So why this final Herculean expedition? Why 129 men? Why waste two unsinkable ships at such phenomenal expense? Why go to so much trouble for something that could have been accomplished for so much less?

Not the Northwest Passage?

I began by saying I intended to present a hypothesis, but that I would lead into it gradually. To do so, I have presented the facts as they are usually told in history books. It was important to establish the history of this subject before overturning that history, to explain what is commonly accepted before proposing an alternate interpretation of the facts.

My hypothesis is simply this: the Franklin expedition was never intended to complete the Northwest Passage. This was not its true purpose. Instead, its true goal was to enter the Arctic in search of something else. What something else? We will get to that soon enough.

In the meantime, such a suggestion demands evidence. After all, if we suppose the Franklin expedition was searching for *something* other than the Passage, certain corollaries arise from this hypothesis. For one, the Navy must already have known about this *something* and must have known where to look, otherwise they could hardly have expected Franklin to find it, no matter how well outfitted his expedition. Thus, it is reasonable to ask: how did the Navy know?

CHAPTER TWO

Victory Point Revisited

> When fishes flew and forests walked
> And figs grew upon thorn,
> Some moment when the moon was blood
> Then surely I was born.
> G.K. Chesterton,
> *The Donkey*

JOHN ROSS' SECOND VOYAGE

As we have seen, sixteen years before the *Erebus* and *Terror* sailed on their final voyage, John Ross returned to the top of the world on his second attempt at the Northwest Passage.

But why, after more than a decade, did Ross now decide he wanted another try at the Passage? Certainly he had always had reason enough to want another go at the prize. Having abruptly (and inexplicably) terminated his first attempt on sighting the imaginary Croker Mountains in 1818, his reputation amongst the Admiralty brass was less than shining. Edward Parry, who had sailed with him on that botched voyage, had gone on to fame and glory (in spite of the loss of the *Fury*), and in the process proven that Ross' mountain range did not exist. It is easy enough to see why Ross might have wanted another try at the Passage. But why now? Why after so long?

Initially Ross sought official support for his venture, but the Admiralty would have nothing to do with him. It refused to support any more quests for the Passage. Just to drive home its point, it cancelled the twenty-thousand-pound reward that had stood available since Ross' first attempt and it eliminated the Board of Longitude whose duty it was to judge such matters.

Ross was determined. So determined that he sank three thousand pounds of his own money into the endeavour before finally securing an additional seventeen thousand from a private source, Felix Booth, Sheriff of London. It wasn't much but it was enough to purchase the *Victory*, a small sidewheel steamer that had been used to run between Liverpool and the Isle of Man.

With a crew of twenty-eight, the *Victory* set out from Woolwich in May 1829. With the weather on his side, Ross breezed through Baffin Bay into Lancaster Sound, then south down Prince Regent Inlet as far as Fury Beach where Parry had abandoned his ship, the *Fury* [see map 4]. After some difficulty, Ross managed to collect some of the provisions left by Parry on the beach, then proceeded south once more.

There were two main goals for this voyage. One was to discover the exact location of the North Magnetic Pole. It wasn't then known that the Magnetic Pole is not stationary but drifts gradually over decades; it *was* known that the Pole lay in the vicinity of Somerset Island and the Boothia Peninsula. Indeed, its proximity rendered compasses virtually useless on this leg of the journey. (The Magnetic Pole is entirely different from the Geographic North Pole, which is the point around which the planet turns and which is fixed at ninety degrees latitude, far to the north of the Magnetic Pole.) The second purpose of the expedition was to discover whether or not there was a strait through the landmass of Boothia-Somerset.

At the time, little was known about this area. Though it was eventually discovered that Boothia is connected at its southern end to the Canadian mainland (making it a peninsula), it was thought at the time that there might actually be a strait separating the two, which would serve as a link in the Northwest Passage. Conversely, it was not known then that there *was* a strait (albeit, not a useable one) separating Boothia from Somerset to the north (making Somerset an island). For the purposes of this book, we will generally refer to Somerset as an island and Boothia as a peninsula, even when speaking of periods when they were not yet identified as such.

Before he could determine whether or not a strait existed along the coast, Ross ran into heavy ice and was forced to take shelter in a harbour, where the *Victory* settled in for the winter. As we have seen, the harbour turned out to be too shallow, trapping Ross for three years and eventually forcing him to abandon the *Victory* and make his escape on foot.

JAMES CLARK ROSS AND KING WILLIAM ISLAND

In early January of the first winter some local Inuit arrived, and it was through their assistance in procuring game that John Ross' expedition survived at all. Furthermore, the Inuit were able to supply details about the surrounding geography.

Ross' nephew, James Clark Ross (who would later gain his fame through explorations in the Antarctic), set out from the *Victory* several times by dogsledge to explore the countryside. During one of the first of these forays, an Inuk named Ooblooria led James Clark Ross across the peninsula to its west coast to show him a strait that, Ross was told, remained ice-free in the summer [see map 5]. Thinking this passage might lead to the Pacific, James Clark Ross set out again in May for this same point on the west coast, taking two dogsleds, three weeks of provisions and a skin boat. He was accompanied by Abernethy, the ship's mate, and three other men.

But, this time, when they reached the western coast, the group crossed out onto the ice. Passing islands as they went, Ross found it difficult to tell the hummock-covered water from the lowlying land. He wrote: "When all is ice, and all one dazzling mass of white — when the surface of the sea itself is tossed up and fixed into rocks, while the land is, on the contrary, very often flat, it is not always so easy a problem as it might seem."[1]

Finally, he reached his destination, a long, low shore he had sighted from Boothia. He named this King William Land, thinking it was likely connected to Boothia somewhere to the southwest. In fact, it was an island. This mistake, more than anything else, has been historically cited as the cause of the Franklin tragedy. Because Franklin was not aware of the strait that separated King William Island's east coast from Boothia Peninsula, he instead attempted to pass the island on its west coast thus running straight into the impenetrable ice stream that flows forever down from the pack in the Beaufort Sea.

With his companions, James Clark Ross sledged directly to the northern tip of the island which he named Cape Felix. Then, steer-

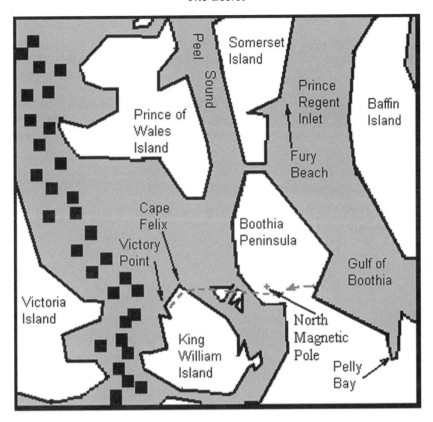

Map 5
James Clark Ross Sledges to Victory Point, 1830

ing a course down its west coast, Ross continued on with only Abernethy accompanying him. Finally, he reached a point of land where he planted the flag and which he called Victory Point. Here Ross erected a cairn, leaving inside a record detailing his expedition's accomplishments to date. In the distance, across a yawning bay, he could make out another headland, which he christened — in what would be the eeriest irony of all — Cape Franklin. About his choice, Ross explained: "If that be a name which has now been conferred on more places than one, these honours, not in fact so solid when so widely shared, are beyond all thought less than the merits of that officer deserve."[2]

With provisions running low, Ross and his companions retreated to the *Victory*, even then nearly failing in the return journey. Only two of the eight dogs survived, and the humans would also have perished if they had not run into Inuit who fed them before sending them on to the ship. Unable to free the *Victory* in the spring, the expedition settled down for a second winter. Early the next year, 1831, James Clark Ross set off once again, this time successfully discovering the location of the North Magnetic Pole on the west coast of Boothia. In the meantime, through information obtained from their Inuit visitors, the two Rosses learned that Boothia was, in fact, a peninsula, and that there was no strait through it leading to the west water. James Clark Ross, however, was unable to prove this definitively during his many sledge trips, and thus the theory of the strait continued long after the expedition returned to England two years later.

AN ASTONISHING COINCIDENCE?

When considering Ross' second expedition, several features stand out. The most obvious is the remarkable coincidence of James Clark Ross' trip to the northwest tip of King William Island, for it was precisely here that Franklin's ships would be trapped during the fatal expedition to come. On the northern tip that Ross named Cape Felix, evidence would be found of a camp established there by the crews of the doomed ships. When the last survivors abandoned their vessels and marched across the implacable ice to shore, they reached the island at Ross' Victory Point. Indeed, they left their final record in the cairn erected by him (or, at least, this is what they attempted).

James Clark Ross visited no other part of King William Island, nor did he return there, even though the *Victory* was trapped for two more winters. Why did he not pay a further visit to the southwest corner of the island? He thought he had found a Passage, but only by going farther south on the island could he have known for certain. Moreover, he had observed massive ice sheets thrust up on the shore as much as half a mile. Even if he thought King William Island was attached to the Boothia Peninsula, why didn't he check the east coast of the island to be certain, knowing that a strait — *any* strait — would have been preferable to that heaving river of ice to the west? Other questions become apparent. There were two main purposes to the expedition: to find the North Magnetic Pole and to determine whether or not there was a way through Boothia-Somerset. Whatever their plans, James Clark Ross could not be certain there would be a second winter. The staying power of any Arctic expedition was unpredictable, none more so than this one. The *Victory* was never made for voyaging in the Arctic ice. They carried provisions for three years (thanks partly to Parry's stocks left at Fury Beach), but food alone was not enough to survive. To combat scurvy required fresh meat, something that only their Inuit visitors could supply. During that first winter, there could have been no guarantee the Inuit would stay another season as they did. Surely, he should have tracked down the Magnetic Pole sometime during the first winter. He had to pass the Pole in order to reach King William Island. The discovery of the Pole was the main reason Felix Booth had sponsored the venture in the first place.

As for the possibility of a strait through the peninsula, James Clark Ross knew the testimony of the Inuit would not be enough. His first priority (after the Pole) should have been to see for himself. Instead, he chose to visit King William Island. Why?

We cannot escape the feeling that he went there because he expected to find something — something more important than the Magnetic Pole or the Northwest Passage. He went there looking for something and, more importantly, he knew precisely where to look. The northwest coast of King William Island. Victory Point. The exact same place where the Franklin expedition would meet its end. The *exact* same.

But how did he know?

CHAPTER THREE

The *Fury* Vanishes

Is he in heaven? – Is he in hell?
That demmed, elusive Pimpernel.
Baroness Orczy,
The Scarlet Pimpernel

PARRY'S DISASTROUS THIRD VOYAGE

Clearly, if it is true that James Clark Ross went to King William Island
expecting to find something there, the next question we must ask is:
how did he know that something was there to be found?

It makes sense, then, to consider the expedition which preceded this
one — the last navy expedition to be sent in search of the Northwest
Passage, after which the government suddenly decided no more should
be sent out and cancelled the twenty-thousand-pound reward. We must
consider William Edward Parry's disastrous third expedition.

Parry also thought there might be a strait through Boothia and
Somerset. With his second expedition, he had tried to reach this passage
from the south by way of Hudson's Strait and the Foxe Basin, only to
find himself defeated by ice in Fury and Hecla Strait. Now he was prepared to try to find it from the north again, using Prince Regent Inlet.

In May 1824, Parry set sail with the two ships he had used on his earlier expedition, the *Hecla* and *Fury*. The expedition reached Baffin Bay
a month later and by mid-July it was already in trouble. Due to the
"quantity, magnitude, and closeness of the ice" the two crews were "constantly employed in heaving, warping, or sawing through it".[1] On August
1st, a storm closed in and caused the grinding ice pans to pile atop one
another. The terrible pressure of the heaving ice forced the *Hecla* on her

beam ends with such relentless strength that Parry was convinced no normal vessel could have survived the onslaught. Nevertheless, by September they were clear and they passed into Lancaster Sound, miraculously almost ice-free. Still, it was merely the lull before the storm.

It was now late in the season; ice gradually formed around the ships and a three-mile-per-hour current forced them steadily backward. Only gradually did they make up the lost ground, before turning south down into Prince Regent Inlet. Unable to proceed farther, they found a suitable wintering spot on the east coast of the inlet, rather than on the west coast as they had hoped. There they spent a bleak, lonely winter, sending out several exploratory missions by sledge to the south, north and east.

Ten months later, the ice floe that had blocked their harbour broke apart and they again set sail, this time determined to reach the coast of Somerset across the inlet, and to find out whether a strait through it existed or not. But no sooner had they reached the opposite shore than the *Hecla* found herself mired in grinding ice and, after wrecking two ice anchors, they had no choice but to drift for two days to where the pack took them. From then on things got worse, as a storm struck the *Fury* and forced the ship up onto the cliff-lined shore of Somerset Island. The crews floated her free, but then both ships were driven aground by the merciless ice. Again they were floated free, but by now the *Fury* was leaking badly and required the constant use of pumps to stay afloat. Again ice forced her onto the shore, with the *Hecla* barely escaping a similar fate.

On surveying the damage done to the *Fury*, it was decided that she would have to be repaired. The crews set about building a basin for her where she would be sheltered by icebergs from the worst of the storm, but once she had been unloaded and moved into the basin the storm blew away the sheltering ice. Quickly she was loaded up again and floated out into open water, but no sooner had she cleared the harbour than the ice delivered the *coup de grace*, forcing her onto the beach for the final time.

Parry later wrote, "Every endeavour of ours to get her off, or if got off, to float her to any known place of safety, would be at once utterly hopeless in itself, and productive of extreme risk to our remaining ship."[2] Her provisions were offloaded in the hopes they might be useful to future expeditions (as, in fact, they were to John Ross) and the battered *Fury* was left there on the beach, which was now, fittingly, given the name Fury Beach. The *Hecla* returned to England alone.

THE COMMON FACTOR

Ever since Parry's brief side trip in 1819, no ship had passed down Prince Regent Inlet until the *Fury* and *Hecla's* ill-starred voyage. After Parry, the next to do so would be John Ross. Is there a connection between the two expeditions? Is there any reason to think the course of one was determined by the other? On first glance, if there is a common factor it is well hidden. Parry's expedition was proposed and carried out as a naval venture. Ross' expedition was privately sponsored precisely because the Admiralty didn't want him going there. There was certainly no love lost between the two men; Parry had made a fool of Ross and Parry was the favourite of the Admiralty while Ross was an outcast. And yet, there does remain one tantalizing link between the two voyages.

JAMES CLARK ROSS

John Ross' nephew had been a midshipman on both of Parry's previous expeditions, and was promoted to lieutenant prior to the third one. He sailed aboard the *Fury*. It is certainly a tenuous link if we are to suggest James Clark Ross visited King William Island during this earlier voyage. After all, according to Parry, that first winter was spent across the strait from Somerset Island and what time was spent on her shores the next year was amply taken up trying to save the two ships. The only sledge trips Ross is recorded as undertaking were on the east side of Prince Regent Inlet, not the west side.

Is it even remotely possible Ross found time to sledge south down Somerset and across to King William Island during the second summer — perhaps while the crews were fighting to save the beached ships? It would unquestionably have been a difficult and lengthy journey, but no more so than many of the journeys undertaken during the later search for Franklin's expedition.

If distance were the only obstacle, we could say it was possible Ross made such a journey. But time is also to be considered. After all, between Parry's ships repeatedly being tossed up on the rocky shore, refloating them and building a basin to repair the *Fury*, little time would seem to have remained for Ross to make this trek.

That is, assuming things happened as Parry claimed they happened.

WHAT REALLY HAPPENED TO THE FURY?

One of the assertions of Parry's story of ice and wind was that he had been forced to unload the *Fury's* provisions and abandon his vessel while she was grounded on Fury Beach. Yet, when John Ross reached Fury Beach four years later aboard the diminutive *Victory*, there was no sign of the *Fury*. Of course, it is possible that the same ice that had grounded the ship in the first place returned in later years and dragged it into open water, where it assuredly would have sunk. And yet, the provisions left on the beach remained precisely where Parry had placed them — undisturbed.

Ross also abandoned his vessel on the same coast. Over the years, the Inuit visited this wreck many times and relics from the *Victory* were found in the possession of Inuit across the eastern Arctic long afterward. Copper from Ross' vessel was made into Inuit mukluks. In fact, the Inuit referred to the harbour where the *Victory* was abandoned as *qilanartot*, meaning "joyful beach", because of the useful materials to be found there.[3] Yet no trace of Parry's ship *Fury* was ever discovered, no relic found its way into Inuit hands, and no wreckage washed ashore. It simply disappeared.

What are we to make of this? Was the *Fury* simply dragged away by the ice? Or is it possible the *Fury* was never there to begin with? If not, why would Parry lie? If the *Fury* was not abandoned on Fury Beach, what really happened to her?

Another point: Parry published official accounts for each of his three expeditions. Unlike the accounts of his first two voyages, his written version of this third expedition filled only a slim single volume. "Reading these excerpts from his journal," commented Pierre Berton, "so much sparser than in previous years — one gets the impression that Parry was growing weary of it all."[4] And perhaps he was. But is it not also possible that this account was shorter for the reason that it was a partial fabrication? In fact, is it not possible that Parry was instructed to make up the story of the *Fury's* grounding on Fury Beach, to conceal the true circumstances of its loss?

But then, what did become of the *Fury*?

A MYSTERIOUS WRECK

In 1929, long after the final resting place of Franklin's crew had been discovered on King William Island, Major L.T. Burwash gleaned from the natives of Boothia Peninsula what David C. Woodman called, "One of the most unlikely of the Inuit tales."[5] From two Inuit, both about sixty years old, Burwash was astonished to learn that they had "for many years been aware of the fact that the wreck of a large vessel lay submerged off the northwestern extremity of Matty Island." [see map 6] Matty Island is a small island nestled in between King William Island and the Boothia Peninsula. By the very nature of its position, it is almost impossible to reach by ship. Yet the Inuit claimed that occasionally bits of wood and metal were washed ashore from this wreck and they showed Burwash some of this flotsam, some of which he thought were "ship's fittings".[6]

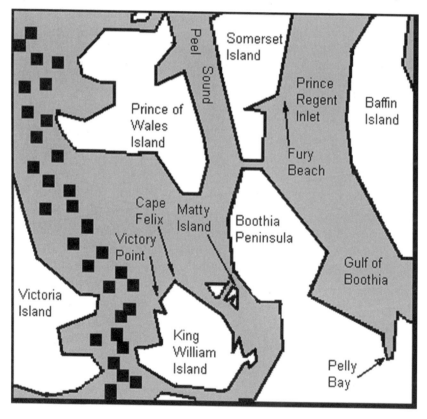

Map 6
A Wreck near Matty Island?

The two Inuit also claimed that, when they were twenty years old, they had visited a cache of provisions left on an island, supposedly deposited there by the crew of the wrecked ship.

When Burwash heard the story of the wreck in 1929, he knew that almost no ship had ever passed by Matty Island and none had sunk there. But, in 1903, Roald Amundsen had passed by Matty Island while traversing the Northwest Passage for the first time in the *Gjoa*. Amundsen briefly grounded on the reefs, splintering his vessel's false keel. He was forced to off-load some provisions to refloat his ship. Noel Wright, in *Quest for Franklin*, concluded that the Inuit story told to Burwash was just a muddled memory of the near-wreck of the *Gjoa*. But there are objections to Wright's conclusion. For one, the Inuit were quite certain there was a wreck "beneath the water", and told of barrels and fifteen-foot planks which washed ashore from the sunken ship. The *Gjoa*, after its near disaster, had continued on its course. Another objection, as Woodman pointed out, is that Burwash's sixty-year-old informants had visited the cache when they were twenty, placing the wreck long before Amundsen's voyage of the *Gjoa*.

Burwash himself believed the wreck could only have been that of either the *Erebus* or the *Terror*, since these were the only ships known to have met with disaster in the general area. But this too presented problems, for it had long before been ascertained from the Inuit that one of Franklin's ships had sunk off the west coast of King William Island, and the other had gone aground further south of that point. Woodman agreed with Burwash and, to get around this difficulty, Woodman suggested that Franklin had tried to pass by Matty Island on the east side of King William Island, run aground, off-loaded provisions, then turned around and attempted to get around King William Island on the west side, where he met with ultimate disaster. The "wreck", Woodman hypothesized, was a ship's boat that was lost while lightening the ship. While possible, it is hard to imagine how such a small boat could be mistaken for the wreck of a ship, or that it would still be tossing up wood and metal so many years later.

Noel Wright also rejected Burwash's theory, but for a different and, from our point of view, very significant reason. Wright observed, "As for the source of the iron said to be washed up by the sea, it has been known for more than a century; for the first mention of it one has to go back to the *Narrative* of Captain John Ross."[7]

Indeed, during the voyage of the *Victory*, it was James Clark Ross himself who told how the Inuit showed them "ironstone ... taken from beneath the water". The Inuk in question, Poo-yet-tah, told how his brother had discovered the iron the previous summer "on the shores of an islet called Toot-ky-yak, which was a day's journey to the northwest." Wright felt this underwater source of "ironstone" combined with the wreck of the *Gjoa* fully accounted for the story told to Burwash.

But now let us take a different tack to the problem. Let us assume Burwash's Inuit informants knew precisely what they were talking about, that there was a shipwreck beneath the water off Matty Island, there was a cache on the shore, and wood and iron pieces were tossed up by the waves over the years. This eliminates the *Gjoa* since it sailed merrily on its way. Previous to the *Gjoa*, no other ship sank in that area except the *Erebus* and *Terror*. But both these vessels met their ends on the opposite side of King William Island, eliminating them as well. Further, if we suppose the "ironstone" shown to James Clark Ross was actually iron from a shipwreck, this places the wreck even before the *Victory*'s visit to Boothia Peninsula in 1829.

The only ship missing at that time was Edward Parry's *Fury*.

The *Fury* had been lost in 1825, supposedly stranded on Fury Beach, but she was not to be found there when Ross arrived only four years later. Is it possible, then, that the shipwreck off Matty Island was the wreck of Parry's *Fury*? If so, we no longer face a problem finding time for James Clark Ross to sledge over to King William Island; instead, we suppose that the Parry expedition actually travelled down Peel Sound, reaching the coast of King William Island, where the *Fury* foundered on the shoals. From there, Ross could easily have visited King William Island.

What he may have discovered on that island, we will discuss in time, but whatever he found was of such importance that the Admiralty decided to keep it secret. Parry constructed a false narrative to explain the loss of the *Fury*, pretending the ice had taken the ship in Prince Regent Inlet, eliminating any mention of the journey to King William Island. As for James Clark Ross, he could hardly have ignored the evidence of the iron shown to his uncle's expedition but, knowing the iron was from the *Fury*, he neutrally characterized it as "ironstone" and left it at that.

CHAPTER FOUR

Never To Return

I have been one acquainted with the night.
Robert Frost,
Acquainted With The Night

GEORGE BACK AND THE TERROR

And what of John Ross?

Why after more than a decade did he decide to return to the Arctic to seek the Northwest Passage? Is it possible that he too had seen something so many years ago, something other than (or even in addition to) a mountain range that wasn't there? If so, we might imagine that he had wondered himself, all those years, if he hadn't imagined the whole thing. That was what everyone else said. No doubt he came to believe it. That is, until his nephew James returned and told him what *he* had seen on King William Island. If John Ross did see something in Lancaster Sound, he could have had no way of connecting it with King William Island, a yet to be discovered island in a totally unexplored region of the Arctic far to the southwest. But with his nephew's tale to finally confirm his vision, perhaps he decided he had to go there himself.

But now, suddenly, the Admiralty wanted nothing more to do with trips into this area. Or, at least, it didn't want private expeditions to try. Though the government cancelled the twenty-thousand-pound-reward to discourage would-be explorers — and John Ross in particular — it did eventually dispatch another naval expedition into the same general area in 1836, three years after John Ross returned. George Back was sent aboard HMS *Terror* — the same ship Franklin would later employ

— to follow the same route Parry had taken during his second voyage: through Hudson's Strait and then up into Repulse Bay, spending the winter there while exploring by sledge to the west.

If Parry told the government about discovering something on King William Island, we may assume that they would be interested in following up his discovery. But Back's voyage certainly couldn't have been intended to reach the distant island. In order to reach Prince Regent Inlet from the south, he would have had to sail up through Fury and Hecla Strait — the strait that had stopped Parry dead in his tracks during his second expedition. More likely, this was merely by way of preparation for the larger expedition yet to come — an attempt to establish the best route to reach the island by water. If so, Back proved spectacularly that this was not the way to go. The *Terror* was caught by icebergs, crushed and dumped on her side. By the time she escaped from the ice she was leaking badly, barely making it back across the ocean, where she beached on the coast of Ireland with only hours to spare.

Just the same, the fact that the *Terror* returned at all, after weathering the worst the ice could offer, was surely a testament to how well she was built. Before being transferred to the Franklin expedition, she would be refitted and made stronger still.

A THIN EXCUSE

Without the government's support, having spent three thousand pounds of his own money, aboard a rickety, jury-rigged sidewheeler, John Ross and his nephew James Clark Ross returned to the Arctic. But all was not well between them. Sharing the same cabin during those prolonged sunless winters on Boothia Peninsula, they fought frequently, though about what we don't know. William Light, the ship's steward, likened the quarrels between them to "the lava in the craters of Vesuvius and Etna" which frequently "terrified the other inmates of the cabin."[1] Whatever the reason for this animosity, it would stain their relations far into the future. John Ross would remain suspicious of his nephew long after they returned, and would attribute dark motives to him during the later search for Franklin.

But it wasn't John Ross who made the trek to King William Island. James was the land traveller, not John. And it was James Clark Ross who, upon reaching the north tip of the island, left the rest of his party behind — all except the ship's mate, Abernethy. Together the two of them trekked to Victory Point where Franklin's doomed crew would come ashore years later. If James Clark Ross was looking for something, did he find it? If he did, this is most likely where and when it happened — as he and Abernethy stood alone at Victory Point with the piled hummocks of ice and the howling wind on the brink of a lonely, frozen, heaving strait named for the Queen of England, Victoria.

We have no evidence that he found anything other than a potential route to the Pacific, no proof that anything out of the ordinary transpired. But after his return to England, James Clark Ross abruptly forsook Arctic exploration and instead turned his attentions to the Antarctic. In command of the *Erebus* and *Terror*, he made his name during a single expedition in which he discovered the Antarctic continent. On returning, he was offered what should have been the greatest prize of all: to lead the final expedition in search of the Northwest Passage. Having taken part in all three of Edward Parry's voyages and both of John Ross' — in essence, every major attempt — now he was being offered the final voyage to which all the others had been leading.

The Passage, it was said, was as good as complete. After John Ross' expedition, Peter Warren Dease and Thomas Simpson had travelled overland and extended the Passage from the west to just south of King William Island. All that remained to be accomplished was to connect Barrow Strait in the north with Simpson's Passage in the south, then on to the Pacific and glory. South past King William Island.

Inexplicably, James Clark Ross declined. Instead, the mission went to Sir John Franklin.

Ross' explanation? He had promised the parents of his new bride that he would never set to sea again. As Pierre Berton commented, "It seems a thin excuse."[2] We can only wonder if there might have been another reason for his refusal to return to that place. As it was, he would soon have no choice but to sail north one more time — to seek the very expedition that he had refused to take part in.

Curiously, his situation was paralleled by Edward Parry's. On returning from his third expedition, after the loss of the *Fury*, Parry was a changed man. He suffered from depression and headaches, conditions that he treated with medications. This change may be understandable considering what he had been through. On the other hand, we have considered the evidence suggesting that the story of the *Fury's* loss in Prince Regent Inlet was a fabrication; the evidence points to a shipwreck off the coast of King William Island. Thus, it may be of some significance that, after the loss of the *Fury*, William Edward Parry, like James Clark Ross, swore never to return to the Arctic again.

Sir John Franklin would prove how spectacularly right they had both been.

CHAPTER FIVE

A Second 1824

And what rough beast, its hour come
round at last,
Slouches towards Bethlehem to be born?
W.B.Yeats,
The Second Coming

JOHN ROSS' CONCERN

Her Majesty's Ships *Erebus* and *Terror* were last seen in Baffin Bay in
1845. They were still secured to an iceberg awaiting a break in the ice to
allow them to enter Lancaster Sound. After that, nothing more was heard
from them. There was no way for those back home to determine their
progress, as first one and then a second winter passed. Had they even
made it to Lancaster Sound? No one could know. Perhaps they had found
themselves frozen out and had turned north to search higher up Baffin
Bay. On the other hand, perhaps everything had gone perfectly and they
were already through the Passage and sailing south in the Pacific. Then
there was the third and more likely possibility: they were somewhere deep
within the maze of straits and sounds of the Arctic, frozen in, waiting for
summer to make a final dash to the Bering Strait and the Pacific.

Under these circumstances, it wasn't strange that there should be
so little concern for the expedition. Franklin had taken enough food to
last three winters, which he could "spin out" to seven years if necessary
(or so he told the captain of one of the whalers he met in Baffin Bay).
John Ross had managed four winters with relative ease. Ross, of course,
had only survived because he had had Parry's supplies at Fury Beach
and because he had had Inuit hunters to supply him for two years.
Also, Ross hadn't had to feed 129 men. But Franklin's expedition was

better supplied than any which had gone before and all but the middle section of the Passage had already been charted. So, by early in 1847, although Franklin had been out of touch for two winters, it was not so odd that the Admiralty wasn't worrying about him.

What is more odd is that John Ross did.

John Ross, from the very beginning, seemed convinced the expedition would meet with disaster. He had spoken with Franklin personally, urging him to set up food caches and small boats along the way. If the ships had to be abandoned, this would give the expedition something to fall back on, just as Ross had fallen back on Parry's provisions when he abandoned the *Victory* in 1832. (In the Arctic cold, remarkably, food can remain edible for many years.) Furthermore, he promised Franklin that if nothing was heard from the expedition by February of 1847, Ross himself would set out to rescue them.

SCIENTIFIC EXPERTISE OVER ARCTIC EXPERIENCE

One of Ross' chief concerns centred on the officers chosen for the expedition. Remarkably, for what was supposed to be an allout, no-holds-barred completion of the Northwest Passage, almost none of the officers had any experience in the waters they were supposed to be traversing. Indeed, the Admiralty seemed to have had other criteria in mind when making its selections.

William Gibson, one time Chief Trader for the Hudson's Bay Company, observed:

"The scientific results aimed at were well evidenced in the selection of officers, the majority of whom were versed in some particular field of scientific investigation.[1] How heavily such qualifications weighed with the Admiralty, may be guessed from the following extract from a letter by Captain Fitzjames, who was interested in the appointment of the surgeon to the *Erebus*: 'Bradford is just the man for the work, being active and energetic, a capital shot, and a pleasant fellow. But he is no "–ologist". He can't stuff birds, give long names to slimy things, or put moss in blottingpaper. However if I have a choice, he is the man.'"

Apparently Fitzjames didn't have a choice. Gibson added, "With such scientific deficiencies outside his profession Bradford did not receive the appointment."[2] Important areas of expertise were oceanography, geodesy, terrestrial magnetism, botany, ornithology, geology, and marine biology.

While it was standard for such expeditions to carry out scientific studies along the way, Franklin's instructions were to do so only in so far as it didn't interfere with the main purpose of his voyage — traversing the Passage. Why then this emphasis on scientific expertise over Arctic experience? Of the officers, only four had been through Arctic waters before. Lieutenant Graham Gore had been on George Back's ill-fated voyage through Hudson's Strait, which ended with the *Terror* barely making it back to the Irish coast. Any knowledge he could have gained during that voyage would hardly have been helpful during the present one.

The two Greenland ice masters both had prior experience. In fact, Thomas Blanky had sailed with John Ross during his visit to Boothia Peninsula, when James Clark Ross visited King William Island, ostensibly for the first time. If James Clark Ross did discover something (or rather, rediscover) on the island, did Blanky know? It would certainly explain his presence on this expedition. Indeed, if Franklin's true purpose was to reach King William Island, rather than to complete the Passage, he would have needed someone on board who could guide him to his target. Was Blanky that guide?

FRANCIS CROZIER'S PREMONITION

Apart from these three, one other officer had experience in Arctic waters. He was Francis Crozier, captain of the *Terror* and thus Franklin's second-in-command. Crozier had not been aboard the *Victory* during John Ross' second expedition, so there is no definite connection between him and King William Island. On the other hand, Crozier was a close friend with James Clark Ross, having sailed with him on all of Parry's voyages. When James Ross travelled to Antarctica, Crozier was his second-in-command and the two of them were close friends with Franklin, having spent time at Franklin's former home in Van Diemen's Land (now the Australian state of Tasmania) both before and after their voyages to the Antarctic. More important, Crozier had been midshipman aboard the *Hecla* during Parry's third voyage when the *Fury* was supposedly lost at Fury Beach.

If Ross really did make a sledge trip to King William Island during Parry's third expedition, Crozier was there as well. And, whatever happened to the *Fury*, Crozier was there to witness it.

This may explain Crozier's feelings regarding his most recent expedition. Other than John Ross, Crozier seems to have been the only one to feel any doubt about the success of the present mission. In a letter written to James Clark Ross, Crozier made a comment that is oddly suggestive in the present context. He wrote that he was afraid the expedition would "make a second 1824 of it."[3] This was a reference to Parry's third expedition and the loss of the *Fury*. Yet according to Parry's account, the *Fury* wasn't lost until the second year of that expedition, in 1825. In 1824, they were supposedly safely wintering on the *east* side of Prince Regent Inlet.

Indeed, Pierre Berton noted, "If one navy wife, Lady Belcher, is to be believed, Crozier told a fellow officer that he didn't expect to come back."[4]

CHAPTER SIX

The Ghost and Lady Franklin

The ghost of Roger Casement
Is beating on the door.
W.B.Yeats,
The Ghost of Roger Casement

JANE FRANKLIN

Early in 1847, John Ross approached the Admiralty for permission to embark on a rescue mission that summer, just as he had promised Franklin he would. The Admiralty, however, refused to let him go. It was convinced, so it said, that there was no possibility the expedition had run into trouble. Ross kept up the pressure, trying again and again to convince his superiors that something had to be done that summer — another year might be too late. A lonely voice crying in the wilderness, he went to the Royal Society, but they too refused to support him in his cause. Confidently, the Admiralty stated that they "have as yet felt no apprehensions about [Franklin's] safety," but conceded that "if no accounts of him should arrive by the end of this year, or, as Sir John Ross expects, at an earlier period, active steps must be taken."[1] With nowhere else to turn, Ross contacted Franklin's wife, Lady Jane Franklin, and told her of his concerns and desire to go in search of the expedition.

Ross could never have imagined then the part that Jane Franklin would soon play in the search for her lost husband. She would become an unstoppable force in her all-consuming drive and devotion to the cause, becoming a mythic heroine in the eyes of the contemporary public, thereby inscribing her own name in the annals of history alongside that of her husband. In an age where women were expected to mind their place, Jane Franklin pitted herself against the full might of the British Admiralty in her unceasing endeavour, forcing them to mount search after search where they would have let the matter rest, and organizing her own expeditions to search where they would not. And, when the bodies were finally found on the bleak western shore of King William Island, it was not one of the many navy expeditions that accomplished the task. It was a voyage organized by Lady Franklin.

Everywhere but the right place

As we will see, it is difficult not to see a darker intent behind the Admiralty's inability to find the lost expedition. How else to explain the astonishing fact that in the eleven years of searching virtually every single island was explored in the Arctic except the right one?

When the *Erebus* and *Terror* entered the Arctic in 1845, little was known about the Arctic islands. Through the overland expeditions of Franklin, Richardson, Dease, and Simpson, it was known that a strait existed along the roof of the Canadian mainland, but no one had yet crossed this strait. Only headlands had been spotted to the north. They were assumed to be separate islands. In fact, they were part of one giant land mass, later to be called Victoria Island. Far to the north, during his amazing voyage of 1819, Edward Parry had crossed in a straight line from east to west discovering Lancaster Sound, Barrow Strait, and Viscount Melville Sound all in one trip. Along the north side of his passage Parry had spotted many different shores, but to the south he had sighted only a single feature, which he named Cape Walker. He assumed Cape Walker was the northwestern corner of Somerset Island, with a wide bay to the east. In fact, Cape Walker was the northern tip of Prince of Wales Island and the "bay" to the east was Peel Sound — the passage which, it would later be deduced, Franklin had actually taken in his doomed voyage to King William Island.

But to the west of Cape Walker, Parry had not seen anything until he had run up against the impenetrable ice stream in Viscount Melville Sound. There, in the distance, he had spotted another shore almost dead ahead, which he called Banks Land. So, between Cape Walker in the east and Banks Land in the west, then south to the passage along the roof of the mainland, all was *terra incognita* — a giant unknown rectangle. Everything farther north was equally unknown territory. Finally, everything beyond Banks Land was also a blank.

Throughout the years of searching for the lost expedition, these areas were filled in — piece by piece, strait by strait, island by island. It was an incredible achievement: they looked everywhere but the right place. Such ineptitude surely stretches credulity. Still, hindsight is 20/20 and the Arctic is, after all, very big. It may seem unfair to be suspicious of the Admiralty simply because they were spectacularly unlucky. And so it might be, were it not for one damning fact.

From the beginning the searchers knew where to look.

FRANKLIN'S ORDERS

Franklin's sailing orders had been specific. He was to reach Cape Walker, then travel south and west by whatever passages might turn up [see map 7]. In short, he was to attempt to find a route between Parry's Passage in the north and the Passage along the roof of the mainland by travelling through the unknown rectangle between the two. He was to start this search at Cape Walker.

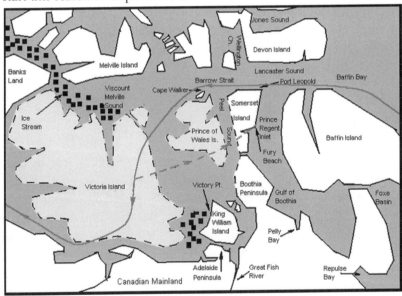

Map 7
Franklin's sailing orders to find a route southwest of Cape Walker

Indeed, it was to the southwest of Cape Walker that Jane Franklin felt certain her husband had gone. Her husband's orders had been explicit. If there was any way to carry them out, he would have done so. Initially, others also argued that this was the first place to look — southwest of Cape Walker.

At the same time, some argued that the search should concentrate on neighbouring Boothia Peninsula. It was believed that if Franklin's expedition really had been forced to abandon the ships anywhere within the unknown rectangle beyond Cape Walker, the crewmen would almost certainly attempt to reach Parry's cache of provisions at Fury Beach. From that point, like John Ross, they could hitch a ride home on a whaler.

But Jane Franklin's certainty was stronger than anyone else's. When the navy later changed the area of search, she remained determined that this was where her husband would be found and the ships that she herself sent out were directed to search this area.

Why was she so certain, when everyone told her she was wrong? If, as we have argued, the search for the Northwest Passage was merely what, in a later time, would be called a "cover story", and if Franklin was secretly instructed to go to Victory Point on King William Island, it is fair to wonder: did Jane Franklin know?

Obviously, as his wife it wouldn't be strange if she had known of his true mission. But, on the other hand, later in the search Jane Franklin did momentarily falter in her conviction, which would suggest that she had not been taken into his confidence.

Why then her certainty?

A GHOST?

Surely one of the strangest stories told about the Franklin tragedy concerns a little Irish girl named Louisa (or "Weasy") Coppin. In May 1849, at the age of four years, Weasy Coppin passed away from gastric fever. A short time later, according to Weasy's shipbuilder father Captain Coppin, the little girl began making ghostly appearances to his three eldest surviving children, and especially to his ten-year-old daughter, Anne — appearances sometimes in the form of a sort of bluish light, other times merely as a presence felt but not seen. The ghostly Weasy apparently communicated with the children by writing on the walls. During one of these strange visitations, the ghost printed: "Mr Mckay is dead." Mr. Mckay was a banker and a friend of the family. Worried by this message, they inquired the next day and were horrified to learn that Mr. Mckay had indeed been found dead that morning, having died in his sleep.

Impressed by this blue light's powers of revelation, an aunt had sister Anne ask the spectre about the whereabouts of Franklin and his men. Immediately Anne was possessed of a remarkable vision, in which she saw spread out on the floor before her "a complete Arctic scene, showing two ships, surrounded by ice and almost covered with snow, including a channel that led to the ships."[2] According to the Reverend Skewes, who later brought the story into the open, "The 'revelation', as if an actual Arctic reality, made [Anne] shiver with cold, and in consequence to clutch the dress of her aunt. This scene in the form of a chart and with much taste [Anne] immediately drew."[3] Anne's chart was particularly impressive since "as far as the father knew, his child had never seen a chart, much less drawn one." But this was not the end of the remarkable vision, as moments later ghostly handwriting appeared on the wall of the room "in large round-hand letters about three inches in length". The message read: "Erebus and Terror. Sir John Franklin, Lancaster Sound, Prince Regent Inlet, Victory Point, Victoria Channel."

If true, the story is astonishing. To specifically pinpoint Victory Point was positively uncanny. As we have seen, Victory Point was the headland which James Clark Ross reached after leaving the rest of his sledge party at Cape Felix on King William Island. More importantly, it would later be found that it was indeed at Victory Point that the crews of the *Erebus* and *Terror* had reached the shore after abandoning their ships in the icy clutches of Victoria Strait (Channel).

How can we possibly explain the improbable accuracy of the ghostly vision given to Anne Coppin?

Assuming we discount the existence of a real ghostly Weasy, a possibility suggests itself. After all, we have supposed that Franklin's real mission was to reach Victory Point, to find and study whatever it was James Clark Ross had seen there during Parry's third voyage and John Ross' second. Inevitably others must have known about Franklin's true mission. The Admiralty may have done all it could to keep the real purpose of the expedition secret, but leaks occur. Is it possible that the children's father, Captain Coppin, had learned of Franklin's mission through channels of his own? If so, surely he would have known that he could never come right out with his information. Who would have believed him? And what would the Admiralty do if they found out?

But then Captain Coppin saw another way. After all, though the testimony of blue lights may seem suspect in our time, it bore much more weight with the public of the mid-nineteenth century. Just the year before the Coppin children saw their vision, across the ocean in the town of Rochester, New York, two young sisters ushered in an era of seances and paranormal visitations that, to some extent, has continued to the present day. They were known as the Fox sisters and they claimed to be able to communicate with the dead through "spirit rappings" — quite literally, the spirits used a sort of Morse code to answer the questions of the living. To Captain Coppin, in possession of a terrible secret he didn't dare openly reveal, the sudden interest in messages from beyond the grave (particularly through the medium of innocent young girls) may have seemed like a godsend. Respected people believed in the Fox sisters, so why not his daughter? It was, after all, Captain Coppin who went to Jane Franklin with this fabulous story. And it was largely owing to this ghostly revelation that Jane Franklin alone sought to search in the correct place, when all the experts assured her Franklin would not be found there.

Of course, there is no proof Captain Coppin had inside knowledge that he sought to reveal through a fabricated story. But the facts remain: Captain Coppin assured Jane Franklin that the lost expedition would be found at Victory Point, and at Victory Point it was found. If we do not believe Franklin was secretly headed for Victory Point, if Captain Coppin was not possessed of special knowledge, then how else are we to explain his daughter's vision?

Ghosts?

Part II
By Unworthy Motives

Outward be fair, however foul within;
Sin if thou wilt, but then in secret sin.
Charles Churchill,
Night

CHAPTER SEVEN

The Deception of James Ross Clark

What cannot a neat knave with a smooth tale
Make a woman believe?
                    John Webster,
                    The Duchess of Malfi

THE ARCTIC COUNCIL

It was now 1848. The ghost of Captain Coppin's daughter would not produce her amazingly accurate vision for another two years. The Franklin expedition had been missing for three winters. Already convinced something had gone wrong, John Ross had been fighting since early the previous year, writing letters to the First Sea Lord of the Admiralty, to the Royal Society, to the Royal Geographical Society, even to the council of the Astronomical Society. At every turn, he was told his concerns for the expedition were premature; the Admiralty had consulted its Arctic experts and had no plans to send out a relief expedition.

Its Arctic experts.

If there is to be a villain in this story, it is to be found among this extremely exclusive, tight-knit group of worthies. Later they would be known unofficially as the Arctic Council. Sometimes they were simply called the "Arctics". The membership of this group was never entirely static, although certain names remained fairly constant throughout the years of the Franklin search — notably, John Ross' nephew, James Clark Ross. How one qualified for membership was fairly vague. Some, like James Clark Ross, had spent time exploring in the Arctic. Others had amassed a sort of honourary expertise though overseeing previous expeditions from the comfort of London. John Ross' former companion, Parry, was a member.

John Ross was not.

He was, in a sense, the father of the modern era of Arctic exploration through that first aborted expedition in 1818. His 1829 (unsanctioned) expedition aboard the *Victory* had spent four full winters on the east coast of Boothia Peninsula without the loss of a single life — a claim no one else could come close to matching. To the public, John Ross was an Arctic hero in the truest sense of the word. Long after the world had given him up for dead, he had come sailing out of the darkness and the ice aboard the whaler *Isabella*, as miraculous a comeback as anyone could have asked for. (More amazing still: as if to fully erase the stain on his career left from his first voyage, the ship that rescued Ross and his crew was the same *Isabella* that he had been sailing when he spotted the imaginary mountain range so long before.) He was as knowledgeable on the topic of the Northwest Passage as anyone could hope to be. Yet, incredibly, he was not included in the sacred circle of the Arctic Council.

The council acted as the official advisors to the Admiralty. At the same time, their opinions were freely given to Jane Franklin — perhaps too freely. The fact that this group — especially James Clark Ross — had Lady Franklin's ear, while John Ross most certainly did not, led John Ross to develop an almost paranoid sense of persecution, even the belief in a conspiracy. At one point he wrote: "The individuals most to be pitied ... were the amiable lady and daughter of Sir John Franklin whose minds had been deceived by the unworthy conduct of their advisors."[1]

Unworthy? Just what precisely was Ross trying to suggest?

JOHN ROSS' DECEPTION?

During his initial push for a relief expedition, it was John Ross' contention that he believed Franklin had intended to "put his ships into the drift ice at the western end of Cornwallis or Melville Island"[2] [see map 8]. As Ross reminded the Admiralty: this was the same ice which had stopped Parry in his first extremely successful voyage and this supposed plan was precisely what Parry had decided should *not* be done at that time. But did Ross really believe this was what Franklin had intended?

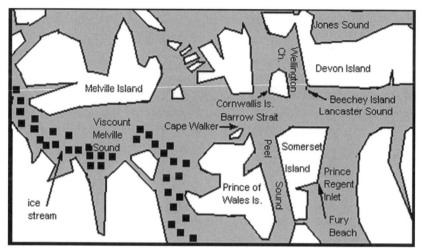

Map 8
The Ice west of Melville Island?

Franklin's orders were explicit: he was to enter Lancaster Sound, then sail through Barrow Strait, "not to examine any channels leading northwards or southwards from Barrow Strait," then, on reaching the longitude of Cape Walker (which was directly north of King William Island) he was to "steer to the southward and westward towards Bering Strait" by whatever path he could manage through whatever lands might lie in that unknown quarter.[3] His orders said nothing about putting in the ice westward of Melville Island. Indeed, to even reach Melville Island Franklin would have had to travel considerably past Cape Walker.

In fact, the very next clause in Franklin's orders stated that, "This route offers the best prospect of discovering a North-West Passage because the ice seen at Cape Dundas, Melville Island appeared to be fixed and very heavy." Either Ross believed Franklin had intended to disobey his orders even before leaving England or Ross was making the whole thing up — the only excuse he could think of to explain his desperate fear for the safety of the expedition.

If it was merely a fabrication it was a good one, for it also gave him ammunition in battling his nemesis nephew.

John Ross was outraged when he learned that the Admiralty's sole response to the absence of any word from the expedition was to offer a twenty-thousand-pound reward to any whalers or members of the Hudson's Bay Company who might offer assistance to

Franklin and his crew. He claimed such an "inefficient [tactic] must have been suggested by unworthy motives, for Sir [James] C. Ross is one of those officers who, in Parry's expedition, was then of the opinion [that entering the ice westward of Melville Island] was imprudent".[4] Again, that odd word, "unworthy". What possible motive could his nephew have had for purposely stalling the salvation of Franklin's expedition?

THE NAVY ACTS

Still, not even the Royal Navy could stall forever. In January of 1848, while Franklin was spending his third winter lost in the Arctic, a ship by the name of *Plover* was dispatched to travel around Cape Horn into the Pacific Ocean and enter the Arctic from the opposite side. The *Plover*'s goal was to search along the northern coast of the continent in case Franklin had gotten that far.

In March, a second expedition was dispatched, this one travelling overland, up the Mackenzie River to explore Victoria Land — a piece of ground located precisely in the southwest path that Franklin would have taken (had he truly been seeking a Northwest Passage), but known only by glimpses of its southern headlands.

Finally, in June a third expedition was sent, this one to follow in Franklin's tracks, entering the Arctic from the east. Though John Ross had advised the use of four small ships (since he had done so well with the tiny *Victory*), this expedition planned to search using two vessels, *Enterprise* and *Investigator*, both even larger than Franklin's *Erebus* and *Terror*. John Ross was probably not surprised when he learned who would command the expedition. Having rescinded his former promise never to return north again, James Clark Ross now set out to rescue Franklin.

JAMES CLARK ROSS TAKES HIS TIME

James Ross' official orders were extremely general. Historian (and Franklin descendant) Roderic Owen observed, "Their brief was so extensive as to be all but meaningless."[5] This was particularly odd, for enough trouble had already arisen interpreting Franklin's specific orders; what would they have done if James Clark Ross had disappeared as well? It would seem the Admiralty wished to give John Ross' nephew plenty of room to manoeuvre. And manoeuvre he did.

Though he carried enough provisions for four years (three years for his crew and an extra for Franklin's crew should he find them), upon reaching Greenland James Clark Ross abruptly sent back word that he would order the *Investigator* back to England if he found he had to spend even two winters in the Arctic. Things did not improve after that.

The ships had been inexplicably late in the season before even setting out from England. After entering Baffin Bay, they were first towed through loose streams of ice, then hindered by light winds until, in the words of historian Samuel Schmucker, "the season had so far advanced as to preclude every hope of accomplishing much, if anything, before the setting in of winter."[6] Battling their way through the ice in Baffin Bay, Ross searched for signs of the lost expedition along the west coast of Greenland, then headed into Lancaster Sound [see map 9]. Running into heavy ice near Leopold Island at the entrance to Prince Regent Inlet, Ross decided to explore the

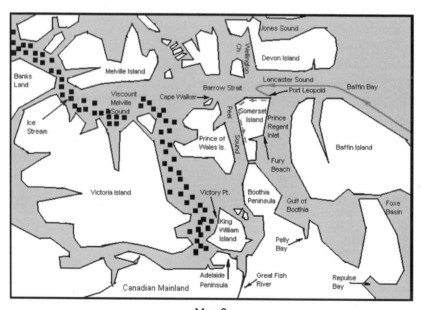

Map 9
James Clark Ross's Search, 1848–1849

north shores of Barrow Strait, travelling as far as Wellington Channel, before again being turned back by ice and finally managing to force his way into Port Leopold.

It was James Clark Ross' claim that "so great a quantity of ice was never before seen in Barrow's Strait at this period of the season."[7] Perhaps, but Ross' uncle later countered, "A witness ... stated that on the 11th September, the day on which the ships entered the harbour, Regent Inlet was perfectly clear of ice."[8] Why then had James Clark Ross not tried to reach Fury Beach, where Parry's provisions from the vanished *Fury* had already served to save the two Rosses? It was widely believed that Franklin, if beset southwest of Cape Walker, would surely try to reach the cache at Fury beach, hoping to hitch a ride with whalers in Barrow Strait just as John Ross had. James Clark Ross himself held to this theory. So why didn't he continue on down Prince Regent Inlet? Once frozen in at Port Leopold, another winter would pass before Ross would get around to checking out Fury Beach by sled. If by chance the Franklin survivors had been there, they might easily have perished in the interim — a result that could hardly have endeared James Clark Ross to the anxiously awaiting public back home.

FURY BEACH, SLEDS AND LEOPOLD McCLINTOCK

Once stuck at Port Leopold, nothing more could be done until the sun rose again in the spring. Perhaps significantly, James Clark Ross seemed oddly bothered by his final voyage to the Arctic. As Pierre Berton put it, "he was no longer the energetic officer who had enlivened the crew of his uncle's *Victory*."[9] Clements Markham, who knew Ross, thought he was "somewhat shaken" by his explorations in the Antarctic.[10] Possibly. But it had been after his voyage with his uncle to this same coastline and his visit to Victory Point that he had vowed never to come north again. Is it not more likely that he was "somewhat shaken" by something he saw on that expedition — something which continued to haunt his dreams all through the long, black winter months of his return?

Ross was not entirely inactive during those winter months, however. The crew trapped foxes alive. Copper collars were fixed around the necks of these animals, bearing the locations of the ships and of caches of provisions placed along the coast. The foxes were then released in the hopes that Franklin's crew might catch them for food. One suspects the procedure can hardly have been healthy for the unfortunate foxes.

Finally, in April 1849 (Franklin now having spent four full winters in the Arctic, assuming he was even still alive), Ross set to work. With a party of thirteen men, he followed the north coast of Somerset, working his way westward. His reasoning seemed fair enough: as Franklin had been ordered to travel to Cape Walker and then turn southwest, Ross felt Cape Walker was the first place to check for a sign of the expedition. While Ross was away, Captain E.J. Bird, who was in charge of the sister ship *Investigator*, sent out three other expeditions: one to do what Ross should have done long ago — check the supply cache at Fury Beach. Since Ross was the commander of the expedition, it isn't clear why Captain Bird should have been the one to dispatch the other search parties. Was Bird acting under Ross' orders or was he acting on his own?

Accompanying Ross on his overland search was an officer who would play an extremely pivotal role in the drama yet to unfold: Lieutenant Francis Leopold McClintock. In light of his later importance, it is ironic he was only on this voyage because he was friends with Ross' friend William Smythe. But his presence on this sled trip with Ross immediately raises an important question: how much did McClintock know?

Based on his later behaviour, there is every reason to believe McClintock was totally free of those "unworthy motives" which John Ross had imputed to so many others. If there was a conspiracy to keep Sir John Franklin from being found, it is unlikely McClintock was a party to it. But how then to explain his participation in this sledge trip? If the party had happened upon any messages left by the Franklin expedition, there could have been no way of keeping them hidden from McClintock — or could there?

In his book, *The Fate of Franklin*, Roderic Owen described how, "The drill was for him [James Clark Ross] to walk along the shore some distance ahead, whilst Lieutenant McClintock led the sledges."[11] Had they happened upon any messages left in cairns by Franklin, it would have been a simple matter for Ross to conceal such messages before McClintock arrived with the rest of the party. And, if Ross had happened upon something too large to hide (bodies, for example), he could easily have returned to the sledge party and led them away from the site, under some quickly concocted excuse. The absence of messages left by the Franklin expedition would be a refrain heard again and again throughout the many years of searching. It was inconceivable that Franklin would not have left records behind to indicate where he planned to go, and yet, other than one record dropped in the ocean before reaching Greenland, the only message ever recovered was the note (actually two, but they were duplicates) left on King William Island at the very end of their journey. Cairns were found, constructed by Franklin's crew to hold messages, yet they were always found to be empty. Repeatedly the searchers would find themselves amazed and bewildered by this absence of messages, completely at a loss to explain it. But, they were not so suspicious as John Ross; it never occurred to them that someone might be deliberately stealing the messages.

That season James Clark Ross and his party trudged westward across the north shore of Somerset Island. Or perhaps one should more properly say "struggled": further suspicions must be aroused by Ross' strange decision to use man-hauled sledges on this trip, rather than dogs, which he had employed with such success on his trip here aboard the *Victory* (including his journey to Victory Point). Expecting men to pull massive sledges across the ice and snow is not only much slower than using dogs, but it was also guaranteed to wear down the party's strength much faster. It was almost as if James Clark Ross deliberately set out to limit the range of his explorations.

WHAT ABOUT CAPE WALKER?

On reaching the northwest corner of Somerset Island, James Clark Ross could see across the wide entrance of Peel Sound all the way to Cape Walker. Of course, Ross still thought he was looking across a wide bay at this point. Yet again, his actions remain puzzling. Cape Walker was possibly the most important place to search for a message left by Franklin, since it had been specifically mentioned in his sailing orders. He was to reach Cape Walker then steer southwest by whatever passages he could find. Surely he would have left a note there.

Yet, incredibly, Ross decided not to cross the ice to Cape Walker. Instead, he turned south and began following the west coast of Somerset along the edge of Peel Sound (which now revealed itself to be a sound rather than a bay). Finally, "having consumed more than half our provisions, and the strength of the party being much reduced" (not surprising, considering the use of man-hauled sledges), Ross returned to the ships having accomplished almost nothing.[12] The party dispatched by Captain Bird to the cache at Fury Beach had likewise encountered no sign of the missing expedition. Ross' entire party was ravaged by the rigors of their journey, all being put on the sick list except McClintock who, like Ross, was not required to actually pull the sledge.

JAMES CLARK ROSS' CONCLUSIONS

Ross now came to two startling conclusions concerning the lost expedition — conclusions that would do incalculable damage to later searches. First, having found Peel Sound to be completely frozen over, he concluded Franklin could never have passed south that way. As Pierre Berton commented, "Astonishingly, in spite of all his Arctic experience, Ross didn't appear to realize that a channel could be frozen one year, open the next."[13]

Ross' second and even more damaging conclusion was that "It is hardly possible they [the lost expedition] can be anywhere to the eastward of Melville Island or within 300 miles of Leopold Island [where Ross spent the winter] for if that were the case they would ... have made their way to that point with the hope of receiving assistance from whale-ships."[14] In other words, Ross was voicing the same opinion which others had held: Franklin, if trapped in the ice southwest of Cape Walker, would try to reach the east coast of Somerset and hitch a ride with the whalers of Barrow Strait. The fact that there had been no sign of Franklin at Fury Beach proved Franklin could not be southwest of Cape Walker. But, if Ross was so convinced of this, why had he waited the entire winter before dispatching someone to check the cache at Fury Beach, where Franklin would have gone?

Ross concluded that Franklin, unable to follow his orders to travel southwest past Cape Walker, had then taken the secondary route by going north up Wellington Channel, as his orders permitted. It was not an entirely unreasonable hypothesis. In fact, ironically enough, Ross was right. Evidence would soon indicate that Franklin had indeed been unable to pass Cape Walker during his first winter and so had travelled up Wellington Channel, before returning for a second try. But, on the basis of the evidence then available to him, Ross had no right to make such a sweeping conclusion.

Even ignoring the possibility that Peel Sound might not be forever frozen, Ross had not bothered to visit Cape Walker where a message might have been left. More importantly, Ross did not even attempt to search to the southwest of Cape Walker where Franklin was ordered to go. If he had, he would have discovered another channel there. Instead, he concluded Franklin could not be southwest of Cape Walker purely on the basis of indirect (and negative) evidence. It did not seem to cross his mind that Franklin's expedition might have perished before they could reach Fury Beach.

We cannot overestimate the damage caused by Ross' conclusions. It was on the basis of his views that the entire search to be conducted by the Admiralty abandoned the area where Franklin had been ordered to go, and instead concentrated all its efforts on Wellington Channel and areas west of Melville Island. We cannot help but wonder if this was the whole purpose of James Clark Ross' expedition — to misdirect any future searches.

KEYSTONE COPS

On August 28, the crew managed to saw a channel through the ice and the two ships left Port Leopold. But very quickly they found themselves stuck in the ice of Barrow Strait and Ross feared they would be forced to spend a second winter in the Arctic (a strange fear given that he had been expected to spend three winters there). But, amazingly, the ice steadily carried the ships back out of Lancaster Sound into Baffin Bay, then southward along the coast of Baffin Island, before finally breaking up and allowing them to return to England.

Ironically, even as James Clark Ross' expedition was being carried down the west side of Baffin Bay, another ship was similarly trapped in the ice on the opposite side of the bay along the coast of Greenland. This ship was the *North Star*, an "old sailing-donkey of a frigate" sent out by the Admiralty and loaded with provisions for Ross' expedition precisely to prevent him from returning home after only a single winter.[15] While it was the Admiralty's decision to dispatch the *North Star* upon the advice of the Arctic Council, it doesn't take much to see Jane Franklin's influence at work.

If the Admiralty had hoped to sweep the Franklin expedition under a rug, it did not reckon with Sir John's wife. We can imagine how she reacted when she learned of James Clark Ross' letter from Upernavik, Greenland, in which he stated his intention to send the sister ship, *Investigator,* home should he have to spend even a second winter in the North. We must remember that Franklin's expedition was believed to have provisions for only three winters. In a pinch he could have stretched this out to four winters, the same amount of time as John Ross' record-setting stay in the Arctic. James Clark Ross' first winter was Franklin's fourth. If Ross returned to England, yet one more winter must pass (Franklin's fifth!) before another expedition could be dispatched. So, while other expeditions might be sent to discover Franklin's fate, James Clark Ross alone stood any chance of actually rescuing the lost expedition while they were still alive. Later would certainly be too late.

Jane Franklin undoubtedly realized this, and she may have had her own suspicions regarding the Admiralty's sincerity in searching for her husband. She was not about to wait dutifully for James Clark Ross to return. Contacting the ambassador of the Imperial Russian government in London, she secured a promise that Russia would send out search parties from the Asiatic side of the Arctic. Then she wrote to the President of the United States. After describing the steps taken by the British to find the lost expedition, she wrote, "I have entered into these details with the view of proving that, though the British government has not forgotten the duty it owes to the brave men whom it has sent on a perilous service, and has spent a very large sum in providing the means for their rescue, yet that, owing to various causes, the means in operation for this purpose are quite inadequate to meet the extreme exigence of the case."[16] Was she suspicious? Probably no more so than anyone might be when faced with obvious bureaucratic bungling and indifference.

But now, with both Russia and the United States taking an interest in Franklin's fate, the Admiralty had little choice but to make at least a token effort to prolong Ross' search in the Arctic. And so the *North Star* was sent on May 15, 1849.

Perhaps we should not be too surprised by what happened next. Not only did the *North Star* fail to catch up with Ross, it failed even to reach Lancaster Sound — something that only one other search vessel did (or didn't do) during all the years of later searching. On September 25th, Ross was freed from the ice and immediately set sail back to England. Four days later, far to the north, the *North Star* put into winter quarters on the coast of Greenland. The Keystone Cops could not have done it better.

Adding to the sense of farce, the Admiralty had announced a second reward of 10,000 pounds, this one to any ship which might discover evidence of Franklin's fate. But, typically, the reward was announced after all the whalers had set out from England, so no one actually knew about it. Thus, as the long dark winter drew closer — Franklin's fifth — not one ship remained to look for him in all the vast eastern Arctic. The Admiralty could not have done a worse job of finding the lost expedition if it had tried.

CHAPTER EIGHT

The Turning of Captain Forsyth

Out flew the web and floated wide;
The mirror crack'd from side to side;
"The curse has come upon me," cried
The Lady of Shalott.
> Alfred, Lord Tennyson,
> *The Lady of Shalott*

TOO CONTEMPTIBLE TO INVITE CRITICISM

That winter, Jane Franklin again wrote to the American President: "A period has now, alas, arrived when our dearest hopes as to the safe return of the discovery ships this autumn are finally crushed by the unexpected, though forced return of Sir James Ross."[1]

It was a cry from the heart. She had allowed James Clark Ross to guide her in her decisions; she had listened to him against the advice of his uncle, John Ross; she had believed that, if any man would find her husband, it was he. His betrayal must have devastated her.

But others were considerably less contained in their criticisms. We have already read of John Ross' accusation that Prince Regent Inlet was still open the day his nephew put into winter quarters. Even more vehement were the opinions of Dr. Richard King. Dr. King had travelled with George Back on a historic journey up the Great Fish River (later called Back's River), which had led them to the top of the Canadian mainland just below King William Island (undiscovered at that point). Dr. King had long been an opponent of sea voyages in search of the Northwest Passage, arguing that the job could have been done much more safely by a handful of men travelling overland. It was also his belief that, no matter where Franklin might be stuck in the ice, the best way to reach the expedition would be by the Great Fish River. If this latter suggestion had been followed, the expedition would have been found. But Dr. King, despite his experience, was in the same boat as John Ross — he was outside the charmed circle of the Arctic Council and no one listened to him.

Still, that didn't stop him from expressing his opinions in no uncertain terms. Of James Clark Ross' expedition he snarled, "By an extraordinary amount of delay, hitherto unaccounted for, he lost the chances offered by his first season, and in his second season his puny efforts ... are too contemptible to invite criticism."[2] Echoing John Ross' cries in the wilderness, King baldly stated that James Clark Ross "can have no intention of searching for Sir John Franklin."

Jane Franklin's William Penny?

In spite of such harsh criticism, the ball game seemed to be over. Franklin, wherever he was, was almost certainly dead. What point was there in continuing the search? The Admiralty must have heaved a sigh of relief. But, again, they had not anticipated the perseverance of Jane Franklin.

No sooner was James Clark Ross back in England than Jane Franklin set to work. Having been so thoroughly betrayed by those she had thought she could trust, she now sought help outside the navy and her former advisors. She approached a whaling captain named William Penny — a man of impeccable credentials, a colourful old salt, respected by one and all. He agreed to search for her husband, refusing even to accept payment. Lady Franklin planned to pay for the expedition using her own finances. Whether the Admiralty liked it or not, she was going to find her husband. The navy did the only thing it could: it made her an offer she couldn't refuse. The Admiralty agreed to pay for the expedition and to allow the use of two of its ships. Jane Franklin foolishly — though understandably — accepted. After all, she wasn't made of money. But now her independent expedition was effectively under the control of the same people who had betrayed her before. It was only through her strenuous efforts that she was able to ensure that Captain Penny remained in command.

Finally, Lady Franklin's American correspondence bore fruit. Henry Grinnell, a wealthy New York merchant, agreed to outfit two vessels to enter the Arctic in search of Franklin. John Ross too, no doubt feeling grimly vindicated, was chaffing at the bit. He had refused retirement back before James Clark Ross' expedition in the hopes that he might be sent out to rescue Franklin. Now he persistently hounded the Admiralty, fighting for a command, always insisting he believed Franklin to be beset around Melville Island. In the end, rebuked at every turn, he had no choice but to again outfit a private expedition, funded by public subscription and the Hudson's Bay Company. From the Admiralty's point of view, it was rapidly losing control of the situation. It responded with its guns blazing.

Along with Captain Penny's expedition, it now proposed to refit the two ships used by James Clark Ross, sending them to the Pacific Ocean to enter the Arctic from the opposite side (which it had already done with the *Plover* — from which no word had yet been received). Then, in a spectacular feat of one-upmanship, it agreed to dispatch an expedition of no less than four ships, under the command of Captain Austin, all to enter the Arctic from the east. To an outside observer, everything that could be done was being done.

JANE FRANKLIN TRIES AGAIN

But Jane Franklin was not so certain.

Having foolishly allowed herself to lose control of Penny's expedition, she now set out to organize *another* private voyage. This time, the Admiralty would not take it away from her. To command the voyage she secured the services of a friend from her days in Van Diemen's Land, Commander Charles Codrington Forsyth. He was, of course, in the service of the Royal Navy, so we may wonder what made her think she could trust him after her previous experiences. But she may have felt she knew him well enough. On the other hand, the fact that she chose as his second-in-command a civilian named Parker Snow, may indicate that she was not entirely comfortable even with Captain Forsyth.

The purpose of the expedition was ostensibly to act as an aid to the government ships. But, in actual fact, it had a far more telling goal —

made clear in the prospectus used to encourage public funds. It was to travel to Prince Regent Inlet and search Somerset Island (and Fury Beach) for signs of the lost expedition. Here we may see some indication of her true suspicions regarding her former advisor, James Clark Ross. She was sending her own ship to go over exactly the same ground as Ross had covered only two years before. Ross can hardly have been pleased.

The need for a search of this area arose because of the behaviour of the other searchers. Now that the Navy controlled Penny, it ordered him to ignore Lancaster Sound altogether and instead explore Jones Sound, located farther north up Baffin Bay. As a location for finding the lost expedition, Jones Sound was a very long shot indeed. By sending Penny there, the Admiralty might as well have told him to stay home. (The Americans were headed for Smith Sound at the northernmost top of Baffin Bay — an even more unlikely spot.)

As for the impressive group of four ships under Captain Austin, their orders were based entirely on the opinion of James Clark Ross: search Wellington Channel and Melville Island, as Franklin could not have gotten southwest of Cape Walker. With John Ross still insisting he believed Franklin had "put into" the ice off Melville Island, it was painfully clear to Jane Franklin that a vast section of the Arctic had been simply written off — the section where Franklin had been ordered to go.

In public, her reasons for searching this area were entirely sensible (although they sidestepped the thorny question of James Clark Ross having already been there). It was the same argument as had been advanced time and time again: if Franklin became stuck southwest of Cape Walker, he would try to reach Somerset because of the cache at Fury Beach and because it was his only hope of meeting with whalers. Jane Franklin also noted that her husband had carried a map with him that clearly showed a strait connecting the southern part of Prince Regent Inlet to the water on the west side of Boothia-Somerset. In actual fact, there was no strait because Boothia was really a peninsula, a fact that James Clark Ross had discovered from the Inuit during his visit there on his uncle's expedition. Many people, however, continued to doubt Ross' claim, as they doubted all evidence obtained from the Inuit. Franklin, though, had written his wife a letter in which he explicitly accepted Ross' findings. Still, there was always the possibility he might have changed his mind — particularly if faced with imminent starvation.

This was her public explanation for insisting on a search of this area. She could hardly have admitted her true reason.

FORSYTH'S SECOND THOUGHTS

It was at this point that Captain Coppin, having learned of Jane Franklin's privately outfitted expedition, first approached Lady Franklin with his incredible story of the ghostly Weasy seen by his daughter Anne. He seemed so certain of the truth of his daughter's vision, one might have been excused for thinking he had seen the apparition himself.

He set it out for Lady Franklin in no uncertain terms: Prince Regent Inlet, Victory Point. This was where Franklin would be found, he told her: his daughter's ghost had said so.

Did it occur to Jane Franklin that the captain's certainty might be caused by something other than a belief in visitations; that perhaps the whole thing was a clever means of revealing inside information without appearing to do so? It was certainly odd that Captain Coppin should have chosen to reveal his story to a private expedition, rather than one of the government ones. But then, by this point Jane Franklin had her own doubts about the Admiralty's sincerity. If she had any doubts about the reality of Captain Coppin's story, she kept them to herself.

She went to Captain Forsyth and told him all about the amazing vision. Prince Regent Inlet, she said. Victory Point. The captain's reaction was strange. When she first related the astonishing story, the captain was "much impressed" and she thought he was a believer. But then, the next day, inexplicably he had changed his mind, pooh-poohing the story as "more surprising than sensible".[3] What had served to change his mind over the course of twenty-four hours? Was this merely the result of sober second thoughts or were there darker influences at work? Based on Captain Forsyth's later actions, there is reason to believe that he, if not originally a party to the conspiracy, eventually became one. Is it possible Captain Forsyth already knew about Victory Point and — taken by surprise by how cleanly Jane Franklin's strange story seemed to hit the nail on the head — he reacted without thinking, revealing his amazement at her knowledge?

Then, the next day, perhaps after consulting with his superiors, had he tried to repair the damage?

Again, we may wonder if Jane Franklin saw anything suspicious in the captain's changed reaction. Though she claimed to hope his "original impressions" might revive with time, she must have had her doubts. Nevertheless, she hadn't chosen a civilian chief officer for nothing. She took her story to Parker Snow, who was also to serve as the ship's doctor, even though he wasn't a doctor. In an eerie midnight meeting entirely suited to her weird tale of ghostly writing, she laid out her haunting narrative. Snow's response was everything Jane Franklin had hoped for. Pleased with herself, she thought, "At all events I succeeded in making his [Forsyth's] Chief Officer, who ... will have great influence over Capt. Forsyth, deeply and seriously impressed with the facts revealed."[4] In the end, though, even Parker Snow's efforts would not be enough.

A TALE OF DEATH AND FIRE

In April, Captain Forsyth and Parker Snow set sail in the *Prince Albert*, a tiny clipper vessel of a mere ninety tons, built the year James Clark Ross had set out on his failed search. Their orders were to travel far down into Prince Regent Inlet past Fury Beach, and winter at Brentford Bay, from which they would send out search parties overland. Had Captain Forsyth succeeded in this plan, he would almost certainly have discovered the remains of the expedition on King William Island. At the very least, he would have received word of the lost ships from the Inuit at the bottom of Boothia Peninsula. Unfortunately, such was not to be the case.

The *Prince Albert* soon encountered the other British ships (Austin's four, Penny's two, and John Ross' two) in Baffin Bay off the west coast of Greenland. At this point, a startling incident occurred which, though only causing a small delay for the ships, continues to haunt historical accounts of the Franklin search like the ghost of Hamlet's father.

On August 13th, three ships — the *Assistance* and the *Intrepid* (two of the four Admiralty ships, the *Intrepid* being a stream-driven tender to the *Assistance*) under Captain Ommanney and John Ross' small schooner *Felix* — spotted three Inuit men on the ice near Cape York, Greenland. Ross dispatched his second-in-command, Phillips, in the ship's whaleboat, along with a native interpreter from Greenland named Adam Beck, to interview the Inuit. Unfortunately, though the Inuit apparently told Adam Beck something of tremendous importance, Beck could not relate the information since he could only translate into Danish! Ross had already continued on up the coast, so the searchers took Adam Beck over to Captain Forsyth's ship, where there was a steward who could translate for them.

The story that came out was astonishing. We will discuss Beck's tale more thoroughly later, but the upshot was this: apparently, two naval ships had been beset in the ice and crushed not far away along the Greenland coast in the winter of 1846. The ships were attacked by a fierce tribe, with some of the crew drowning and others being killed by darts and arrows. The ships had been set afire.

Considerable controversy erupted over this story at that time and again later. A second translator was found who proceeded to interview one Inuk, producing a completely different translation from Beck's, "whom, as we are told, he called a liar and intimidated into silence; though no sooner was the latter [Beck] left to himself than he again repeated his version of the tale, and stoutly maintained its accuracy."[5] It was learned at that time that the *North Star*, sent out with provisions for James Clark Ross' expedition, had spent the winter in the area and departed only the month before. Though it was generally thought the story had more to do with the *North Star* (a view still held by many historians) than with the lost expedition, ships were nonetheless dispatched to the area indicated by Beck's version of the story, Wolstenholme Island.

When nothing was found to support Beck's tale, he was viciously assailed from all sides, with only John Ross standing by his interpreter. Sherard Osborn, one of the searchers, voiced the general consensus when he said, "Adam Beck ... an Equimaux half-breed — may he be branded for a liar."[6] Ten years later, Charles Francis Hall, searching for relics of the Franklin disaster, encountered Beck in the north. Beck continued to insist he had told the truth, though by then he was emotionally ruined by his ordeal. When the final proof of the expedition's last days was discovered on King William Island, of course, no doubt remained. Either Beck had lied or, as

Pierre Berton wrote, "it was poppy-cock, a distorted rumour based on the death of a single member of the transport *North Star*."[7] It is difficult to imagine how a single "old sailing-donkey of a frigate" could multiply into a pair of three-masted naval vessels, nor how a single death could be turned into a massed assault involving darts and arrows. Still, we will have more to say about Adam Beck's amazing tale at a later time.

BETRAYAL OF THE BLACKEST HUE

Meanwhile, the little *Prince Albert* — Jane Franklin's ship — continued on course into Lancaster Sound. Reaching the mouth of Prince Regent Inlet, Captain Forsyth found heavy ice around Port Leopold (where James Ross had wintered). He sailed down into Prince Regent Inlet, just as Lady Franklin had instructed. But that was as good as it got. Approaching Fury Beach, the *Prince Albert* encountered more ice. Captain Forsyth decided nothing more could be done and promptly opted to return to England.

It was betrayal of the blackest hue.

There would be no winter at Brentford Bay, no sledge trips along the coast, no interviewing the Inuit. Jane Franklin had lavished a fortune of her own money on this expedition; she might just as well have flushed it down the loo. After Forsyth's strange about-face regarding her story about Captain Coppin's ghostly daughter, she had hoped his "original impressions" might revive; she had hoped in vain.[8] His was the only ship sent to search this area of the Arctic and now he prepared to turn around and sail home as if the mission entrusted to him by Lady Franklin had been no more than a passing fancy.

Jane Franklin may already have harboured some doubts about the captain's sincerity. She had reason enough to be wary of anyone attached to the Navy. She had seen to it that his chief officer was a civilian, Parker Snow. But, though she had hoped Snow might have a "great influence" over the captain, what influence he had wasn't enough. He begged Captain Forsyth to remain. He felt he could reach Fury Beach by ship's boat, then take up the search by sledge along the coast — just as they had promised Lady Franklin. But the captain insisted the ice was too heavy and Snow didn't feel competent enough to argue the point. As they returned back up Prince Regent Inlet, Snow must have been racked with a miserable sense of failure, remembering that eerie midnight meeting when Jane Franklin had told him of the ghostly vision: Victory Point... They were so close, and yet there was nothing he could do. In desperation, he suggested they might land at Port Leopold and search overland from that point. Predictably, they discovered that harbour still frozen as before.

DISCOVERY AT CAPE RILEY

Leaving Prince Regent Inlet, they met one of the American ships, *Advance*, also casting a discouraged eye over Port Leopold. By this point, all the search ships, American and British, were sailing in the waters of Lancaster Sound and Barrow Strait. Because of ice, the Americans had been unable to enter Smith Sound, far to the north in Baffin Bay, and Captain Penny had been saved from purgatory in Jones Sound when that entrance was found to be blocked by ice as well.

Following the *Advance*, Captain Forsyth and Parker Snow crossed to Devon Island (on the north side of Barrow Strait), with the intention of picking up mail from the other ships before returning home [see map 10]. On the way they spotted two cairns on a thin limestone jut named Cape Riley, on the southwest corner of Devon Island at the entrance to Wellington Channel. Parker Snow went to investigate.

Notes found inside the cairns revealed that one had been built by the crew of the British vessel *Assistance*, captained by Ommanney, which had been there only two days before. The other had been left by the American ship *Rescue*, which had arrived along with the *Assistance*. Ommanney's note explained, "This is to certify that Captain Ommanney, with the officers of Her Majesty's ships Assistance and Intrepid, landed upon Cape Riley on the 23d August, 1850, where he found traces of encampments, and collected the remains of materials, which evidently proved that some party belonging to her Majesty's ships had been detained on the spot." Then, more tantalizing still: "Beechey Island was also examined,

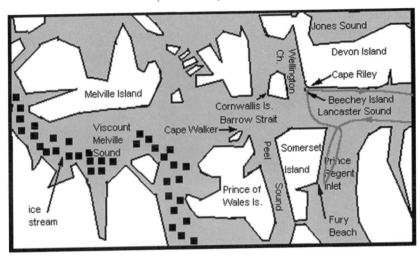

Map 10
Charles Codrington Forsyth's search and visit to Cape Riley, 1850

where traces were found of the same party."[9] The note concluded with the report that Ommanney had set out for Cape Walker.

Looking around, Parker Snow found the remains of a camp, most likely set up by Franklin's crew to make magnetic observations. He collected some rope, canvas, and beef bones scattered about, then returned to the *Prince Albert*. Under the circumstances, Captain Forsyth might have been expected to hurry over to Beechey Island, to see what had been discovered there. Instead, he was determined to wring every last ounce of failure out of Lady Franklin's sacred trust. Insisting the little *Prince Albert* could never survive the coming winter, he turned east and sailed back to England. When he faced Lady Franklin, Forsyth couldn't even tell her what had been found at Beechey Island. All he had to show for his efforts (and her money) was the meagre discovery at Cape Riley, and Adam Beck's dubious story of violent death on the Greenland coast.

Sophia Cracroft, Jane Franklin's niece, wrote bitterly to Parker Snow's wife. "The men had the highest wages ... the best equipment, moreover the season had been an extra-ordinarily favourable one ... Every advantage seems to have been thrown away."[10] Did Captain Forsyth betray Jane Franklin? Is it possible he never had any intention of performing the search, but was acting under the orders of his naval superiors to effectively sabotage the only expedition dispatched to search in the right place? It seems the only way to explain his astonishing behaviour, carried out even in the face of his civilian chief officer's opposition.

In modern terms, we would say: they got to him.

CHAPTER NINE

The Deception of John Ross

> For when the One Great Scorer comes
> To write against your name,
> He marks (not that you won or lost)
> But how you played the game.
>> Grantland Rice,
>> *Alumnus Football*

JOHN ROSS PLAYS THE GAME

And what of John Ross?

Ever since the spring of 1847, with Franklin gone for a mere two winters, the grand old man of Arctic exploration had fought a terribly one-sided battle, fighting, pleading, and cajoling to be sent out after Sir John Franklin. Jane Franklin hadn't listened when he said he believed her husband was in trouble. She hadn't listened when he said his nephew could not be trusted. No one had listened. Now, at long last, recognizing the futility of ever expecting the Admiralty to give him command of an expedition, John Ross — like Jane Franklin — decided a private expedition was the only way to go.

Funded by public donation as well as by the Hudson's Bay Company, Ross set out in April, 1850, aboard the 120-ton schooner *Felix*, accompanied by his own tiny 12 ton yacht *Mary*, acting as tender. In June, he stopped at Holsteinborg, where he acquired the unfortunate Adam Beck as interpreter. By August 10th he was in Baffin Bay along the Greenland coast, where he encountered the four-ship naval flotilla under Captain Austin. Three days later, the three Inuit men were spotted near Cape York, from whom Adam Beck may or may not have elicited a story of a massed attack on two naval ships frozen in the ice near by. But though John Ross bravely defended his interpreter against the accusations of his co-searchers, he nonetheless reported, "In the meantime it had been unanimously decided that no alteration should be made in our previous arrangement, it being obvious that while there remained a chance of saving the lives of those of the missing ships who may be yet alive, a further search for those who had perished was postponed."[1]

His argument was strange; was he suggesting that Franklin, after having lost a number of his crew to an attack by Greenland natives (and one ship burning!), would still have continued on into Lancaster Sound? The others thought Beck was making the whole thing up; their decision to continue on seems reasonable. But Ross?

Is it possible Ross knew something the rest of them did not, something that allowed him to view Adam Beck's story in a different light? Perhaps he thought the story was true, but believed it did not refer to a location on the Greenland coast. Over the years, others have considered this possibility and searches have been undertaken in places considerably closer to King William Island. Is it out of the question that Ross may have had the same such thought?

But where did Ross intend to search? Thus far, Ross consistently maintained he believed Franklin would have "put into" the ice off Melville Island, even though Franklin's orders had advised against that. If he had wanted to lull the Admiralty into a false sense of security, this was the perfect cover story; on James Clark Ross' advice, the Navy was planning to restrict its own searches to Wellington Channel and Melville Island. On the other hand, if John Ross knew about Victory Point, James Clark Ross knew he knew; this would go a long way toward explaining the Admiralty's obstinate refusal to give John Ross a ship: they weren't fooled one bit by his act.

GETTING THERE FROM HERE

One possible clue to John Ross' true intentions might be found in the man chosen to act as ice-master during this expedition. That man was Thomas Abernethy. Back in 1830, when James Clark Ross had left the rest of his sledge party at the northern tip of King William Island while he continued on to Victory Point, it was this same Abernethy who had accompanied him. Only two men in the whole world had ever stood on the lonely, ice-battered shore of Victory Point. The one was John Ross' nephew; the other was his ice-master. If James Clark Ross truly did see something extraordinary during that brief visit, Abernethy saw it too. And if John Ross wanted to return to Victory Point, there was no man alive better prepared to take him there.

Yet, even if John Ross was lying, planning all along to make his way to Victory Point, how was he to get there? Thus far, the only way anyone had ever reached Victory Point (apart from Franklin, of course) was by travelling overland from Prince Regent Inlet. If there was another route, it was as much a mystery now as it had been when Franklin set sail five years before. The most probable route was the one Franklin had been ordered to follow — to Cape Walker, then southwest. Apart from that, there remained the slim possibility of at least two water passages from Prince Regent Inlet through Boothia-Somerset. James Clark Ross had been told by the Inuit that there was no lower passage, but that still left the higher one (which did, in fact, exist). It's most probable that John Ross would have tried to follow the same route as Franklin. Unfortunately, there is no proof to be found here as to whether or not he was lying to the Admiralty about his destination. Whether he was headed for Melville Island or Cape Walker, his course would have been the same. Only if he had turned south at Cape Walker might we have known for sure, and before that question could be put to the test Ross received word of the Beechey Island find.

Immediately, he altered course for Beechey Island. What thoughts went through his head? Even if he knew about Victory Point, even if he knew the dangers awaiting there, the possibility still remained that something had happened to the expedition before they could reach their objective. There was no doubt that the Arctic was filled with dangers aplenty, dangers of a more mundane sort, perfectly capable of wrecking even the strongest of ships and the hardiest of men. As well, could Ross be certain the danger he feared at Victory Point was contained to that locale? After all, it was in Lancaster Sound that he had so mysteriously fled at the sight of the supposed Croker Mountains, rushing past his sister ship "as if some mischief was behind him"[2].

WHAT HAPPENED TO THE NOTE?

The British tender *Intrepid* had been the first to spot the stone cairn perched high and conspicuous on tiny Beechey Island. The island was connected to the vastly larger Devon Island by a slender causeway, a mere six feet wide at its narrowest, so it technically wasn't an "island" at all [see map 11]. Going ashore, the landing party immediately found evidence that Franklin's expedition had been there, but all their efforts were directed toward examining the cairn. It had obviously been set up to contain a message, and yet, though the searchers took it apart stone by stone, no note was found. It was a refrain to be played again and again in the following years: why would Franklin build a cairn, then forget to leave a message? In his book *Quest for Franklin*, Noel Wright wryly commented, "It almost seemed that an imp of mischief had delib-

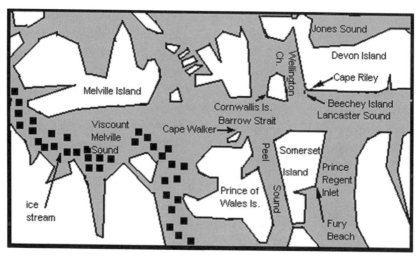

Map 11
Beechey Island

erately confused the trail."[3] But historians have been loath to delve too deeply into the implications wrought by this puzzle, though the obvious solution could not help but cross their minds from time to time.

Surely the only explanation is that someone stole it.

It was one of the British navy ships which had first happened on the cairn and, in the scramble to tear apart the stone pillar, it would have been all too easy for one of the officers, under Captain

Ommanney's orders, to hide any message found lead-sealed in its metal cylinder — and to later open it in secret aboard the ship.

Indeed, it was Captain Penny's irate opinion that this was exactly what had happened. According to historian Leslie Neatby, "In an unpublished letter to his father, [Elisha Kent] Kane [doctor on the American ship, *Advance*] tells how when Penny arrived and learned from the Americans of the traces discovered and the empty cairn, he broke into a rage declaring that the cairn must have contained a notice of Franklin's intended course and Ommanney suppressed it to keep the others searching in wrong directions."[4] This was obviously a serious charge to make, particularly since Penny, though originally hired by Lady Franklin, was effectively employed by the Navy for the duration of the search. Did he have concrete evidence to back up his suspicions of foul play or was he merely guessing? We don't know; but this wasn't to be the end of Penny's charges against his naval co-searchers.

John Ross shows his hand

After leaving a report of the find made at nearby Cape Riley, the British set off toward Cape Walker.

Incredibly, within mere days, three of the five expeditions had arrived at Beechey Island: Penny, the two American ships, and of course, John Ross. A search was begun as men fanned out across the barren, cliff-backed island.

At the same time, Penny took up the search from Cape Riley with the crew of his second ship. Quickly he found evidence of a shooting station at Cape Spencer on Devon Island on the opposite side of the causeway from Beechey. There were the remains of a stone hut, scraps of newspaper dated to the year before Franklin had set out, a torn piece of paper bearing the words "until called", but no indication of anything more than a brief visit.

Ross could see for himself that Franklin was not to be found on Beechey Island. The navy ships would soon return. If he truly believed Franklin had gone to Victory Point, Ross would never have a better chance to set out than now. He told Elisha Kent Kane that he intended to sail over to inform Lady Franklin's ship *Prince Albert* of the Beechey Island find.

He expected to find them in Prince Regent Inlet.

Why? Kane himself (aboard the *Advance*) had encountered Captain Forsyth *leaving* Prince Regent Inlet. They had still been together when Forsyth learned of the Beechey Island find from the cairn on Cape Riley. Ross must surely have known that Forsyth was not to be found in Prince Regent Inlet, that the *Prince Albert* was already headed back to England. Was this merely a ruse, an excuse to allow Ross to winter in Prince Regent Inlet, and from there seek one of the passages through Boothia-Somerset? With Captain Austin's ships between Ross and Cape Walker, that route would no longer have been an option. As well, he may already have realized, as Austin discovered, that the ice was too thick in the west, preventing any ship from reaching Cape Walker.

We can only wonder if this was the moment when Ross would finally have revealed his true intentions, because, even as Ross was returning to his ship, a crucial and frightening discovery was being made by one of Penny's men. John Ross' plans, whatever they might have been, were once again waylaid.

CHAPTER TEN

The Dead of Beechey Island

Full fathom five thy father lies;
Of his bones are only coral made:
Those are pearls that were his eyes:
Nothing of him that doth fade,
But doth suffer a sea-change
Into something rich and strange.
William Shakespeare,
The Tempest

GRAVE WARNINGS

"Graves, Captain Penny! Graves! Franklin's winter quarters!"
And graves there were, three of them all neatly set in a row, with three headstones, each "made after the old orthodox fashion of gravestones back home", in the words of Elisha Kent Kane.[1] As the searchers gathered around to read the inscriptions, they must have shivered in a way having nothing to do with the howling wind. Two of the men — John Torrington and John Hartnell — had died within only four days of each other, even though they had served on separate ships. The first, Torrington, had been lead stoker stationed aboard the *Terror*, while Hartnell was an able seaman from the *Erebus*. Torrington had died on New Year's Day, 1846. The third grave belonged to Private William Braine, a Royal Marine also serving aboard the *Erebus*. He had died in the early spring of the same year, April 3rd, 1846.

These dates told the searchers what they most wanted to know: Franklin had camped on Beechey Island during the winter of 1845-46, his first in the Arctic. Dr. Kane and the others must have noticed how closely the second death had followed the first and wondered whether there might be a connection. If so, it would have been difficult to imagine what; the two men had different professions and served on different ships. And then there was William Braine to consider. Three deaths during a first winter was odd by any standards. Provisions would still have been plentiful and scurvy — the bane of Arctic travellers — should not have set in. What could have happened?

But by far the strangest and most disturbing discoveries were the two chilling Biblical passages inscribed on Hartnell's and Braine's headstones. On the first stone the grim message ran: "Thus saith the Lord of Hosts, consider your ways." The marine's similarly ominous inscription instructed: "Choose ye this day whom ye will serve." Understandably, the searchers were puzzled (and unnerved) by such dark and frightening sentiments, and they wondered if these hinted at some terrible incident which had led to the two men's deaths. Had there been a mutiny, perhaps?

Franklin was very much a Bible-quoting man, and it was suspected that he had most likely been the author of the inscriptions. But, as everyone knew, it was vital for the commander of an Arctic expedition to do what he could to keep up his crew's spirits during the long, black winter months. Great lengths were taken to ensure that gloom and despondency didn't have a chance to settle over the men, as expeditions organized plays and balls, and printed satiric newspapers; the two ships of Franklin's expedition had even carried two hand organs, one of which played fifty tunes. A crewman's death could act as a dangerous catalyst, planting seeds of fear and depression in the others. At such times, what could possibly have caused Franklin to place such frightening quotations on the graves of the two men?

William Braine's inscription grows more eerie still when seen in the context of the full passage from which it was taken: "If it seem evil unto you to serve the Lord, chose ye this day whom ye will serve; whether the gods which your fathers served which were on the other side of the flood, or the gods of the Amorites, in whose land ye dwell."

The gods of the Amorites? In whose land ye dwell?

It was, to put it mildly, bizarre. What could Franklin have been thinking of?

Still, as weird and inexplicable as this might have been, the searchers could never have imagined how much stranger still were the contents of those graves around which they solemnly gathered. Nor could they have guessed that it would be a full 134 years before another searcher, still doggedly following the track of Franklin's lost expedition, would finally dig up those three graves, revealing for the first time their amazing occupants, and study them with technology which would have seemed little short of magic to the seaman of that ancient era. Had they known what lay below the frozen gravel beneath their feet, perhaps more than a few of them would have had second thoughts about their quest for the lost expedition.

The Autopsy of John Torrington

But every one of those men went to his grave without knowing the secret of those three graves. It was not until August 17, 1984, that Owen Beattie, a physical anthropologist with the University of Alberta, set about the difficult task of exhuming the first of the three graves, that of John Torrington. Beattie recounted his remarkable experiment in his excellent book *Frozen in Time* (co-written with John Geiger). As he explained, "Because of his special interest in forensic anthropology, Beattie had assisted in numerous investigations conducted by the medical examiner's offices, the Royal Canadian Mounted Police and other police forces."[2] It was his hope that by applying the same modern methods of physical anthropology to the ancient problem of the Franklin expedition, it might be possible at long last to find some explanation for why the voyage had met with disaster.

On August 17, having finally received permission to begin the exhumation (having already dug down through 1.5 feet of frozen permafrost), Beattie and his party set to work. As their digging was on the verge of exposing the buried coffin lid, something strange occurred. Suddenly a great black cloud gathered over the camp and the wind rose, almost as if the forces of the Arctic itself were rearing up, bent on hindering their mission. Beattie wrote, "The conditions had suddenly become so strange that Kowal observed, 'This is something out of a horror movie.'"[3] Though they tried to continue, the weather rapidly grew worse. In spite of all their scientific expertise, the group was so unnerved by the experience that Beattie was forced to call a halt to the excavation, postponing the operation until the following day. Before finally blowing itself out, the storm vented its fury during the night in the form of a violent gust of wind that wrenched up the tent covering the half-dug grave, heaving it disdainfully onto the adjacent ridge of beach. If Beattie had been inclined toward a belief in the supernatural, he would surely have taken this as a very inauspicious omen.

The following day, the team finally succeeded in uncovering the coffin. On the lid was a tin hand-painted crest that read: "John Torrington died January 1st, 1846, aged 20 years". By shearing the nails holding down the lid, the team was able to open the coffin. Inside they found a solid block of ice, which had to be melted using buckets of warm water. But once this was done, they found the body of Torrington to be incredibly well-preserved after 138 years in the ground.

Beattie thought, "John Torrington looked anything but grotesque. The expression on his thin face, with the pouting mouth and the half-closed eyes gazing through delicate, light-brown eye lashes, was peaceful."[4] One can admire Beattie's sensitivity, but the photographs taken of Torrington's corpse produce an altogether different impression. The life-like preservation was incredible, but the effects of so prolonged a time in the ice had still had a profound effect. The discoloured lips were hideously curled outward, like the mouth on an ancient Greek theatrical mask, exposing the yellow teeth clenched in a simulation of a ghastly snarl (the jaws were held closed by a polka dot handkerchief wrapped under the chin). The nose and forehead were darkly stained from a blue cloth that had been found covering the face and the eyes had a disturbing half-lidded gaze, like the blind stare of a Hollywood zombie.

After removing Torrington's body from the coffin, an autopsy was begun. Unfortunately, because of Torrington's 138 years of frozen burial in the high Arctic, the results of that autopsy were not easy to interpret. Beattie found Torrington to be incredibly thin and wasted, with very few fat reserves. Beattie felt this was evidence that Torrington had been ill for some time before his death. But how much might this be blamed on the effects of prolonged freezing and dehydration? No one could say for sure, because no one had ever dug up a body under these precise circumstances before. Most of the corpse's cellular structure had been broken down, then further dissolved by the cells' own enzymes. Beattie could find no food in either the stomach or the bowel, nor were there callouses on the stoker's fingers. All this seemed to confirm Beattie's theory that Torrington had been ill for a considerable period. On the other hand, no bed sores were found on the body, which might have been expected if Torrington had been so ill that he couldn't eat. The lack of callouses might also be explained if, for some reason, Torrington had been punished with a prolonged stay in the brig.

Tissue samples were taken, including samples from the brain, to be analyzed by Roger Amy at the University Hospital in Edmonton, but "despite careful study of the organ samples ... a specific cause of death could not be established."[5]

Plenty of evidence was found, however, indicating that Torrington had never been a healthy man (which makes one wonder what he was doing on the expedition in the first place), including signs of emphysema and tuberculosis. Based on scarring around the lungs as well as some fluid found within the lung, Beattie surmised that Torrington had perhaps died of pneumonia. But of far greater importance was Beattie's discovery of elevated levels of lead both in Torrington's bones and in his hair.

Beattie had previously wondered whether lead poisoning might have played a part in the Franklin disaster after he had found elevated levels in bones recovered from King William Island. Now this further evidence seemed to bolster his unusual hypothesis.

A DISTURBED GRAVE

Beattie did not return to Beechey Island to exhume the other two bodies, those of Hartnell and Braine, until two years later. On their previous visit, Beattie's team had gone so far as to partially excavate the grave of John Hartnell, and they had been surprised to find unmistakable evidence that someone had dug down to the coffin before them. The coffin lid had been badly damaged and cloth had been pulled out from the right side.

During the two intervening years, Beattie learned that it was Captain Edward Inglefield and Dr. Peter Sutherland who had dug down to the coffin in September 1852 (two years after the graves were first discovered by Ross, Penny, and Kane). Inglefield was at Beechey as captain of the *Isabel*, a steam yacht bought and outfitted by Jane Franklin with public funds, there to take on mail from a five-ship naval flotilla sent in search of Franklin.

In a strikingly mysterious omission, there is no mention of the exhumation in Inglefield's published journal. Beattie observed that "there is a blank period in it covering the time between when he

[Inglefield] and Sutherland finished dining with the officers of the *North Star* and the departure of the *Isabel* from Beechey Island shortly after midnight", the precise period during which the exhumation occurred.[6] It is a curious oversight given the obvious importance of this undertaking. As a result, Beattie only learned of the operation through an unpublished letter from Inglefield to Rear-Admiral Francis Beaufort. Incredibly, Inglefield claimed that they worked only by moonlight so that it was through touch alone that he determined Hartnell had died of a "wasting illness".

Beattie commented that, based on his experience, it would have taken three people twenty hours to dig down to the coffin, from which he surmised that Inglefield's crew had actually been digging all that day, while their captain was aboard the *North Star*. He further argued that the entire operation must have been carefully planned in advance, because of the short amount of time during which Inglefield remained on Beechey Island. And yet, we are to believe Inglefield didn't think to bring a lantern? Knowing how much might depend on what he found in the grave, does it really make sense that Inglefield would have been content to use touch alone to determine the cause of death?

But why should Inglefield lie about such a thing? What reason could he have had for omitting mention of the exhumation in his journal? Is it possible he discovered something in the grave, something which he felt he could not make public? If so, then what?

A DISTURBED CORPSE

The answer to that question may have been provided in part by Beattie's exhumation of able seaman Hartnell.

The body of John Hartnell was found, like Torrington's, to be exceedingly well-preserved. Also, like Torrington, the lips had curled outwards in the same grotesque fashion, exposing the clenched teeth. The eyes, though, had suffered considerable damage, both sinking back into their sockets — a result, Beattie believed, brought about by the brief periods during which the body had been thawed both by Inglefield and by Beattie's team during their previous excavation. Hartnell's arms had been bound to his body using a light-brown woollen binding, but the right arm had been removed from the binding — presumably by Inglefield — and left loose beside the body.

This time, Beattie had brought along a portable X-ray machine. Once Hartnell's body was removed from the coffin, the corpse was X-rayed, only to reveal something very odd. The brain would not show up properly on the X-ray because it had frozen into a solid block of ice. This became stranger still when the X-rays of William Braine would reveal no such solid ice in his head even though he had been buried under the same conditions as Hartnell.

Yet, what amazed the team even more was the discovery that "[Hartnell's] internal organs appeared uncharacteristic and of unusual and varied densities."[7] Apart from his skeleton, very little could be distinguished on the exposures. While it was possible that the unusual conditions under which the X-rays were taken might have had something to do with the problem, the team was nonetheless bothered by the unexpected find. But an explanation was soon discovered, when they undressed the body in preparation for an autopsy.

To their astonishment, they found Hartnell had already been autopsied. And yet, they noticed a curious anomaly about this autopsy. In standard autopsies a Y-shaped incision is made, with the arms of the Y starting at the shoulders and coming together at the base of the breastbone, the straight part then extending down to the pubic bone. In this case, the Y was upside down. The arms began at either hip, came together at the belly button, then the straight part ran up to the top of the breastbone. Was this just the way autopsies were performed back in the mid-1800s? No one knew. Beattie wrote, "The procedures for autopsy technique in the mid-nineteenth century are not well-represented in scientific literature."[8] But even more puzzles awaited the team as they set about reopening the sutured incision.

They originally thought that perhaps the upside-down incision indicated the doctor responsible was mainly interested in examining the bowel. However, once inside the body it became clear that whoever had done the procedure had concentrated on the heart and lungs — the bowel had not even been touched. The heart had been removed and then two cuts had been made, one into each ventricle. The roots of the lungs had been dissected and then the liver as well. None of this was especially odd, although it was unclear why the ship's doctor should have decided to autopsy Hartnell when he hadn't autopsied Torrington who had died only days before.

What *was* astonishing was what had been done at the conclusion of the autopsy. The organs had simply been put back in the body in "one mixed mass".[9] This was why they hadn't shown up on the X-rays. Even more bizarre, the front part of the ribcage, which had been removed to allow access to the lungs and heart, had then been put back *upside down*.

WHO DID IT?

It is difficult to imagine a ship's doctor, even under trying circumstances, treating a shipmate in such an oddly uncaring manner. The doctor aboard the *Erebus* was Dr. Harry Goodsir. Would Dr. Goodsir really have so callously dumped the organs back into Hartnell's body in a mixed mass? More importantly, would any doctor have put the ribs back in upside down? And yet, if not Dr. Goodsir, then who?

Perhaps there is another clue. When first exhuming Hartnell's body, the ice that had frozen over his chest area was found to be brownish in colour. It became evident to Beattie that the brown staining the ice was caused by blood and body fluids that had seeped out of the incision between the time Hartnell was buried and the point at which the water froze in his coffin. And yet, is there not another explanation? Is it possible the autopsy was performed while Hartnell was already in his grave? Could someone have dug up Hartnell and performed an autopsy on the spot at some time long after Franklin and his crew had already left Beechey Island?

Obviously, Dr. Sutherland seems the most apparent suspect, since we already know he and Captain Inglefield did exhume Hartnell in 1852. We have already found reason to question Inglefield's account of what took place under that crisp Arctic moon, but why should he lie about performing an autopsy? Why autopsy Hartnelland then pretend he had been unable to even see the body, relying instead on touch alone? Of course, perhaps more to the point, why would Dr. Sutherland be any more likely to replace the ribcage upside down than Dr. Goodsir would have been? And, if this isn't reason enough to remove Sutherland and Inglefield as suspects, there is also a question of time. In order to autopsy the body,

Sutherland would have found it necessary to thaw out each organ before it could be removed, as Beattie did. It is doubtful there would have been time enough for the entire procedure before the *Isabel* sailed at midnight.

Unfortunately the list of suspects ends with Dr. Sutherland, leaving us with a truly unnerving question still unanswered. But, if someone really did exhume and autopsy Hartnell's body sometime after he was already buried, a further question to be asked is this: had the autopsy already been done by the time Inglefield exhumed Hartnell in 1852? For that matter, is it not a strange coincidence that, of the three bodies, Inglefield just happened to choose the one which had been autopsied? Is it possible Inglefield had some reason to think something odd might be found in Hartnell's grave before he even arrived at Beechey Island? Could he have exhumed Hartnell's body because of information gleaned from a message left by Franklin in the Beechey Island cairn?

There is a curious comment made by Inglefield in his unpublished letter to Rear-Admiral Beaufort. He begins by describing the process of digging through the frozen earth. "The pale moon looking down upon us as we silently worked with pickaxe and shovel at the hard-frozen tomb, each blow sending a spur of red sparks from the grave where rested the messmate of our lost countrymen. *No trace but a piece of fearnought half down the coffin lid could we find.*"[10] [my italics] No trace? No trace of what? (Fearnought is a coarse fabric.) Clearly Inglefield had expected to find something, but what? Was he merely hoping a message might have been left with the body? It seems unlikely; Franklin would hardly have buried a message deep under the perpetually frozen ground sealed in a coffin.

Whatever Inglefield was searching for, if his letter is to be believed, he never found it. But he may have found something else, something totally unexpected and, because Inglefield harboured suspicions regarding its true significance, something which could not be revealed to the public. So, he omitted mention of the entire episode when it came time to publish his journal. That something would have been the strange autopsy conducted on Hartnell. In pursuing this line of reasoning, it is not too hard to imagine Inglefield, on finding the upside down Y incision, grimly ordering Dr. Sutherland to reopen the body. After silently noting the curiously uncaring manner in which the organs had been placed in the body, and seeing the astonishing way in which the ribcage had been replaced upside down, Inglefield would have instructed Sutherland to suture closed the incision, after swearing all present not to speak of what they had seen.

WILLIAM BRAINE, TOO?

As strange as the discoveries made in Hartnell's grave were, there was yet more to come when the team exhumed the body of Royal Marine William Braine. Braine died in the very early spring, almost three months to the day after the death of Hartnell. Braine's facial features seemed less grotesque than those of his crewmates. His lips had been held down by a red cloth over his face, so that they did not curl outward in the same weird way, but seemed drawn tight across his teeth, almost as if laughing. His features seemed smoother and more alive, and even his eyes seemed less zombie-like, perhaps because they were squinted, making it more difficult to notice the damaged eyeballs within.

Even before the body had been removed from the coffin, it was clear that something was wrong. One arm, which at first seemed to be missing, was found to be twisted awkwardly beneath the corpse, while the head and body were both poorly positioned. As well, one of the undershirts had been put on the corpse backwards. All of this led Beattie to conclude Braine had been placed in the coffin in a hurry, without time being taken to properly dress or arrange his body. But, again, perhaps another possibility presents itself.

Is it possible that Braine's body, like Hartnell's, had been exhumed by someone prior to Beattie's visit? Beattie had found obvious signs of Hartnell's exhumation; the coffin had been damaged and fabric had been pulled out. But this damage was almost certainly caused by Inglefield's party. If someone else exhumed and autopsied Hartnell prior to Inglefield's visit, perhaps they exhumed Braine at the same time, but took greater care to leave no trace of their work behind. (As an added note: Hartnell was found to be dressed only from the waist up. Beattie had been puzzled by this and supposed there had been a public viewing aboard the ship with the lower body covered by a shroud. But, as with Braine's backward undershirt, this could be further evidence that Hartnell had been exhumed, stripped, autopsied, then half-dressed in the same strangely careless way as his organs and ribs had been replaced.)

More evidence in support of this theory would turn up during the autopsy. First though, Braine's body was X-rayed just as Hartnell's had been, but this time with better results, because he had not been previously autopsied.

Before beginning the autopsy, something curious transpired. As the team prepared for the task, abruptly the entire party began to experience severe headaches. They grew dizzy and some even felt physically ill. They concluded the problem could only have been caused by breathing carbon monoxide produced by the two stoves they had used to warm water during Braine's exhumation, the gas presumably filling the tent covering the grave pit. It was a poor omen before beginning their job on the final body, in some ways reminiscent of the weird and sudden storm which had sprung up so vengefully to wreck the tent over Torrington's grave on the first day of digging two years before. Stranger still was the fact that the gas had somehow gathered in the tent even though the tent flap had been open, with a breeze blowing in all the time they worked.

On removing Braine's clothing, it was discovered that, in contrast to the previous two bodies, green discolouration was to be found, indicating that the body had begun decomposing some time before burial. This suggested that the body had been kept in a warm location, a considerable feat of ineptitude while in the high Arctic in April. Beattie commented that "the body could easily have been placed in a cool or even freezing part of the ship where the amount of observed decomposition would have been far less likely to occur."[11] Indeed, the improbability of such a mistake suggests another possibility. If someone exhumed Braine's body (along with Hartnell) sometime before Inglefield arrived, might they have done so during one of the six short Arctic summers between 1846 and 1852? In which case, the warmer temperatures to be found in August might have caused the decomposition during the time that the body was under study.

Almost as a final dash of spice to add flavour to the mystery, strange lesions were found on Braine's body. They occurred on his shoulders, around the groin area, and on his chest, and involved damage not only to the skin, but even to the muscles beneath. On closer examination, it was found that the lesions were teeth marks. Beattie concluded the marks had been made by rats, which often stowed away aboard ships. It is, of course, the most likely explanation.

A CHANGE IN THE MYSTERY

Still, when all this is taken together it is all tantalizingly suggestive. When we consider all the evidence, we may find ourselves dimly sensing a change in the mystery before us, as if suddenly discovering the blue pieces of a puzzle are not parts of the sea but of the sky. When we think about the curious unexpected evidence of an autopsy, possibly conducted long after Hartnell had been buried, the oddly callous way his organs were returned to his body, his ribcage astonishingly replaced upside down; when we consider the possibility that Braine too may have been exhumed, examined, then returned to his grave, hastily positioned, one arm twisted beneath him, his undershirt on backward; when we reflect on the strange teeth marks, the evidence of decomposition, Captain Inglefield's journal omission; finally, when we append the additional discovery, commented on by Beattie but not elaborated upon, that in John Hartnell's veins there was no blood, only clear ice — we may find ourselves tempted to change the nature of our search and the form of the question asked. We may be excused for wondering not *who* autopsied John Hartnell, but *what*.

CHAPTER ELEVEN

The Cashmere Gloves

They are all gone into the world of light,
And I alone sit lingering here.
Henry Vaughan,
They Are All Gone

THE CAIRN OF CANS

As those first searchers congregated solemnly around the three lonely
graves in 1850 — John Ross, William Penny and Elisha Kent Kane —
they could not have known the strange contents of those graves. They
knew only that evidence at last had been discovered of Franklin's expedition, evidence of his first winter in the Arctic. If any of them had
been well versed in Biblical passages, they might have wondered at the
curious quotations marking the headstones of Hartnell and Braine (the
two who, in our scenario, were exhumed by persons unknown) and
recalled the passage from which the latter's was taken. The gods of the
Amorites, in whose land ye dwell.

But there were other discoveries to consider, and their attention
soon shifted from the graves to the surrounding terrain set in the
shadow of brooding, broken cliffs. As Penny's sailor had rightly surmised, there could be no doubt that they had happened on
Franklin's winter camp. All around them was scattered evidence of
a prolonged stay on this barren heap of wave-washed rubble. There
were the foundations of some sort of storehouse, in one part of
which was discovered coal sacks, while in another part wood shavings indicated where carpentry work had been performed. Near the
beach, cinders and scrap iron showed where a forge had stood, and

tubs for the men to wash in had been constructed out of salt-meat casks. In one area, tents had been erected and a shooting range had been set up in a nearby gully, with stones marking the distances and a "Soup and Bouilli" can as the target, found riddled with holes. Captain Sherard Osborn, with the Royal Navy flotilla, was particularly impressed by the remains of a garden: "its neatly shaped oval outline, the border carefully formed of moss, lichen, poppies and anemones, transplanted from some more genial part of this dreary region, contrived still to show symptoms of vitality."[1]

While wandering amongst this abundant proof of Franklin's winter sojourn, the searchers happened upon a weird and disturbing find. A strange cairn was discovered built of 600 to 700 meat tins, each one carefully filled with gravel. As with the earlier cairn, this too was taken apart; each tin was emptied and searched, but again, suspiciously, there was no sign of a message.

What did it mean? Had the gravel-filled tins been used as ballast, as some speculated? Or was there a darker significance? It was suggested that there might have been a problem with the meat carried on Franklin's expedition; perhaps some of it had spoiled and been thrown out. The navy had previously had complaints about the packager, Goldner. It was argued that there were far too many tins to be accounted for by a single winter. Had Franklin constructed this curious monument just to let later searchers know the meat had spoiled? Surely a simple note would have sufficed.

THE GLOVES

But perhaps the most eerie find of all was reserved for Captain Osborn's searching eyes — eerie for precisely the reason that it at first seemed so mundane. He discovered a pair of cashmere gloves neatly set out to dry on a rock, small pebbles placed in each palm to keep them from being blown away by the unrelenting wind. So much had been left behind by Franklin's expedition, there could be no doubt their departure had been hasty. But this discovery must surely have aroused a slight thrill of unease even in Osborn's unflappably British breast. Four years before, one of Franklin's officers had laid out those gloves, precisely as Osborn saw them now.

On a sunny day, he had set them there, left them to dry and then, inexplicably, never returned.

CHAPTER TWELVE

Penny Versus Austin

And then it started like a guilty thing
Upon a fearful summons.
William Shakespeare,
Hamlet

FROZEN IN WELLINGTON CHANNEL

If John Ross had hoped to set off for Prince Regent Inlet before the naval ships returned, it was not to be. Since his departure had been postponed by the discovery of the graves and Franklin's winter encampment, he was still at Beechey when Captain Austin came back the next day after being prevented from reaching Cape Walker by heavy ice. Then Ross found himself called upon to unload provisions from the British tender *Pioneer*, which, having run aground, needed to be floated free. In the end, the Arctic winter closed its chill, dark fingers, hardening the waters and trapping every one of the expeditions in the Beechey Island area.

With Jane Franklin's ship *Prince Albert* retreating back to England, this left the four British ships under Captain Austin, the two ships under Penny, the two American vessels, and John Ross' schooner, *Felix*, with its tiny tender, *Mary*. What should have been an all-out search encompassing every corner of the Arctic had become an over-crowded gathering in the mouth of Wellington Channel.

In April, sledge parties set out across the hummocky ice in no less than eight directions, but, of course, the main areas of interest were Melville Island in the west, and areas further north up Wellington Channel. Leopold McClintock was placed in charge of the Melville

Island search. He had previously assisted James Clark Ross on the very first search for the lost expedition. There was reason enough at that time to believe McClintock was innocent of any "unworthy motives" and now, again, his actions are understandable enough. He was under orders from Captain Austin to carry out a search of Melville Island. All the experts were in agreement that this was a likely place to find the lost seamen, even though Franklin had been advised in his sailing orders to keep away from the heavy ice off Melville Island. Who was McClintock to question such lofty authorities?

Just as James Clark Ross had so inexplicably insisted on using the slower man-hauled sledges despite having previously employed dogs with such success, again the navy expeditions spurned the use of dog sledges, greatly limiting the size of the areas any one party could hope to cover. Only Captain Penny, the whaling captain championed by Jane Franklin, employed dogs for the sledge that he used to search Wellington Channel. At the very least, the navy's efforts were conveniently flawed.

Having failed to reach Cape Walker the previous year, the navy now tried again, this time sending a sledge party over the ice-covered surface of Barrow Strait.

Cape Walker, at last

The history of Cape Walker reflects the poor understanding of the area's geography that resulted from the hindering effects of the implacable ice. Its initial importance lay in its being the westernmost point of land yet sighted along the south side of the entrance to the Arctic. It was initially thought to be the southwest corner of Somerset Island, rather than the northern tip of an entirely different island, soon to be named Prince of Wales (or more properly, the tip of a small islet now named Russell Island, just north of the northern tip of Prince of Wales Island). The waterway between Prince of Wales Island and Somerset Island, eventually to be named Peel Sound, had formerly been identified as a bay; although James Clark Ross had concluded it might be a sound, no one could yet be certain. For these reasons, it had seemed reasonable to conclude that if there was a waterway connecting the northern part of the Northwest Passage to the more southern route, it was to be found somewhere beyond Cape Walker.

Of course, the same reasoning would hold if someone wished to reach Victory Point on King William Island. James Clark Ross had stood on Victory Point and gazed out over an ice-choked waterway to the west which he called Victoria Strait, a waterway located directly south and slightly west of Cape Walker. No matter what Franklin's real plans were, Cape Walker had beckoned like the Pillars of Hercules.

Because of its prominence in Franklin's orders, everyone had believed a message would be found there. To quote one of the searchers (Ommanney): "Cape Walker was the spot on which it was almost universally believed that Sir John Franklin would have left a cairn, if proceeding in that direction."[1] Of course, this had not stopped James Clark Ross from steering away from Cape Walker at the very last moment in 1849; nor had it been reason enough to convince Captain Forsyth to land boats the previous winter. But now, at long last, with Franklin having been lost for six years, an expedition was sent to Cape Walker to find a sign.

What they found was nothing. There was no message at Cape Walker, not even a cairn to hold a message as there had been on Beechey Island. Later, after the final evidence was discovered on King William Island, it would be concluded that Franklin had sailed, not southwest past Cape Walker, but southeast, down Peel Sound. If true, it is impossible to understand how he could have failed to leave a message on Cape Walker, telling of his change in plans.

Franklin had carried two hundred cylinders to place messages in; and yet we are to believe that he failed to leave even a single message in the one place where everyone felt certain he must?

We have nothing more than suspicion and supposition. Those who searched Cape Walker insisted that neither note nor cairn was discovered. They may have told the truth. On the other hand, it was a naval team which made the claim, and the commander in charge was Captain Ommanney — the same captain who had overseen the discovery and search of the cairn found so prominently displayed (and so inexplicably empty) on Beechey Island; the same man Captain Penny had accused of "suppressing" a message found there.

WRITING OFF THE SOUTH

Still, message or no message, the searchers were finally on the right track. Having reached Cape Walker, Captain Ommanney now decided to divide his sledge party into two groups: one, under Willy Browne, to explore to the southeast of the Cape down into Peel Sound; the other, led by Ommanney himself, to explore to the southwest [see map 12]. At long last, they were doing what should have been done from the start — following the course Franklin had been instructed to take past Cape Walker.

Very quickly, Captain Ommanney discovered that there was indeed water to the southwest, but water frozen into rugged hummocks and "pygmy ravines", making for less than ideal sledging conditions.[2] Working their way south, they came upon a deep bay, where the party

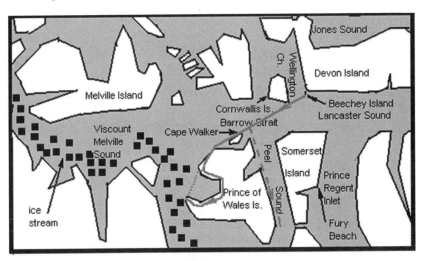

Map 12
Navy Sledges search Prince of Wales Island, 1851

The ships -- Austin, Penny, Ross, and Americans

<u>Navy sledges</u>

Ommanney ————————➤——————————

Osborn · · · · · · · · · · · ·

Browne — — —➤— — — — —

divided into two: one, under Sherard Osborn, to cross directly south to the opposite side of the bay; the other, under Ommanney, to take the longer path, tracing the bay's deep arc. Again, if Franklin had left any record of his travels, Ommanney would have found them. Osborn reached the south side of the bay, then travelled just a little further along the coast before finally turning back, having found the wind and fog too much to handle.

Meanwhile, to the southeast of Cape Walker, the other searchers had similarly run afoul of poor weather, and were driven back by a furious blizzard after only exploring Peel Sound for a short distance. All the searchers returned to the ships.

What had been accomplished? No message had been found at Cape Walker, but it had finally been proven that water (albeit frozen water) was to be found to the southwest of the Cape. This meant there were no less than two possible routes Franklin might have taken in his bid to reach the southern passage, provided either waterway was ever clear of ice. But it was the contention of the Peel Sound searchers that *the east passage* was frozen to the bottom and so was "rarely, if ever, open to navigation."[3] Peel Sound was now officially discounted as a place to search for Franklin.

The same went for the waterway to the southwest. In this case, Ommanney was almost certainly correct in believing no ship could possibly manage the massive, heaving pack off the west coast of Prince of Wales Island. This was a continuation of the gargantuan ice channel which Edward Parry had run up against off Melville Island so many years before and which Franklin had been advised to steer clear of. It was the southernmost extent of this river of ice which James Clark Ross had looked upon from Victory Point years before.

It was decided that the case had been proven beyond a shadow of a doubt: Franklin could not have gotten south as his orders stipulated. From now on, the navy would consider the entire southern area over and done with. Of course, this could hardly be said to constitute a change in tactics.

ACTING IN CONCERT?

While Austin was sending out his sledge parties, Captain Penny had been doing some sledging of his own. He had sent several parties up

Wellington Channel, and used his dog-team to explore that direction himself. He had even discovered two pieces of wood which he believed must have come from the lost ships (and which almost certainly did come from Franklin's ships which, it would later be learned, had explored Wellington Channel before wintering at Beechey). Believing he was on the verge of discovering the lost expedition, Penny went to Captain Austin and asked to borrow one of the navy's steamships, to push through the ice further north. Then an astonishing thing happened.

Austin refused.

Amazingly, he now claimed to think Wellington Channel should be abandoned; instead, he wanted to return to Baffin Bay to explore Jones Sound. This was the same water route Penny had previously been ordered to search, but which he had found frozen.

Austin's decision is incomprehensible. The discovery at Beechey Island proved Franklin had entered the Arctic through Lancaster Sound and had already gotten as far as Wellington Channel; Penny's discovery of wood in the upper reaches of Wellington Channel was further evidence that Franklin had gone up there. What was the point in effectively leaving the Arctic and starting again by a different route?

If Penny had had his suspicions regarding the empty cairn, now he was confirmed in his belief. He challenged Austin, "You say we have been acting in concert. Let us prove the sincerity of that concert."[4] But Austin wouldn't give Penny the steamer he needed to complete the search and Penny told him, "Then I know the truth of your sincerity and will have nothing more to do with you."

What was Austin's purpose in abandoning the search of Wellington Channel when it was nearly complete? Historian Noel Wright remarked, "Subsequently, Austin must have regretted rejecting Wellington Channel, virtually a 'bird in the hand', for the uncertainties of Jones Sound."[5] But Austin's reasoning seems all too logical if, indeed, he had been ordered to ensure Franklin's expedition was not found. Believing Franklin to be trapped to the south off King William Island, Austin had been happy to let Penny explore Wellington Channel to his heart's content. But the discovery of wood pieces in Wellington Channel may have caused Austin to wonder whether perhaps Franklin hadn't become stuck up there after all. With no way to contact his superiors in London, Austin may have panicked and decided his safest course was to abandon the entire area.

Finding Jones Sound sealed by ice, Austin returned to England in September. All the other expeditions — Penny, Ross and the Americans — also returned as soon as the ice broke up in the summer. Penny was not content to let the matter rest, and a committee was organized to consider the question of whether or not Austin had acted properly in refusing Penny a ship and abandoning the Wellington Channel area. Not surprisingly, the committee ruled in Austin's favour, in spite of the fact that the Admiralty would soon send yet another fleet of ships right back out to search Wellington Channel. Though displeased by the verdict, Captain Penny — originally hired by Jane Franklin — applied for command over another expedition.

He was told his services were no longer required.

CHAPTER THIRTEEN

The Canadian and the French Lieutenant

Down to Gehenna or up to the Throne,
He travels the fastest who travels alone.
Rudyard Kipling,
The Winners

JANE FRANKLIN TRIES AGAIN

The previous October, Jane Franklin had been shattered by the inexplicable return of her private expedition under Captain Forsyth. The *Prince Albert* had been expected to spend at least one winter at Brentford Bay in Prince Regent Inlet; instead, in spite of Parker Snow's strenuous objections, the naval captain had turned tail and fled back to England — the only one of the five expeditions to do so. For all her trouble and expense, nothing had been accomplished. Captain Forsyth could tell her something had been found on Beechey Island, but he couldn't tell her what. He hadn't waited long enough to find out.

But Lady Franklin was not one to throw in the towel. It must have seemed as if the forces opposing her were enormous. First James Clark Ross had betrayed her; then she had unwisely relinquished control of Penny's expedition to the Admiralty; now Captain Forsyth — her close friend from Tasmania — had proven to be less of a friend than she had thought. The temptation to give up must have been strong, but she resisted it with an iron will. She resolved to send out the tiny *Prince Albert* once again. This time she was taking no chances. This time there would be no navy involvement.

KENNEDY AND BELLOT

For the captain, she chose a Canadian fur trader, formerly with the Hudson's Bay Company, named William Kennedy. Kennedy was a man after Franklin's own heart, religious to the core and a strict teetotaller. He had considerable experience in the cold north, having spent eight years on the chill Labrador coast. His mother was Cree, and Kennedy had quit the Hudson's Bay Company because of his outrage at the damage the "Honourable Company" was causing by selling liquor to her people.

Kennedy crossed the ocean to volunteer his services for Lady Franklin's search for her lost husband. To her upper-crust acquaintances, choosing a "mixed-race" Canadian fur trader to command her expedition seemed odd, to say the least. But odder still was her choice for Kennedy's chief officer.

After some hesitation, Lady Franklin accepted the gallantly offered services of a charming sub-lieutenant on loan from the French Navy, by the name of Joseph-René Bellot. First a Canadian fur trader, now a Frenchman — it was as if she had given up on England altogether.

KENNEDY HEARS THE GHOST STORY

Like Kennedy, Bellot had come to England of his own accord, seeking out Lady Franklin to offer his assistance in the search. The mysterious Captain Coppin — of the ghostly vision — encouraged Lady Franklin to accept.

But this wasn't the end of Captain Coppin's influence. For some time now, Jane Franklin had sought a meeting to speak with Coppin's daughter Anne about the vision provided by his dead daughter Weasy. But Coppin had been strangely reluctant to allow such a face-to-face encounter to take place, preferring instead to speak on his daughter's behalf. His reasons were varied: his wife was an invalid; daughter Anne was "retiring in disposition"; a visit from the famous wife of John Franklin would draw too much attention and "cause no small stir".[1] His hesitation is understandable if, indeed, he had merely invented the story of his daughter's vision to explain his own certainty with regard to Victory Point. If so, he must have finally decided he could trust his daughter to play her part in the charade. At Lady Franklin's request, he agreed to allow William Kennedy to visit his home in Londonderry and to personally meet with his daughter.

Kennedy stayed at the Coppin home for three days. Was he convinced by whatever Anne had to tell him? Based on his later actions, it is fairly safe to say that all of Captain Coppin's efforts were wasted on the Bible-reading, teetotal fur trader from Canada. He may have believed Moses parted the Red Sea, but apparently his belief in miracles stopped somewhere short of blue lights and ghostly writing on a wall.

THE CANADIAN EXPEDITION

Still, whether Kennedy believed or not, his sailing orders were clear: sail down into Prince Regent Inlet, seek a winter harbour, then cross and travel down the entire west side of Boothia-Somerset by sledge — in other words, what Captain Forsyth had failed to do [see map 13]. This would have placed them directly to the east of King William Island, where they might have encountered Inuit with news of the one hundred plus men lying dead in the snows just across the island.

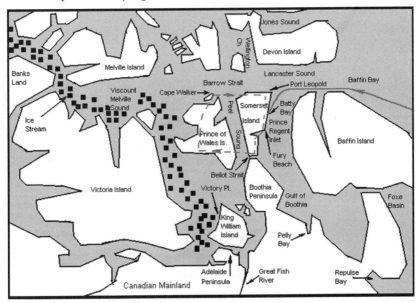

Map 13
Kennedy and Bellot's Search, 1851–1852

For this journey, the diminutive *Prince Albert* had been refitted and strengthened to better withstand whatever she might encounter. Jane Franklin didn't want to hear any more excuses about poor ice conditions.

Apart from Kennedy and Bellot, the crew consisted of sixteen men, a mixed bag of Orkneymen and Canadians, each used to hard work in the biting cold. With a Canadian captain and several Canadian crew members, this second voyage of the *Prince Albert* was effectively the first and only Canadian voyage to take part in the search for Franklin.

Provisioned for two years, they set out from Aberdeen on May 22, 1851, and reached Baffin Bay by the first of July, stopping briefly at Upernavik to pick up a team of six sledge dogs. They would not have the excuse of men wearied from hauling at the traces. Following the Greenland coast northward, they ran into the two ships of the American expedition, the *Advance* and the *Rescue*.

The Americans had been through a truly horrendous ordeal. Having become locked in the ice in Wellington Channel, they had been inexorably carried all the way out into Baffin Bay over the course of eight months and twenty-four days, being finally released when the pack broke up in early July. Yet, in spite of their harrowing journey, the Americans had promptly crossed over to the Greenland coast and started north again, intending to re-enter Lancaster Sound and resume their search.

It was while the Americans were waiting for a clear path through the ice that Kennedy and Bellot happened upon them. For a month, the three ships hung together, the ice thick in their path. In the end, the delay cost them dearly. By the time the *Prince Albert* reached Prince Regent Inlet, all the harbours were choked with ice, including Fury Beach. They barely managed to find a safe haven at Batty Bay, twenty miles south of Leopold Harbour, where they settled in for the long, dark winter.

But, unlike James Clark Ross, Kennedy wasn't about to wait until the sun came again in the spring before visiting that most holy of holies: Fury Beach. By the light of a January full moon, Kennedy and Bellot set off southward along the base of brooding cliffs, accompanied by four men. But, when they reached the supplies at Fury Beach, they found them untouched; there was no indication Franklin had ever been there. Frustrated, they grimly returned to the ship.

The rest of the winter was spent exploring their immediate sur-roundings and positioning provisions caches for the coming search. The weather was relentlessly brutal; in Samuel Schmucker's words, "There seemed to be but one gale during the winter around the ship; but that gale blew when she came, and continued till she departed."[2] During one such trek, Kennedy and Bellot found themselves completely blinded by the snow. In desperation, they released the sledge dogs, who promptly vanished and returned to the ship without their masters. By sheer luck, the party happened upon the ammunition dump (stored on land away from the ship, for obvious reasons) and so worked their way back to the *Prince Albert*, their faces "puffed and scarred as if by blows of the fist."[3]

It may have been that this near-fatal brush with the merciless forces of the north dampened Kennedy's enthusiasm for their quest. The next day, he made a fateful decision. He no longer believed it was possible to travel all the way down the west coast of Boothia-Somerset. They were berthed too far north. Instead, he now planned only to travel as far south as James Clark Ross' cairn left at the North Magnetic Pole.

Thus, on February 25, Kennedy and Bellot set off with four men and a seven-man relief team. Though they did not know it, every other expedition sent by the British to the eastern Arctic had returned home with the summer thaw. Penny's two ships, Austin's four, even doggedly determined John Ross — all had sailed back to England, with nothing to show for their troubles but the discovery on Beechey Island and the bitter feud between Penny and Austin over Wellington Channel. In all the eastern Arctic, only the crew of the tiny *Prince Albert* remained to continue the search.

AN ILLUSION?

They reached Fury Beach on March 5, then on March 29 they were off again, leaving the relief team behind, headed south for Brentford Bay — the bay where Forsyth had been expected to spend the winter. On reaching Brentford Bay, they entered its deep bite in the east coast. Kennedy was in such a hurry he wouldn't allow Bellot time to properly determine their positions. Before long, they found themselves looking westward across a frozen sea and they realized they had crossed fully to the west side of Somerset Island. It would not be until later that Kennedy, on looking over their measurements, would realize that they had just passed along a waterway cutting clear through Boothia-Somerset. They had finally found a water passage connecting Prince Regent Inlet to the waters to the west. Somerset was an island after all, and the strait was named after Bellot.

But now both Kennedy and Bellot made a strange mistake. Looking north, they thought they saw land connecting Somerset Island to Prince of Wales Island. In other words, they thought they saw solid land where in fact there lay only the open passage of Peel Sound. First James Clark Ross had rejected Peel Sound because it was frozen; then the sledge team sent under Willy Browne had made the same claim; now Kennedy and Bellot made the biggest mistake of all — Peel Sound, they said, was a dead end. Franklin could never have come south by that route.

How could they have been so mistaken? What did they see as they gazed into the white distance? An illusion? Refraction of the light? They were neither the first nor the last to be misled by the astonishingly real vision of land where there was no land. So common is the phenomenon in the north that it has been given a name: the fata morgana. Just as John Ross apparently spotted an entire mountain range spread across Lancaster Sound, so have many other visitors to the North spotted looming peaks spread across the horizon, visible one trip, then gone the next. These ghostly ranges are only part of a wide variety of odd sightings reported over the centuries, from "mock suns" to even weirder objects sighted hovering in the Arctic skies. It is a topic to which we will return.

Whatever they really saw, Kennedy and Bellot were fooled into thinking Peel Sound was blocked off at its southern end. This led Kennedy to a second change in plans. Believing Franklin could not have come south down Peel Sound, he decided there was little point in proceeding south to the North Magnetic Pole. Instead, he opted to travel directly westward to see if he could find a passage southwest of Cape Walker. Southwest of Cape Walker was where Franklin had been told to go, and southwest was where Kennedy now planned to search.

Crossing the ice, Kennedy and Bellot reached Prince of Wales Island, an island already searched by Ommanney's sledge parties. For thirteen days they continued westward across the level island, with no sign of a passage. Finally, Kennedy decided they had travelled far enough. He turned north, sledging up to Cape Walker under the belief that he might find a message left there by Franklin. Of course,

Ommanney's sledges had already visited here too, and if there ever was a message left by Franklin, it had long since disappeared.

Frustrated by their failure, Kennedy and Bellot crossed Peel Sound, returning to the ship on May 30, 1852. On August 6th, they left Batty Bay and set sail up Prince Regent Inlet, then over to Beechey Island, where they encountered the *North Star,* the same ship which had been previously sent to provision James Clark Ross.

The *North Star* had returned to Beechey Island as part of a new Admiralty effort to explore Wellington Channel. In a final heroic gesture, both Kennedy and Bellot (and two other men) volunteered to transfer to the *North Star* to continue the search for another winter; but, significantly, on being informed they would have to place themselves under the command of the navy, they changed their minds. Kennedy accepted the latest dispatches for the Admiralty and headed back to England.

Kennedy's motive?

Essentially nothing had been learned of Franklin's fate. Kennedy and Bellot had merely gone over ground that others had searched before them. Worse, Kennedy had decided at the last moment to completely alter his plans.

Why? He had known the navy ships were searching in Barrow Strait; surely he could have assumed they would have searched for a passage to the southwest of Cape Walker. Surely he could have assumed they would have visited Cape Walker itself. In the absence of other searchers, Kennedy's strategy makes some sense, but not if he thought that the navy sledge teams were operating in the area.

Eight years later, Kennedy would pen a letter of apology to Captain Coppin to explain why he hadn't listened to the Captain's daughter about Victory Point: "Lady Franklin herself was so possessed with the matter that Sir John had gone up Wellington Channel that most people were carried away with the same impression. I was amongst this number and so did not attach the importance to these revelations that I ought to have done."[4] It was certainly true that in the November after Kennedy had set out, Jane Franklin was quoted in the *Nautical Magazine* as saying, "I am persuaded now that it is pretty well proved that my husband could not have penetrated south west ... but that he has taken the only alternative their instructions presented him by going up the Wellington Channel."[5] But this opinion was, in historian Roderic Owen's words, "as over-stated as it was newly acquired."[6] She may well have believed it, but this statement was made soon after the Beechey Island ships had returned, in the heat of the battle between Penny and Austin over why Austin had so suddenly abandoned Wellington Channel with the search nearly resolved one way or the other.

As well, there is the matter of Jane Franklin having sent Kennedy to spend three days interviewing Anne Coppin about her ghostly vision. Would Lady Franklin have done so, if she was really "possessed" by the Wellington Channel route? What's more, Kennedy had not been sent anywhere near Wellington Channel; he had been sent to Somerset Island. His explanation to Captain Coppin rings hollow indeed.

But what other explanation can there be?

Kennedy's actions make no sense since he must have known the British expedition would explore the areas he planned to search. On the other hand, his actions make perfect sense, if Jane Franklin *did not trust Austin to honestly search Cape Walker and the area to the southwest.*

Is it possible Kennedy had been secretly instructed to search to the southwest of Cape Walker and to search Cape Walker itself because Jane Franklin did not trust the navy to honestly search those areas? Perhaps she, like Captain Penny, suspected the navy searchers might go so far as to conceal any messages found and she hoped Kennedy might get there first. Kennedy's and Bellot's offer to transfer to the *North Star* might then be seen as an attempt to further keep an eye on naval activities, but one which they abandoned once they realized they would have had to place themselves under the navy's command.

CHAPTER FOURTEEN

Captain Collinson and the *Enterprise*

What was he doing, the great god Pan,
Down in the reeds by the river?
Elizabeth Barrett Browning,
A *Musical Instrument*

WITHOUT A TRANSLATOR

Incredibly, even as the Canadian expedition set sail back to England, another vessel was making its way through the summer ice on a course which couldn't help but lead it to the lost ships. More amazing still, the vessel was Royal Navy.

Back in 1850, slightly before Penny, Austin, John Ross, Forsyth, and the Americans had all set out on their combined search, with the Beechey Island find still in the future, James Clark Ross' two ships, *Enterprise* and *Investigator*, had been refitted and dispatched with the task of entering the Arctic by way of the Bering Strait — the west end. A previous expedition, the *Plover*, had been sent the same way but hadn't turned up any sign of Franklin along the north coast of the continent.

Once again, the Admiralty chose to ignore the probable in favour of the improbable.

The most obvious course for the *Enterprise* and *Investigator* would have been for the ships to extend the *Plover's* search along the southern passage — the passage Franklin had known would lead him out of the Arctic if he could only get to it. Instead, both ships were instructed to make for Banks Land farther north. Banks Land was the western-most land mass sighted by Parry during his spectacular voyage so many years before. It also lay on the other side of the impassable ice barrier that Franklin had been specifically ordered to avoid. In this respect, the searchers were taking the same course as every other expedition except Jane Franklin's *Prince Albert*: forget Franklin's sailing instructions; search north or west, but not south.

In command of the expedition was Captain Richard Collinson, aboard the *Enterprise*, the faster of the two ships. In charge of the *Investigator* was Robert McClure, destined to go down in history as the first man to finally discover the Northwest Passage ... sort of.

His triumph was diluted by several factors: for one, he was forced to abandon his ship in the ice and complete the Passage on foot; for another, later evidence would indicate Franklin's crew had discovered *another* Northwest Passage to the south shortly before they perished.

On setting out from England, the *Enterprise* and *Investigator* had parted company with the understanding that they would regroup off the Alaska coast. However, they met again having just reached the Pacific Ocean by way of the Strait of Magellan. At this point, an astonishing thing happened. Before setting out from England, a missionary from Labrador, of the Moravian Brotherhood, had been recruited to assist the expedition in translating any news they might obtain from the Inuit in the western Arctic. But there had been no berth available on the lead ship, *Enterprise*, so the missionary was placed on the *Investigator*. Now, meeting again off the tip of South America, Collinson asked the missionary to transfer to the lead ship, where a berth had been prepared for him.

Incredibly, the missionary refused. He didn't want to get his books wet in the wind and rain while crossing over to the other ship. McClure concurred and Collinson easily gave in. Instead, Collinson said, the missionary could change ships when they met in Honolulu. It was to be a fateful mistake, for by the time McClure reached Honolulu, Collinson had decided to continue on without his translator after a stop of only four days. They had missed each other by twenty-four hours.

Collinson's decision to proceed without his translator was a remarkable oversight, which would have grave consequences later. Still, it is possible he planned to pick up the Moravian when the ships met off the Alaskan coast and on its own this oversight would not be reason enough to question Collinson's motives for the search. But there would soon be more.

FIT TO BE TIED

Even though Collinson was ahead and in the faster ship, McClure suddenly saw a way to take advantage of his enforced isolation and beat Collinson to the Arctic. Being in no great hurry, Collinson took the longer route to Alaska, circling around the treacherous Aleutian Islands. McClure decided to head directly through the islands, even though this was generally thought to be a risky venture. The move paid off and McClure handily beat Collinson to their meeting point off Kotzebue Sound. There he was met by the *Plover* and, when told Collinson had not yet arrived, he feigned disbelief, arguing that the *Enterprise* must have passed in the fog. Off he went, only to be stopped again by another Royal Navy ship, the *Herald*. Again, McClure pretended to believe he was hurrying to catch up with the *Enterprise,* and the captain of the *Herald*, though seeing through the pretence, wasn't prepared to order McClure to wait for his superior. Had half this much initiative been shown by the Franklin searchers, the lost expedition would have been found right off the bat. Unfortunately, McClure wasn't interested in discovering the fate of Franklin's lost crew; McClure had eyes only for the Northwest Passage. So, off he went again, headed for Banks Land and destiny.

When Collinson finally reached Alaska, he was astonished to learn McClure had already been there and gone on without him. Collinson's officers told him there was still time to catch up with the *Investigator*, but Collinson refused to heed their advice. Desperately they suggested he winter at Point Barrow on the Alaska coast; again he refused. Instead, he turned around and sailed back to Honolulu to spend the winter, apparently seeing his rescue mission as something less than urgent.

The next summer, while Kennedy and Bellot were entering the Arctic from the east, Collinson penetrated the northern waters from the west, hard on the trail of his insubordinate subordinate. But, again and again, Collinson ran into ice, becoming trapped in waters which should have been easily traversed. He wouldn't listen to his ice master, Francis Skead; he wouldn't listen to his own officers. Unable to comprehend his commander's strange behaviour, Skead bitterly wrote, "As we make so little progress when there are so few obstacles to our advance, I am afraid to think of what we shall do if we meet with difficulty from ice."[1] It was as if Collinson was deliberately set on wasting an entire season. "Poor Sir John!" Skead bemoaned. "God help you — you'll get none from us."

After coasting the southeast and southwest shores of Banks Land and finding messages left informing him that McClure had already been that way, Collinson finally sought a winter harbour on the west coast of "Prince Albert Land", which was actually the western shore of the massive Victoria Island, a gargantuan land mass stretching all the way across the southern Arctic until its eastern shores looked out upon King William Island itself.

Once again, Collinson was inexplicably lax in pursuing the search for the lost expedition. Though the ocean didn't freeze-up for another five weeks, he adamantly refused to budge from his haven. As Pierre Berton commented, "In that time, he could have found a wintering harbour farther south, putting himself in a better position for the thrust to the east the following spring."[2] But then, in his every decision, Collinson had made it perfectly clear he was in no hurry to find the lost expedition — this in spite of the possibility, at that time, that Franklin might still be alive. Skead found he could not remain silent in the face of Collinson's inexcusable negligence, "considering Franklin was perishing for food and shelter."[3] He continued to fight the captain, until finally Collinson had him placed under arrest for the duration of the mission.

But Skead wasn't the only member of the *Enterprise* fit to be tied. When Collinson finally departed the Arctic in 1854 and returned to Honolulu, the *Illustrated London News* reported that he had either placed under arrest or suspended every single one of his officers during the course of his voyage. Collinson had made certain that he alone determined where the *Enterprise* sailed and what she found once she got there.

THE RIGHT DIRECTION

The next summer, as Kennedy and Bellot set sail for home, the *Enterprise* resumed her journey. But this time there was a striking difference to her course; this time she was headed in the right direction.

Collinson decided to follow the southern passage along the roof of the continent [see map 14]. The path had already been explored and

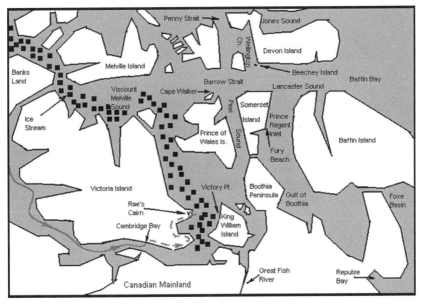

Map 14
Richard Collinson's Search, 1850-1855

mapped — by John Richardson, by John Rae, and by Peter Warren Dease and Thomas Simpson — but all had come overland through Canada; no one had yet tried to pass this way by ship. Indeed, the famous Arctic explorer Roald Amundsen would later praise Collinson highly for this feat of navigation; Amundsen had difficulty passing through the same waters even in a far smaller ship.

It was this southern passage that Franklin had (ostensibly) hoped to reach somehow by a route to be found somewhere southwest of Cape Walker. Collinson explicitly stated his reason for taking this route was to place his ship in a location "where we should be in a good position to succour any parties who might have come to mishap after entering the strait between Capes Bunny and Walker"(in other words, Peel Sound.[4] If Collinson had kept going on his course he would eventually have run smack into King William Island and the scattered and grisly remains to be found there. But there wasn't time to travel farther than Cambridge Bay on the south shore of Victoria Island. Again, the *Enterprise* put into winter quarters. This time, however, the answers they sought were finally within sledge distance.

IGNORING THE EVIDENCE

"It would almost seem," commented Noel Wright, "that during the ship's long stay in Cambridge Bay Captain Collinson's reasoning faculty became numbed by the conditions of cold."[5] Having "deliberately isolated himself from the companionship of his officers," Collinson now proceeded to do everything in his power to ignore what was quite clearly staring him in the face. He had said it himself: he was there to succour parties trapped coming down Peel Sound. And yet, on seeing the heavy ice in Victoria Strait to the east of Victoria Island, he decided there was no point in crossing over to King William Island, but settled for a search of the immediate coast.

Local Inuit were encountered, but having left his only interpreter aboard the other ship, communication was difficult. Just the same, an officer named Arbuthnot managed to convince an Inuk to draw a picture of the east coast of Victoria Island, which depicted the lost ships in Victoria Strait. Incredibly, Collinson claimed not to believe it. The drawing did not match the coast he had travelled over, he said; the Inuk was merely repeating back the questions put to him. A sledge party found a piece of door frame with a latch attachment nearby, almost certainly from one of the lost ships; but again Collinson dismissed it as unimportant. Ice master Skead, still under arrest, could only grind his teeth in disgust. Why was Collinson there if not to follow up what few leads he could find?

Why indeed?

WHAT WAS HE DOING?

If we accept that Collinson was part of the conspiracy to keep the lost expedition from being found, we have to ask ourselves one vital question: why had he dared to come this close? His relationship with his officers would indicate that he had not shared whatever secrets he may have been privy to. No matter how tight a rein Collinson kept on his officers, the risk of discovery must surely have been enormous. Why would he chance it?

Perhaps the answer is to be found in a sledge trip undertaken by Collinson in April. Setting out from his winter berth at Cambridge Bay with two main and one supporting sledge, Collinson travelled up the east coast of Victoria Island until he came upon a cairn left by the explorer John Rae two years before. Rae, Collinson discovered, had come overland in the summer of 1851, then briefly visited that same coast by small boat. Rae had been unable to cross over to King William Island because of the ice. Collinson now continued on a little farther, even crossing out onto the ice until he was a mere fifty miles away from the place where the answers lay: Victory Point. Then he turned back and returned to the ship.

Apart from Rae's cairn, it was during this sledge trip that Collinson's party happened upon what Noel Wright described as "three rather mysterious cairns, which contained no documents or clues to their builders."[6] Were these cairns erected by Franklin's crew? If so, Collinson's motive becomes instantly clear. Just as Captain Ommanney may have "suppressed" whatever message was left in the cairn at Beechey Island, as well as whatever may have been deposited on Cape Walker, Collinson too had come, not to succour the lost expedition, but to seek, remove, and conceal the records they had left.

CHAPTER FIFTEEN

A Study in Contrasts

Trifles light as air
Are to the jealous confirmations strong
As proofs of holy writ.
William Shakespeare,
Othello

AS SAFE AS HOUSES

It was April, 1852, and Franklin had now been lost for seven years. In the western Arctic, McClure was solidly trapped in the ice on the northeast shore of Banks Land. Though he had discovered a Northwest Passage, that impassable ice stream sat squarely in his path, preventing him from making good on his discovery. Collinson, further south on Victoria Island, had just placed his ice master, Skead, under arrest for suggesting he might do more to find Sir John. In the eastern Arctic, the Canadian expedition under Kennedy and Bellot was doggedly sledging over Prince of Wales Island.

Now, sailing from England, came the Admiralty's most impressive flotilla yet — what her commander, Edward Belcher, grandly called, "The Last of the Arctic Voyages".[1]

It was nothing of the kind. It was, however, the last of the navy's voyages to be sent in search of Franklin. Edward Belcher would see to that.

The plan, as initially formulated, was as simple as it was hypocritical. No less than four naval ships were to enter and explore Wellington Channel. Ever since the previous expeditions had returned, a battle royal had raged between the "Pennyites", who insisted Captain Austin should have loaned a steamer to Captain

Penny, and those who said Austin had been perfectly correct in writing off Wellington Channel. The navy, true to form, had stood by its man, supporting Austin all the way. Though Penny had offered his services for further searches, the navy wanted nothing more to do with the spirited whaling captain. It was the Admiralty's contention that enough was enough; they had tried to find Franklin and had failed. Let him rest in peace.

But the pressure, both from the public and from Lady Franklin, was as unyielding as the Arctic ice. After all, Franklin's winter encampment had been found; graves had been discovered; success seemed so close. The navy gave in, after a fashion. Not surprisingly, after Penny's find the public was now pushing for Wellington Channel. The Admiralty agreed to send a full flotilla of four vessels, all of them to enter and explore Wellington Channel and nothing else. After the navy's defence of Austin, it was an astonishing turn around. But perhaps not so astonishing if Wellington Channel had always been nothing more than misdirection. The issue had become Wellington Channel or nothing. No one was even discussing Peel Sound.

But then the issue grew more complicated. It was pointed out that McClure and Collinson had not been heard from since they had entered the western Arctic. McClure had been in the ice two winters. No one wanted to contemplate the horror of losing those expeditions as well.

It was decided something should be done. Instead of sending four ships up Wellington Channel, only two were sent to search that area while two others would sail down Barrow Strait into Viscount Melville Sound to search for the searchers on Melville Island and Banks Land. To further facilitate the search, a fifth ship was added to the roster, that "old sailing-donkey" the *North Star*, which would remain at Beechey Island to be used as a fallback position and storage depot between the two wings of the flotilla [see map 15].

Wellington Channel and Melville Island — the navy was essentially using five ships to repeat Austin's search of the previous year. The secret of Franklin's fate was safe as houses.

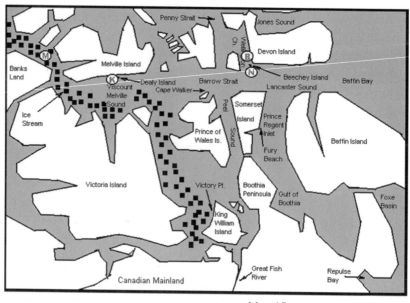

Map 15

Belcher's two ships Ⓑ
Kellett's two ships Ⓚ
McClure's one ship Ⓜ
The <u>North Star</u>   Ⓝ

Sir Edward Belcher's "Last of the Arctic Voyages,"
1852–1854

FINDING MCCLURE

No one was entirely certain why the Admiralty chose Captain Sir Edward Belcher to command so difficult a mission. It was acting under the advice of the Arctic Council, who of course had their own reasons for doing things. Belcher was an elderly officer without a shred of experience in the Arctic, thoroughly detested by all who served under him. But not even his harshest critics could have foreseen the unparalleled disaster that was to follow.

Before disaster there was success; but a success that could only cast further doubt on the navy's sincerity in their search for Franklin. While hindsight may be 20/20, it is impossible not to notice the striking contrasts between the bungled efforts made to find Franklin and the swift, almost effortless recovery of McClure's expedition.

Where Franklin's sailing orders were twisted, misquoted and reinterpreted to suggest he might have gone just about anywhere except where he had been told to go, McClure's instructions were taken to mean precisely what they said. He had been told to sail for

Banks Land, so as to enter the northern passage at Viscount Melville Sound. The two search ships, *Resolute* and *Intrepid*, were dispatched to search Banks Land.

The lead ship, *Resolute*, was under the command of Captain Kellett, who coincidentally had been the officer (then in command of the *Herald*) who had tried so hard to keep McClure from entering the Arctic ahead of Collinson. The *Intrepid* was a screw steamer, which proved of immense value in towing the *Resolute* through the heavy ice and shallow waters of Viscount Melville Sound. Her captain was none other than Leopold McClintock. Having served on that first sledge journey with James Clark Ross in 1849 and then done more sledging on Melville Island under Austin, McClintock returned once again to bring his considerable experience to bear on the McClure search.

Perhaps the most amazing aspect of this other search was that the *Resolute* and *Intrepid* succeeded in reaching their destination at all. It was a spectacular voyage that had not been accomplished by any other ship since Parry's miracle journey back in 1819. Since the navy had found it impossible to sail even as far as Cape Walker because of heavy ice only two years earlier, this would seem to suggest one of two possibilities — the first being that the search for McClure was blessed.

In stark contrast to the tangled scenarios dreamed up to confuse the Franklin search, it was instantly assumed that McClure, if he met with trouble, would leave a message at the cairn erected by Edward Parry at Winter Harbour on Melville Island. Kellett was unable to reach Winter Harbour because six miles of pack ice drifted offshore, but once the ships were safely berthed on Dealy Island slightly to the east, a sledge party visited Winter Harbour and, sure enough, McClure had left a message.

McClure reported that he was stuck fast in the ice on the north shore of Banks Land on the opposite side of the ice river. The next spring, sledges were promptly dispatched. They set out earlier in the year than any of the sledge trips sent in search of Franklin (except for the Canadian expedition).

More significantly, sledge dogs were employed.

DOGS VERSUS MEN

Much has been written about the navy's inexplicable aversion to the use of dogs to pull their sledges. It has been argued that cultural snobbery was at work; a racist conviction that the Inuit could not know more about travelling in their own backyard than the cream of the British Royal Navy. Or else, it has been said that a romantic mythology developed, whereby the brave men shattering their health hauling in the traces acted the parts of modern knights, struggling valiantly against impossible odds. To varying extents, both factors came into play. At the same time, we can't help but notice the navy was remarkably selective in this particular aversion. The same spring that a dog team rushed speedily across Viscount Melville Sound to the aid of the ice-mired McClure, ponderously slow man-hauled sledges grimly slogged their way in search of Franklin in the very same area (having set out a full month *after* the McClure-bound team).

McClintock had concluded on his previous visit that Franklin was not to be found here, but he resumed the search as ordered. He even found ways to improve the efficiency of the task, developing the practice of employing smaller "satellite" sledges to explore areas around the paths of the main sledges. But he could not escape the limits imposed by the use of men in the traces. McClintock became the officially recognized master of naval sledgers, travelling 1,328 miles that spring. While this was certainly a record distance as far as the navy was concerned, it had been handily bested the year before by the Canadian team of Kennedy and Bellot, who had, of course, used dogs.

Lieutenant Bedford Pim and two companions, Robert Hoyle and Thomas Bidgood, mushed across the frozen waters of Viscount Melville Sound to find the crew of the *Investigator* badly ravaged after three winters in the ice. Under Kellett's orders, McClure and his crew abandoned their vessel and crowded aboard the *Resolute* on the other side of the ice stream.

Quickly, Kellett organized a sledge party to transport the most sickly members of the *Investigator* to the *North Star* at Beechey Island, where they were subsequently taken home aboard the supply ship *Phoenix* (which had been dispatched from England to re-provision Belcher's expedition). When the ice began to break up in the summer, the *Resolute* sailed from its berth at Dealy Island, only to stick fast in the ice after travelling a scant 100 miles. Nothing could be done to free the ship, and once more the sun slipped from the sky and the Arctic night closed like a curtain. As yet, none suspected what disaster awaited in the spring.

CHAPTER SIXTEEN

How to Lose a Flotilla

> This time it vanished slowly, beginning with the end
> of the tail, and ending with the grin...
> Lewis Carroll,
> *Alice's Adventures in Wonderland*

MEANWHILE, IN THE EAST

While Kellett was busy saving McClure and McClintock was making a vain effort to continue the Franklin search, Sir Edward Belcher, in command of the entire expedition (if not entirely in control), was busy pushing forward with the search up Wellington Channel. The previous year he had found a safe haven for the ships on the Grinnell Peninsula, where the north end of Wellington Channel enters Penny Strait. This allowed him to explore even further north, where he discovered a new land which he named North Cornwall Island, but no sign of Franklin was discovered.

Now, in the spring of 1853, sledge parties were dispatched to the west of Penny Strait while Belcher himself supervised the search in the east. Unlike Kellett, Belcher had managed to make enemies with just about every officer serving under him. Indeed, there are striking similarities between Belcher's command and Collinson's aboard the *Enterprise*. Like Collinson, Belcher refused to listen to the advice of his subordinates and did not hesitate to arrest anyone who dared question his tactics, a group which would eventually include his sister ship's commander, Sherard Osborn.

Still, by the time all the various search parties had returned to the two ships in Penny Strait, they had virtually completed the map of the entire northern Arctic archipelago. Geographically speaking, the Belcher expedition was a triumph; the British Royal Navy had successfully defined the roof of the world. Unfortunately, Franklin was (to stretch the metaphor) in the basement, and only Collinson was looking there.

Like Kellett, Belcher now took advantage of the summer thaw. The *Assistance* and *Pioneer* slipped from their harbour and sailed triumphantly down Wellington Channel, headed for home. Also like Kellett, they ran up against unexpectedly resistant ice. Before Belcher knew what was happening, he was forced to seek a second winter harbour, this one fifty miles up Wellington Channel from where the *North Star* was still patiently waiting at Beechey Island.

The second winter was worse than the first. Belcher's first lieutenant, Walter May, was relieved of his duties for the use of subversive language and Sherard Osborn was placed under arrest. At one point, Belcher even cut off all communication with his sister ship as a form of punishment. But, as astonishing as all this was, a far greater madness lay just around the corner.

BELCHER'S MADNESS

In the early spring Kellett dispatched a sledge to Beechey Island to learn how Belcher was faring in the search. The sledge team returned with dispatches and a private communication from Belcher. In an official dispatch, Belcher instructed Kellett to "meet me at Beechey Island, with the crews of all vessels, before the 26th of August."[1] Kellett was mystified; he was quite certain his two ships could break free of the ice in the summer, but the 26th of August? In the private communication, Belcher left no doubt of his meaning. He told Kellett to abandon both the *Resolute* and the *Intrepid*. Belcher was going home one way or the other.

Kellett couldn't believe what he was reading. There was no reason to abandon two navy ships (three, when you included McClure's *Investigator*) under the circumstances and anyone who would do so deserved "to have their jackets taken off their backs."[2] Immediately, Kellett wrote a reply to Belcher's bizarre request, telling his superior that he could not act on the instructions as given and would require an official order from Belcher. Kellett gave the reply into the keeping of McClintock, who carried it speedily to Wellington Channel to argue strenuously against Belcher's proposed hasty retreat. All Kellett's officers were certain their ships could be freed in the summer, McClintock told him; there was no need to leave them. But Belcher was adamant. Back McClintock sledged, this time with an official order.

But Belcher's madness grew steadily more surreal by the moment. Not content to order Kellett to abandon three vessels, Belcher himself had decided to desert both of *his* ships in Wellington Channel as well. In the whole history of Arctic exploration, it was a disaster equalled only by the loss of the Franklin expedition itself. Of the five ships sent north under Belcher's command, four of them were to be deserted, without cause or reason.

On top of everything, two records were recovered which had been deposited in cairns by Collinson of the *Enterprise*. He had now been in the Arctic three full winters, the same number as McClure's expedition had suffered through when Kellett found the crew of the *Investigator* in such a terrible state. Surely Belcher couldn't desert Collinson?

Belcher could and did. His officers pleaded with him to reconsider, offering to stay on and continue the search while he returned to England. For a moment, it seemed McClintock had convinced him to allow the master sledger to take full command of the expedition. It would have made perfect sense. This expedition wasn't facing the same perils as had previous voyages to the Arctic; with the *North Star* stationed at Beechey Island and transports arriving each summer with provisions, the ships could have remained in the ice as long as the job required. But, for Belcher nothing less than a complete withdrawal would suffice.

This astonishing decision to abandon five ships, to desert Collinson, to squeeze six crews aboard the *North Star* (miraculously relieved when two supply ships arrived at the last moment), to throw away everything, has remained unexplained down to the present day. What was going through Belcher's head? Why the sudden hurry? Was it merely that Belcher had had enough and wanted out, as historians have assumed? But why then did he refuse to leave McClintock to carry on without him?

KELLETT'S PLAN

If an explanation is to be found for Belcher's abrupt departure, it is to be found the previous spring. Kellett had been sent to the western

Arctic primarily to rescue McClure. As we have already noted, what efforts were made to find Franklin were noticeably lacking when contrasted with the exertions made on McClure's behalf. In this though, Kellett may still have been acting under Belcher's orders. Once McClure was safely aboard, and McClintock had returned without finding any sign of Franklin, Kellett made a bold and unexpected decision, based on McClintock's recommendation. If the ships got free in the summer, Kellett would sail back out into Baffin Bay to the coast of Greenland, and once again investigate Adam Beck's story of a massacre. On the other hand, if the ships were forced to spend a second winter in Viscount Melville Sound (as they were), in the spring Kellett planned to send sledge parties far to the east to travel down Peel Sound [see map 16].

Peel Sound?

Frozen to the bottom it might be; blocked by land at its southern end, perhaps; but Kellett was resolved to see where it led just the same. And where it would have led was straight to King William

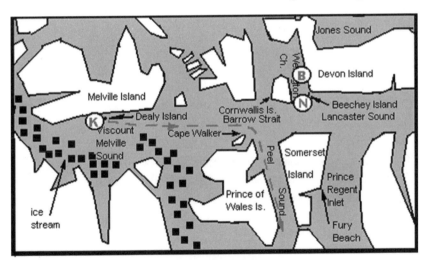

Map 16
Kellett's plan to sledge down Peel Sound

Belcher's two ships Ⓑ
Kellett's two ships Ⓚ
The <u>North Star</u> Ⓝ

139

Island and the answer to Franklin's fate — had Kellett been permitted to pursue that course.

Belcher would have learned of Kellett's plans from dispatches brought to Beechey Island by the refugees from the *Investigator*. He must have been astonished. The sledge journey Kellett contemplated was truly epic; Kellett had been assigned to the western Arctic to search the western Arctic. How could anyone have anticipated the man would decide to mount an expedition to search Peel Sound in the east? Had Belcher wintered with Kellett he could have kept control of the situation, just as he controlled the officers in Wellington Channel; but he was not with Kellett and, because of the stretched lines of communication, Kellett was free to act virtually under his own command.

Belcher had only one option open to him and he took it. As early as possible in the spring, before Kellett could mount his proposed expedition to Peel Sound, Belcher ordered his subordinate to abandon ship and return to Beechey Island. Kellett might still have sent a sledge to Peel Sound, but he now needed his sledges and, more importantly, his best sledger, McClintock, to talk Belcher out of his madness.

A LESSON TOO REFINED

In the end, Belcher could not be swayed and the swift and wholesale abandonment of the ships and of Collinson was carried out as ordered. On reaching England, a court-martial was convened, as it had to be in the event of even one lost ship. Belcher's officers, though, were out for his blood. Sherard Osborn was still under arrest when the ships docked. Historian Roderic Owen noted that Commander Richards "actually feared for his life, and in case his fears proved justified he prepared a secret dossier of Belcher's misdoings which to this day has not been made public."[3] Sophia Cracroft, Jane Franklin's niece, had spoken to the officers and learned that Belcher's "sole object was we are told 'to make a catastrophe for the public in England'."[4] The entire blame thus landed fully on Belcher's elderly shoulders; it never occurred to any of them that Belcher might have been acting under orders from his superiors — orders to ensure Franklin was not found, whatever the cost.

The court-martial acquitted Belcher, but it was said his sword was returned to him in chilling silence. To observers this silence was interpreted as a chastisement, and they were mystified that Belcher did not seem to recognize it as such. Dr. Richard King called it "a lesson too refined for the man".[5] But we may perhaps wonder if there was another significance to that moment of silence, an exchange of glances, common understanding and the secret bond of conspirators joined by unworthy motives. Certainly the ruling of the court-martial, in the present context, lends itself to an interpretation considerably different from the one placed on it by Belcher's enemies. For, after all that he had done wrong, the court-marital seemed able to find but one reason to rebuke him. It was suggested only "that he should have consulted with Captain Kellett previously."[6]

Chapter Seventeen

The Ghost Ship

"Quaff, oh quaff this kind nepenthe and forget
this lost Lenore!"
Quoth the Raven, "Nevermore."
Edgar Allan Poe,
The Raven

Out of the darkness

It had been a fantastically complex and, at times, costly dance of deception. If we are correct, the Victory Point Conspiracy had been carried out over thirty years, ever since Edward Parry's *Fury* entered the Arctic in 1824, there to vanish forever. We have argued that James Clark Ross, during that disastrous voyage, first began to suspect something was to be found on King William Island, returning later aboard his uncle's ship, *Victory*, to confirm his discovery. Eventually, the navy had outfitted a spectacular expedition — the *Erebus* and *Terror*, a sort of pre-atomic Manhattan Project — and dispatched it into the unknown; then, when the expedition had so obviously met with disaster, the navy found itself increasing forced to extremes in an effort to cover-up the entire thing.

It had very nearly succeeded. But, in the end, it was a secret too big to remain hidden, even in the vastness of the Arctic. Within a month of Belcher's return, word finally arrived which pointed the way at last: King William Island. Not surprisingly, the news had come from the one source that many people had suggested but none had tried: the Inuit.

But the British Navy wasn't yet done in its machinations. There was testimony, but only Inuit testimony, translated and imperfect. Artifacts had been found that provided proof that disaster had overtaken the expedition, but, as yet, the secret of King William Island itself had not been breached. If Franklin had left records behind — in the cairn on Beechey Island, at Cape Walker, or in the three cairns on Victoria Island — those messages had long since been "suppressed", as Penny said. Time was on the navy's side. Victory Point remained a long way from England, and every year that passed was another year during which evidence might be eradicated by the ceaseless fury of the Arctic weather. All they had to do was wait.

But then, out of the blue-white north, as if guided by the ghosts of those they had sought so long to bury without honour, sailed Kellett's ship, *Resolute*. It was a voyage impossible to explain. Without a crew, her hatches sealed, her rigging white with rime, the *Resolute* had broken free of the ice in the summer, navigated the shoals and heavy ice of Viscount Melville Sound, passed through Barrow Strait and then Lancaster Sound, and finally glided into Baffin Bay, where she was sighted the next year by Captain Buddington of the whaler *George Henry*.

It was but one more inexplicable event in the weird chain of happenings that made up the story of the lost Franklin expedition. Only two expeditions had ever successfully travelled the track followed by the *Resolute*: Edward Parry's in 1819, and Captain Kellett's. Kellett had only succeeded because he had the screw steamer *Intrepid* to pull the wind-driven *Resolute* out of the shallows and off the grinding ice pans. If it had not happened, we would have said it was impossible.

Nonetheless, the proof was there for all to see as Buddington, taking the ghost ship in tow, led her proudly to New London, Connecticut. To Buddington's surprise, the British government immediately laid claim to their abandoned vessel, but then reversed their decision and returned her to her salvager. We might well wonder if this wasn't just an excuse to allow the Admiralty time to search and recover any compromising documents still aboard her.

But events were rapidly assuming a momentum all their own. The American Congress stepped in and purchased the vessel for $40,000. She was sent to an American naval yard to be refitted. One year later she sailed again, this time on a voyage back to England, as a gift to the Royal Navy from their friends across the pond. It was understood by one and all that she was being returned for the purpose of fulfilling her destiny in the Arctic. The American ambassador referred to her as "a consecrated ship". Henry Grinnell, the man behind the American expedition (actually, expeditions, since there had been a second one sent while Belcher was still in the Arctic, which had come to nothing), wrote to the British government at Lady Franklin's behest. The Royal Irish Academy passed a motion that the *Resolute* be employed in one final voyage to King William Island. Jane Franklin, gathering support wherever she spoke, talked of the *Resolute's* "sacred mission". The Queen, Prince Albert, The Prince of Wales, and other Royals greeted the ship when she arrived at Cowes. Even the Prime Minister was onside. It seemed nothing could stand in the way of this last inevitable push to discover once and for all the true fate of Sir John Franklin.

So the navy, hardly known for its subtlety, did the only thing it could. Under the orders of Sir Charles Wood, First Lord of the Admiralty, the *Resolute* was dismantled and "run up on the mud".[1]

It was a stunning slap in the face to the Americans and a ruthless stab in the back to Lady Franklin. It was a last, desperate play made by an Admiralty backed into a corner and determined to see that no force on earth would resurrect the *Resolute* a second time. But it was also the end of the game. Even the destruction of the *Resolute* could not stop what had grown to be inevitable. Before the strength of will shown by Lady Franklin, all the lies, all the misdirection were no more than temporary setbacks. She would soon find her husband's expedition, though not her husband. She was only one woman, but the navy could not stop her.

Yet, there remains the possibility that the cover-up did succeed in its principle aim. After all, for all the evidence ultimately discovered strung in a grisly trail down the west coast of King William Island, we will never know what was lost to the wind and the blowing snow, to the cold and the ice, during the many years the secret lay silent and undiscovered under the northern lights. There were clues enough, as we will soon see; but what else might those first searchers have found had they reached Victory Point back in 1849, when the disaster was only a year in the past? We will never know; and in this the Victory Point Conspiracy was a success.

There was a final epilogue to the story of the *Resolute*, a last little twist to the tale that somehow reads like the punchline to a very dark joke, a final detail to render complete a story of conspiracy and cover-up.

After the *Resolute* was dismantled, a desk was fashioned from her oak beams, which was then given to the American president, Chester A. Arthur, as a gift. The desk was eventually placed in storage, where it sat in dust and darkness for a century. Then, almost like the *Resolute* itself, the desk was discovered and resurrected, being dragged out into the light of a world which had survived two world wars and now trembled in the shadow of the Hydrogen bomb. The desk had been found by the wife of another American president and, under her care, it was restored and resumed its place in the White House. It was said to have been the President's favourite desk, and its polished oak surface must often have reflected his features like a dark and clouded mirror.

That president was John F. Kennedy.

PART III
Into the Darkness

"Is there anybody there?" said the traveller,
Knocking on the moonlit door.
            Walter de La Mare,
            The Listeners

CHAPTER EIGHTEEN

John Rae

And the highwayman came riding –
Riding – riding –
The highwayman came riding, up to the
old inn-door.

> Charles Howard, Duke of Norfolk,
> *The Highwayman*

THE HONOURED DEAD

It was autumn, 1854, and Jane Franklin must have wondered if she had finally been defeated in her quest. Belcher's "last of the Arctic voyages" seemed almost certainly to have been precisely that.

A staggering tally of six naval ships had been left and lost to the crushing caress of the relentless ice, all within the past two years. McClure's *Investigator* had been abandoned at Banks Land; Belcher's ship *Assistance* and Osborn's *Pioneer* had been deserted in Wellington Channel; Kellett's *Resolute* and McClintock's *Intrepid* had suffered the same fate in Viscount Melville Sound (though *Resolute* would eventually rise like a phoenix from the ashes, for the moment it seemed safe to write it off for good); and, finally, there was the *Breadalbane*, a transport ship dispatched the previous year with provisions for Belcher's expedition. Off Beechey Island, the *Breadalbane* had been suddenly holed by an ice pan, her crew barely having time to save themselves as she settled beneath the icy waters in only fifteen minutes. (Amongst all these ships, it is somewhat ironic that the one to achieve a degree of immortality was the lowly sunken transport. In August 1980, Dr. Joe MacInnis headed a Canadian expedition that relocated the wreck under 340 feet of water in Barrow Strait.)

As far as Jane Franklin knew, Collinsonand the *Enterprise* were still searching in the western Arctic, but she didn't hold out great hope for that expedition. In actual fact, Collinson had already slipped back out of the Arctic the way he came in, and was now heading quickly for Hong Kong.

Finally, the American Grinnell expedition (the second such voyage) remained in Arctic waters, ostensibly searching for signs of Sir John; but again the Americans had unaccountably chosen to explore Smith Sound at the top of Baffin Bay, about as far from the probable region of Franklin's grave as you could hope to get.

But the unkindest cut of all had come in March. Though the deed itself was unexpected, the perpetrator was par for the course. The Admiralty ruled that as of March 31, all 129 men who had entered the Arctic nine years before aboard HM ships *Erebus* and *Terror* were officially to be listed as dead. The navy made this callous decision at a time when Belcher's five vessels were still supposedly searching, Collinson had yet to be heard from, and the Americans, whatever the odds against their finding anything in Smith Sound, were still hard at work.

It was perfectly true that no stretch of the imagination, no matter how desperate or contrived, could concoct a scenario whereby Franklin's crews could subsist on their provisions for nine years. On the other hand, Franklin wasn't exactly lost on the moon. John Ross could never have lasted four years on the provisions he had taken with him to Prince Regent Inlet in 1829, but he had found the Inuit more than happy to supply food for those first two winters. Perhaps Franklin had likewise encountered Inuit to hunt game for his crew. Failing this, it was even suggested that a few survivors might have sought refuge among the Arctic peoples; perhaps even after nine years some of Franklin's crew were to be found living in igloos in some tiny, out-of-the-way Inuit encampment, alive but unable to communicate with the outside world. And then there were all those supply caches to consider: no longer just the one at Fury Beach, but the many that had been established since then. If Franklin had managed to reach one of them, perhaps ... perhaps ...

But the Admiralty could not be swayed. The crews of *Erebus* and *Terror* were dead and that was the end of it. Even Sir John Franklin, the greatest hero of all, was written off as easily as the navy would soon write off her six lost ships. It is difficult to find a suitable comparison from our own age, but it was as if NASA were to have lost contact with Neil Armstrong on the moon, then declared him dead, while there was still a possibility his radio was merely malfunctioning.

With the return of Belcher's overcrowded expedition in September, whatever hope had remained for Jane Franklin must have been crushed as swiftly as the *Breadalbane* itself. Six ships lost — how could she convince the navy to send out another expedition after such a disaster?

Quite obviously she couldn't. Belcher's inexplicable abandonment of his ships had effectively driven the nail into her husband's coffin. For a terrible moment, Lady Franklin perched on the brink of a cruel future, a future reaching on and on until her death, never to know what fate had befallen her husband. The Admiralty very nearly won.

Then, in late October, barely a month after Belcher's return, word reached England — Franklin had been found. More incredible still, the man who had happened upon the lost expedition seemed to have been about the only person in the Arctic not actually looking.

Tarzan of the Barren Grounds

He was Dr. John Rae, the same man who had visited Victoria Island ahead of Collinson, and he is certainly one of the most colourful figures to grace the pages of Canadian history books.

John Rae was a sort of Tarzan of the Barren Grounds. Employed by the Hudson's Bay Company, he travelled staggering distances through the Canadian North, sometimes alone, sometimes accompanied by a few native companions. Occasionally he used dog sleds, other times he ate up the snow-clad miles on snowshoe, averaging as much as 24 miles a day. He had Inuit snow goggles shielding his eyes, and he carried what he needed on his back. He needed surprisingly little. So long as he had enough ammunition for his rifle, Rae could supply all the nutritional needs of himself and his companions, gaining weight in bleak northern regions where any other European would have starved to death.

Rae was born in the Orkneys, where bitter weather served as a sort of overseas kiln, smelting strong, able lads to staff the Company "factories" on the bleak shores of Hudson Bay and the even lonelier posts farther inland. He first entered the service of the "Honourable Company of

Adventurers" as a surgeon aboard the supply ship *Prince of Wales*, on its annual run over to Moose Factory, but he made such a good impression on the Chief Factor that the Company promptly offered him a permanent position. It wasn't long before his remarkable talent for lengthy, snowshoe-clad treks through the Canadian brush earned him a reputation. He was placed in charge of the Rupert River District and then offered a shot at the history books.

ROYAL CLEARANCE

As a condition of its original charter, the Hudson's Bay Company, back in 1670, had been expected to search for a Northwest Passage in addition to trapping beavers for profit. The Company had been fairly lax in pursuing the former, but now, with the growing public interest in the Royal Navy's efforts, the Company took up the cudgel.

In 1836, George Simpson, the Company's governor, had dispatched his younger cousin, Thomas Simpson, along with another company employee, Peter Warren Dease, to venture up the Mackenzie River and then up the Coppermine. Their goal was to map the southern passage along the roof of the continent, a passage already partly delineated by Franklin, and later to be sailed through by Collinson. In their second expedition, Dease and Simpson travelled east from the Coppermine and discovered a strait directly south of King William Island, a passage which Simpson believed had to continue eastward, cutting directly through Boothia [see map 17]. In other words, Simpson believed there was a water passage connecting the Gulf of Boothia at the bottom of Prince Regent Inlet with the western waters under King William Island. He thought Boothia was an island.

On the other hand, James Clark Ross and John Ross had already visited the area aboard the *Victory*. Having spoken to the local Inuit, the Rosses were convinced that no such passage through Boothia existed: Boothia was a peninsula.

Who was right? Everything might hinge on the answer. If Simpson was right and Boothia was an island, then his strait would effectively be the final link in the Northwest Passage. If the Rosses were correct and Boothia was a peninsula, then the Passage, if it existed, would have to be sought farther north.

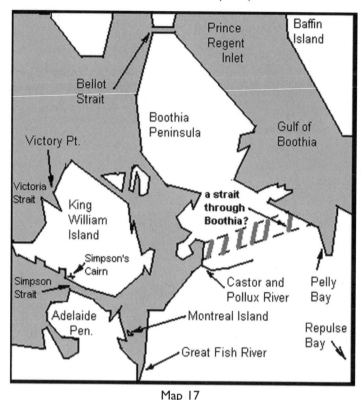

Map 17
Thomas Simpson's proposed strait through Boothia

In 1846, one year after Franklin had set sail on his doomed expedition, the Honourable Company asked John Rae to resolve the question once and for all. Was Boothia an island or a peninsula? To do this, Rae decided to attack the problem from the east, rather than from the west as Simpson had. In two twenty-foot boats named *Magnet* and *North Pole*, he set out from Churchill and sailed up the west coast of Hudson Bay to Repulse Bay. Arriving too late to begin his explorations that year, Rae calmly settled in for the winter, naming his little camp Fort Hope.

The next summer, Rae set off to the north and west, exploring and mapping the southern reaches of Prince Regent Inlet and the Gulf of Boothia. Travelling along the east coast of Boothia, he found no indications of a water passage from the west, and concluded, rightly, that Simpson had been wrong; Boothia was a peninsula, connected to the continent. The Northwest Passage was to be found farther north — if at all.

But what did the Admiralty think of Rae's explorations? After all, we have assumed Franklin's orders were to proceed to King William Island, only a short distance from Rae's area of inquiry. While his visit coincided with Franklin's, Rae had no plans to cross Boothia, and there was no reason his expedition should have encountered Franklin's. The Admiralty may not have given it any thought. On the other hand, when Rae wrote up his adventures for publication, the publisher submitted the manuscript to the Admiralty for clearance. The navy held onto Rae's book for three years, before returning it to him so completely rewritten that he grumbled, "I did not know my own bantling when it reached me."[1] Why did a book describing the purely geographical explorations of an employee of the Hudson's Bay Company require clearance from the British Royal Navy?

LESS THAN ADVERTISED

In 1848, as concern began to grow for the welfare of Franklin's expedition, Rae was again asked to travel to the Arctic waterways, this time as part of a navy search team. In charge of the party was Sir John Richardson, who had previously trekked with Franklin on the explorer's two earlier journeys.

In a foreshadowing of things to come, the expedition seemed determined to fail even before setting out from England. Richardson planned to reach Arctic tidewater at the end of August, in spite of knowing that previous land expeditions had been forced to turn back before then. Governor Simpson felt "some degree of alarm and apprehension"[2] on seeing how ill-prepared the men were, and Rae himself felt that "almost everything connected with the Expedition was a makeshift for such work — the men included."[3] At about the same time, in Baffin Bay, James Clark Ross was dispatching word to England of his intention to severely truncate his own search, so we should hardly be surprised if Richardson's expedition was also less than advertised.

Travelling up the Mackenzie River to its mouth, the party searched slightly eastward along the Arctic coast before turning back and retreating to Fort Confidence on Great Bear Lake to spend the winter, having accomplished exactly nothing. In the summer, Richardson returned to England, while Rae tried again. During two journeys, Rae managed to explore the east coast of Victoria Island by boat, from which position he could look across the ice-choked Victoria Strait toward King William Island. But Rae wasn't equipped to cross the strait, so he settled for leaving a record of his trek, which Collinson happened upon two years later.

Not the slightest hope

The search for Franklin, such as it was, continued without the assistance of John Rae. Ships shuttled back and forth through black leads, man-hauled sledges ground over heaving hummocks, collared foxes scampered over the snow and ice, Franklin's winter camp was discovered on Beechey Island, and the search moved ever northward.

His part in the drama apparently played, Rae requested permission to return to Repulse Bay once again. His goal this time was pure exploration and only marginally different from his previous expedition. Kennedy and Bellot had recently returned from the Arctic with the report of a water passage dividing Boothia from Somerset Island — Bellot Strait. Unfortunately, Kennedy had only recognized it for what it was after returning to the *Prince Albert*, and Bellot, ironically, wasn't convinced they had discovered a strait at all. But if Bellot Strait existed, it might prove to be the final link in the Northwest Passage. Rae proposed to explore the west coast of Boothia starting from the farthest point reached by Dease and Simpson at the Castor and Pollux River, work his way north up to the mouth of Bellot Strait, then trace that strait to Prince Regent Inlet, thereby completing the Northwest Passage [see map 18].

Along the way, Rae had two subsidiary goals. The first was to prove once and for all that Boothia really was a peninsula and not an island. True, Rae had thought that question was settled by his earlier expedition, but the navy would not be convinced until someone mapped the west coast as well. In addition to this, Rae wanted to explore the hitherto unexplored area between King William Island and Boothia. At that time, it was still thought that King William Island was actually King William Land, forming a sort of bulbous outcrop from Boothia, instead of being separated by a strait.

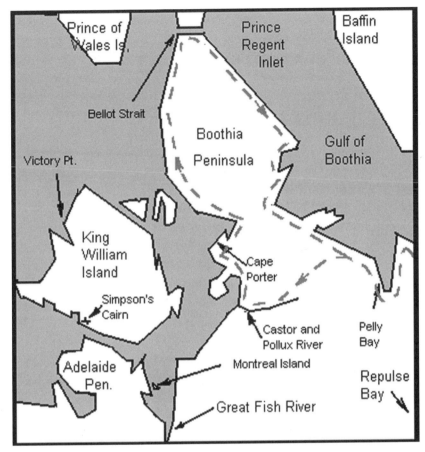

Map 18
John Rae's intended route to Bellot Strait

In August 1853, while Belcher's flotilla prepared for a second winter far to the north, Rae returned to his little winter haven on Repulse Bay. In a letter published in *The Times* the year before, he had written, "I do not mention the lost navigators, as there is not the slightest hope of finding any trace of them in the quarter to which I am going."[4]

CHAPTER NINETEEN

Cannibalism and Other Relics
of the Lost

"'The time has come,' the Walrus said,
"To talk of many things ...:"
Lewis Carroll,
Through the Looking-glass

THE ARTICLE IN THE TIMES

The British public first learned of John Rae's discovery in late October, 1854, from an article printed in *The Times*. The article was Rae's report, which he had sent on ahead to the Admiralty before his arrival in England. It was a remarkably frustrating tale composed partly of solid indisputable evidence and partly (far too much, most people felt) of anecdotes gleaned from Inuit interviewees who had themselves gathered their stories from others. Indeed, Rae's own report hardly encouraged unflinching acceptance when he wrote, "None of the Esquimaux with whom I have conversed had seen the 'whites', nor had they even been at the place where the bodies were found, but had their information from those who had been there and had seen the party travelling."[1]

Still, solid evidence there was, the kind that left no room for doubt. There was a gold watch engraved with the name of the *Erebus*' ice master, James Reid. There were silver knives, forks, and spoons, ownership again confirmed by the initials engraved on the handles. There were eight silver watchcases, surgical instruments, coins, a silver pencil case — in all, something like forty-five separate objects. And then, as if a final gift was cast out of the north to ensure there could be not a shred of doubt remaining, Rae brought home Franklin's own Hanoverian Order of Merit.

THE PELLY BAY INUIT

The lost expedition had indeed been found — but where? And what had happened to cause this disaster? Rae's story was infuriatingly incomplete, built on second-hand evidence.

In the spring of that year, Rae had set out with his six travelling companions and headed northwest from Repulse Bay in order to cross over to the west coast of Boothia to begin his explorations [see map 19]. But, while still on the Gulf of Boothia, Rae encountered a group of seventeen Inuit at Pelly Bay. Here a very strange thing occurred. Even if he didn't expect to find Franklin in the area, Rae had sense enough to ask questions wherever he went; but here he found that "they would

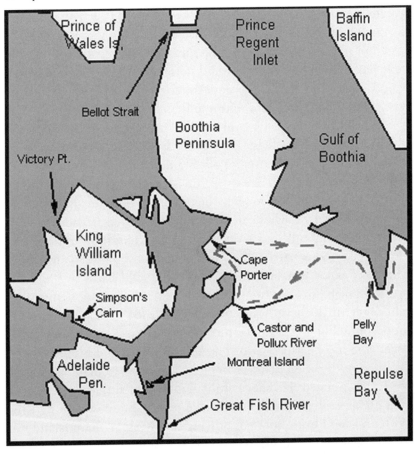

Map 19
John Rae cuts short his explorations at Cape Porter

give us no information on which any reliance could be placed and none of them would consent to accompany us for a day or two, though I promised to reward them liberally. Apparently there was a great objection to our travelling across country in a westerly direction."[2] Even stranger, after speaking with these Inuit, Rae's own interpreter suddenly attempted to run away and had to be chased down and brought back. In fact, Rae believed the interpreter had done his best to conceal whatever it was he had been told by the other Inuit.

What were the Inuit afraid of? Were they concerned that they might be blamed for the deaths of the white men scattered in a ghastly trail in the west? Or was there some other reason they tried to keep Rae from travelling into that country? Strangely, twelve years later, a searcher named Charles Francis Hall would reach Pelly Bay following the same route taken by Rae, while headed for King William Island in search of relics. Like Rae, Hall also met with stiff resistance from the Pelly Bay Inuit. The Inuit told weird stories of a fierce tribe inhabiting King William Island, and the stories so frightened Hall's party that he was forced to turn back and return to Repulse Bay.

Rae did not turn back, and a little farther west he encountered two Inuit dragging a sledge. He noticed that one, named In-nook-poo-zhee-jook, was wearing a gold braided cap-band from the uniform of a naval officer. Rae asked the man where he had come by the cap-band. In-nook-poo-zhee-jook told Rae that the gilt band had come from a place where nearly forty white men had died on an island in the mouth of a river in the west. The Inuk himself had never been there personally and could not show Rae on a map where the place was. Rae then bought the gold band and told the two Inuit to pass along the word that he would purchase any other relics they might have found once he returned to Repulse Bay. He then continued westward to the mouth of the Castor and Pollux River (the most eastern point reached by Dease and Simpson) and explored up the west coast of Boothia according to plan, as if nothing had happened. He successfully demonstrated that Boothia was, after all, a peninsula, and also discovered Rae Strait separating King William Island from Boothia, proving that King William Island was indeed an island. But he interrupted his explorations before reaching Bellot Strait as he had intended and instead returned to Repulse Bay. There he was met by a great many Inuit eager to trade Franklin relics and information, some of the Inuit being from the group he had found so uncooperative at Pelly Bay.

From these Inuit, Rae purchased the vast assortment of watches, cutlery, coins, and the like, which left no doubt that Franklin's ships had been abandoned nearby. He also learned enough to conclude that at least some of the crew had perished on Montreal Island, in the mouth of the Great Fish River just south of King William Island. Because the summer was fast approaching (and, unlike the sea-going expeditions, Rae needed frozen water to travel), Rae decided there was no time to investigate this new information. Instead, he broke camp and headed south. He quickly sent his story to the *Montreal Herald*, where it appeared a month before it exploded across the pages of *The Times*. He hurried to England, claiming his only desire was to prevent other expeditions from being sent to the wrong place.

CANNIBALISM AND DISINFORMATION

If Rae had expected a hero's welcome, he was soon disillusioned. The accusations were soon flying thicker than the flakes in a blizzard. Why, people wanted to know, had he not stayed to investigate? Rae insisted he had not known where to look until his return to Repulse Bay, by which point it was too late in the season. But surely, they insisted, even without knowing the exact location, after learning of the dead white men from In-nook-poo-zhee-jook he could have scouted around? He claimed he hadn't initially thought the story of forty dead seamen had anything to do with Franklin's lost expedition. As Pierre Berton asked, "Who else could they be *but* Franklin's crew members?"[3] Chief Trader for the Hudson's Bay Company, William Gibson, commented in 1937, "It may be a cause of speculation why Dr. Rae did not proceed to Back's Great Fish River to investigate on the spot, before returning to his base at Repulse Bay."[4]

At the same time, Rae had other matters to contend with. Along with various other details supplied by his informers, Rae passed along an extremely unpleasant revelation, one that promptly had the effect of the proverbial bull in the china shop. He reported, "From the mutilated state of the corpses and the contents of the kettles, it is evident that our wretched countrymen had been driven to the last resource — cannibalism — as a means of prolonging survival."[5]

The contents of the kettles? Good God. Apparently, as far as the Tarzan of the Barren Grounds was concerned, Victorian sensibilities could be damned. As Peter Newman remarked, "This went directly against the strictly held tenet of the Royal Geographical Society that English gentlemen do not devour one another."[6]

Sensibilities or no, Rae had shown remarkably poor judgement in publicly disclosing so sensitive a suggestion — and a suggestion, after all, was all it really could be. His own Inuit informers were merely relating stories told to them by others. None of them had actually seen these kettles, and Rae certainly hadn't. Clearly it was a judgment call; Rae could hardly have kept quiet about so important a discovery. But he was talking about, not just the cream of the Royal Navy, but men who had been elevated nearly to sainthood through the efforts of the devoted Lady Franklin. To suddenly suggest that they had calmly gone about the task of cutting up and eating (and cooking!) those of their number who had fallen by the way — Rae was either astonishingly naive or remarkably callous.

But perhaps Charles Dickens was closer to recognizing the true state of things when he penned a furious response to Rae's report in the pages of *Household Words*. Dickens argued that Rae had been perfectly correct in reporting the cannibalism story to the Admiralty, but the famous author wondered why the Admiralty had been so eager to see that story publicly displayed in *The Times*.

He may have been closer to the mark than even he suspected. It was certainly a curious situation; surely a first of some sort. The Admiralty hadn't even waited to interview Rae in person, but had rushed into print his story of mutilated bodies and kettles while the fur trader was still at sea. Not only was the Admiralty not trying to contain the damage to its reputation, it seemed positively eager to spread the word.

It would be many years yet before the term "disinformation" would enter the English lexicon.

THE ANDERSON EXPEDITION

Of course, hot on the heels of Rae's revelations came offers to do what he apparently had not thought important enough to do: travel to the mouth of the Great Fish River and search for firm evidence of the expedition's final trek (and evidence of cannibalism, naturally). Dr. Richard King, who had previously explored the Great Fish River with George Back, made such an offer after heaping abuse on Rae and even going so far as to question the Orkneyman's geographical discoveries. Since Dr. King had argued all along that Franklin's crew would be found by going up the Great Fish River, he had the distinction of being the only person to be proven absolutely correct, at least who was not also basing their conclusions on the word of a blue light.

But the Admiralty was admirably quick off the mark this time. On October 30, within four days of Dr. King's offer and a week after the publication of Rae's report, the Admiralty announced that it had asked the Hudson's Bay Company to dispatch an expedition down the Great Fish River under the direction of Chief Factor James Anderson. In making this pre-emptory move, the navy once again saw to it that the ball remained comfortably in their court.

On the other hand, the expedition was being handled by the Hudson's Bay Company; what could possibly go wrong? Quite a bit, apparently. The Admiralty seemed to have a sort of reverse Midas Touch. Voicing that off-key refrain sung so often before, Roderic Owen observed, "The Anderson Expedition started off under one handicap."[7] While they reported they had read George Back's narrative of his explorations of the Great Fish River, they made no mention of Dr. King's. Given that King had been proven unquestionably right, one might have thought any information he could supply regarding the journey they were about to undertake would have been much sought after.

But a lack of knowledge regarding the area of search wasn't the only handicap weighing down the Anderson Expedition. A far more serious omission was the lack of an Inuit interpreter. Rae had only learned what he had because of information received from the Inuit. Yet now Anderson, like Collinson before him, cheerfully pushed up the Great Fish River in search of Franklin's last resting place with no way to ask questions of those he might find in the area.

On top of everything else, the boats carried along on the expedition were wholly unsuited for the icy conditions they would meet in the Arctic tidewater. Anderson explained the lack of an interpreter and the useless boats by stating that there had not been sufficient time to properly prepare, in spite of the fact that the expedition, promptly announced in October 1854, didn't actually set out until late June 1855. Even then, the expedition departed so late in the season Anderson told Lady Franklin that he "did not expect to reach the sea at all, much less search the coast."[8]

As anticipated, almost nothing was accomplished. Anderson's party encountered a group of Inuit near the mouth of the Great Fish River who had fashioned useful items from wood obviously taken from a ship's boat. From these Inuit they purchased various relics: a letter-nip dated 1843, a broken saw, a chisel, a tin soup tureen. But without an interpreter, there was no way to ask where these things had been found. On Montreal Island (which was the island Rae believed his informers had referred to), Anderson's party found only wood shavings, indicating they had discovered the place where the ship's boat had been cut up by the Inuit. On one wood fragment, the name "Terror" was legible.

The Inuit that Rae had spoken to had told him Franklin's men had been seen retreating from the ice-locked ships down the coast of King William Island. But without proper boats, Anderson was unable to cross Simpson Strait to investigate the island. Having proven only that Rae was correct in placing the disaster somewhere in the area, but having failed in his primary mission to actually find the place, Anderson returned home.

He had accomplished absolutely nothing, but on his return he presented Jane Franklin with a piece of backgammon board that was found on Montreal Island and which she herself had placed aboard one of the ships before sailing. It was small consolation.

CHAPTER TWENTY

Lady Franklin's Decision

Now who will stand on either hand,
And keep the bridge with me?
Lord Macaulay,
Lay's of Ancient Rome

THE NAVY'S MISTAKE

It would not be too unfair to say that the only thing accomplished by
Anderson's expedition was to delay other searches — private searches
— for another year.

In June of 1856, two years after Rae had returned with his relics,
he was rewarded with the 10,000 pounds offered to any party able to
discover the fate of Franklin's crew. The Admiralty had waited for
Anderson's return before handing over the reward to the fur trader —
a curious action in its own right. After all, if they felt Rae's evidence
was compelling enough to earn him the reward, why did they require
Anderson to double check? Nor could it truly be said that Anderson
had confirmed Rae's discovery; he had merely proven that something
had happened in the general area. But what?

For the answer to that question, they had only the second-hand stories supplied by Rae's Inuit informers. Why would the Admiralty suddenly take the word of the Inuit now, when it had doubted them
before? James Clark Ross had been told Boothia was a peninsula by the
Inuit; the navy refused to take that as proof. Then there were the other
dubious stories which littered the years of search: Adam Beck's tale of
massacre on the Greenland coast, for instance. Now, suddenly the
Admiralty considered the second-hand Inuit tales of cannibalism

among the Royal Navy's legendary officers to constitute final proof of their fate?

Jane Franklin, as always, remained a force unto herself. With Anderson's return, she was again pushing for another expedition, this one to do what she had been trying to do for so many years: send a ship down Prince Regent Inlet to winter on the Boothia Peninsula, and from there dispatch search parties across to King William Island.

We can only wonder what horror of mind and soul she must have suffered on first hearing Rae's revelations. Perhaps if she had been seeking her husband in the wrong place, she could have consoled herself with the thought she had simply made a mistake. But the horror was that she had been searching in the right place from the start. She and she alone had stood any hope of reaching Franklin's crew, and she had failed. If only she had not listened to James Clark Ross; if only she had chosen someone other than Captain Forsyth; if only she had been more adamant with Captain Kennedy (or, if only she hadn't instructed him to check up on the navy's search — if indeed she did); if only she had tried harder. She would have to live with the horror for the rest of her life.

It was at this point that the Americans gallantly returned the resurrected *Resolute*, newly repaired after a year in dry dock. She was a "consecrated ship". She too was meant to complete a job left undone. And yet, like the Anderson Expedition, her mere existence acted as a source of further delay, drawing Lady Franklin's resources and energy to an effort which ultimately proved futile. Another year passed, a year of furious lobbying and letter writing, handshaking and trembling speeches, all directed toward seeing the *Resolute* dispatched on a seemingly inevitable voyage to Prince Regent Inlet.

And then, with startling suddenness, everything changed. We might say that after carrying out its carefully orchestrated conspiracy for so long, after so successfully setting false trails, emptying cairns, determining the search areas, controlling and concealing, misleading and covering-up, after all the deceit and all the cunning trickery, the Admiralty finally made a mistake.

It destroyed the *Resolute*.

Everything else could be rationalized away. Jane Franklin could tell herself that she had been cursed with terrible luck, that the navy was simply incompetent, that coincidences happen. She could blame the unpredictable weather or the lack of preparation; she could curse the name of individual officers (like Belcher) or curse herself for her personal choices (like Forsyth); she could put anything and everything down to cruel fickle Fate, and wish to God things might have been different — were it not for the destruction of the *Resolute*. This wasn't an act of incompetence or poor leadership; it wasn't the fault of ice conditions or an Arctic blizzard. The *Resolute* had been destroyed in a clear and deliberate act designed to keep her from doing what so clearly had to be done: reach her husband. And it had been destroyed by order of the First Lord of the Admiralty. Against the wishes of the Americans who had restored the ship, against the wishes of the public, against even the wishes of the Prime Minister, Lord Palmerston, the *Resolute* had been dismantled, and for that crime there could be no excuse.

If there was a point of revelation in this story, a precise moment when Lady Franklin at long last realized the nature of the thing she faced, it must have been now. The enemy was not Fate; her enemy wore a uniform. Her enemy carried a sword and saluted smartly, all the while weaving a web of lies and deceit. Her enemy had made only one mistake but it was enough. It must have been so clear to her.

She wasted no time; that was the navy's game. With the year well under way and the Arctic sailing season fast approaching, she purchased the *Fox*, a 177-ton schooner-rigged screw-yacht that had only been used once before on a trip to Norway. It cost her 2000 pounds. Once again financing flowed from private sources, totalling nearly 3000 pounds, of which 5 pounds was donated by "The brothers and sisters of the late John and Thomas Hartnell of H.M.S. Erebus"[1] (the former lying in a somewhat disturbed state on distant Beechey Island. To this sum, Lady Franklin added a further 7000 pounds of her personal wealth, which was now considerably smaller than in earlier days. In Aberdeen, the *Fox* was refitted and strengthened to face the ice.

And then there was another matter to decide.

ONE MAN

If the Franklin search were to be made as a motion picture, this would be the moment when the music would soar, the moment of truth and vindication to which all else had been steadily leading. For so many years, Jane Franklin had found herself the naive victim, betrayed by those who had seemed her friends, betrayed by men of honour and repute, betrayed by nearly everyone. She was a woman besieged, surrounded by the faceless enemy, deep in its home, beaten at every turn. And so she turned to the only man left who had not betrayed her.

One last time she invited Captain Coppin into her home. She "spoke painfully of her previous selections".[2] She asked him a fairly simple question: who should she send this time?

As simple as the question was, it was nonetheless remarkable for the person to whom it was directed. Captain Coppin wasn't an Edward Parry or a James Clark Ross; he wasn't a member of the illustrious Arctic Council to which she had so often turned in the past; he was a lowly shipbuilder whose sole claim to her ear arose from his daughter having seen words written on a wall by a ghost. Yet, his advice had guided her for so long, urging her to send ships down Prince Regent Inlet when the Admiralty and its experts insisted there was no need. Captain Coppin had been proven right and, more importantly, Captain Coppin had known it all along. He had never claimed to have seen the ghostly vision, yet he had acted as certain as if he had. He had been reluctant to allow Jane Franklin to speak with his daughter personally; he had refused to have his story made public in a proposed book by Charles Dickens, bowing out "for sacred family reasons".[3] Yet, all along, working quietly in the background, he had been insistent: Victory Point. There, he said, Franklin would be found. How could she not have suspected a secret truth beneath the ghost story?

If so, Captain Coppin must surely have recognized this. Perhaps there was a moment of silent understanding, a meeting of eyes, the moment unconsciously echoing that strange instance when Captain Belcher was handed back his sword in silence — a small conspiracy of their own. It takes little imagination to see the true meaning of the question put to Captain Coppin; a squint of the eye and the significance grows clear as if momentarily glimpsed through thinning fog on the Arctic sea. Jane Franklin wasn't just asking him who to send, she was asking him who in all of England she could trust. Captain Coppin took a piece of paper and scrawled a name.

Francis Leopold McClintock.

CHAPTER TWENTY-ONE

The Voyage of the *Fox*

Down these mean streets a man must go
who is not himself mean; who is neither tarnished
nor afraid.
                    Raymond Chandler,
                    The Simple Art of Murder

SO UNACCOUNTABLY CIVIL

The *Fox* set sail in early July 1857 with a crew of twenty-five, seventeen
of whom had been involved in previous Franklin searches, all of whom
had been hand-picked by McClintock.

Captain Collinson, formerly of the *Enterprise* in its voyage to the
brink of success and back, took charge of the business end of things.
Was this atonement perhaps? A way of making up for the part he had
played in turning a blind eye to the evidence of Sir John Franklin's lost
ships in Victoria Strait, perhaps while emptying a cairn or two (or
three) along the way? Collinson had spent much of that hapless earlier voyage drunk in his cabin. Had he been something less than a willing accomplice to the machinations of his superiors?

As for McClintock, his command of this voyage seems somehow
entirely fitting, inevitable even. It was McClintock who had travelled
with James Clark Ross over the north shore of Somerset Island and
down Peel Sound way back in 1849, the first of the Franklin searches.
During that journey, McClintock had hung back with the men who
hauled the sledges while Ross scouted the terrain ahead. McClintock
had returned to the Arctic with Austin's four-ship flotilla in 1850,
where he had set sledging records travelling west along the shores of
Melville Island. Then in 1852 he had again returned to Melville

Island, this time in command of his own ship, the steamer *Intrepid*. Again his sledgers had not turned up a sliver of wood to indicate Franklin's crew had met with disaster in that area. It had been on McClintock's suggestion that Captain Kellett had planned to dispatch a sledge party down Peel Sound in the spring of 1854, an expedition that McClintock would certainly have been ordered to command. When Sir Edward Belcher's orders to abandon all ships came through early that spring, McClintock offered to remain behind and continue the search — a request which was denied. It was as if his entire career had been steadily guiding him toward this one final voyage.

The Admiralty itself seemed remarkably complacent, once Lady Franklin's expedition became a *fait accompli*. Permission was granted for McClintock's chosen officers to join the private venture. McClintock, however, clearly had his own reasons to feel uneasy, though what he believed we can only guess. Before accepting Lady Franklin's request to command the *Fox*, McClintock wrote to James Clark Ross, his former commander: "What I would wish to ask you is how far I might expect the countenance of the scientific bodies ... and in how far the Admiralty sanction ought to be obtained, as I do not wish to be so impolitic as to act counter to their wishes." He then added, "I have not mentioned this subject to anyone and should [the voyage] not take place we would be better not to let it be known that I'd ever contemplated accepting."[1]

But McClintock's concern seemed unfounded. The Admiralty did grant him permission. The Royal Navy even went so far as to supply some three tons of pemmican, powder for ice blasting, and rockets, all left over from previous expeditions. It was all so unaccountably civil. As the tiny *Fox* slowly dwindled over the western horizon off the Orkneys, Lady Franklin might well have found herself wondering if she wasn't waiting for the other shoe to drop.

CHANCES UNKNOWN

Upon reaching the Greenland coast, McClintock promptly purchased ten sled dogs at Godhaven. Noting that he would require twenty more, his interpreter, Petersen (who had been Captain Penny's interpreter back in 1850), directed him to a small settlement named Proven where more dogs were bought. It was a striking affirmation of intent and determination, and a bold split with the naval expeditions which had gone before. McClintock had made his reputation with man-hauled sledges. Yet, now, for the first time, he used dogs. His message was clear: the navy was no longer calling the shots. This time there would be no excuses.

Then, after such a defiantly determined start, the expedition ran into trouble with a capital "I". The ice had not cleared in the upper part of Melville Bay, contrary to what he had been told by whalers. He became trapped, and was forced to spend a terrifying winter locked in the grinding pack. Finally, on April 25th, 1858, after 242 days, the ice broke up and the *Fox* made its way into Lancaster Sound.

Having used up most of his coal battling his way across Baffin Bay, McClintock now steered a course for Beechey Island, where a coal cache had been left by the *North Star* [see map 20]. While at Beechey he erected a monument to Franklin and his crew that had been deposited undelivered at Godhaven by the last American expedition in 1855. The inscription noted that Franklin and his men had "suffered and perished in the cause of science and the service of their country"

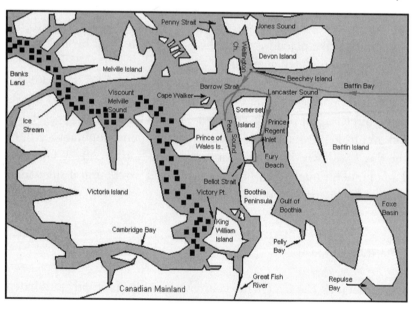

Map 20
McClintock's Voyage of the *Fox*, 1857–1858

and that the monument was to commemorate the grief of their coun-trymen and friends "and the anguish, subdued by faith, of her who has lost, in the heroic leader of the expedition, the most devoted and affec-tionate of husbands." It was somehow entirely appropriate that the woman who had fought against impossible odds to discover her hus-band's fate, but who had nonetheless shunned personal publicity so much so that few photographs were ever taken of her, did not think to place her own name on this monument to her grief.

During his brief stopover at Beechey Island, we may wonder if McClintock took time to visit the three lonely graves with their inscribed headstones — monuments of a less heroic nature. Casting his eye over those two strange Biblical passages, he might well have felt an unaccountable chill. "Thus saith the Lord of Hosts; consider your ways." "Choose ye this day whom ye will serve." What happened in this place during that lonely, sunless winter so long ago? How did these three men die? What was Franklin trying to say with those two dark quotations? Were they messages left for others to decipher?

Perhaps for the first time, standing over those graves, the grim real-ity of his situation may have closed around McClintock like an Arctic fog. The last two times he had come this way, he had been part of naval flotillas: four ships under Austin, five under Belcher. This time, McClintock had no supply transports to depend upon, no depot ships to fall back on; unlike John Ross' *Felix* with its tender *Mary*, McClintock had brought no ship to transfer to if anything happened to the *Fox*. For all intents and purposes, it might as well have been 1845 all over again. But, Franklin had travelled with a pair of powerful (and Antarctic-proven) bomb-ketches manned by 129 seamen, their decks heaped with provisions, libraries stocked with three thousand books, two hundred canisters for messages, and two railway steam engines for screw-propulsion. McClintock had one small steam-yacht which had travelled to Norway and back. With this and twenty-five men, he planned to venture into the unknown Arctic.

True, it was now known that Franklin had found his way down to King William Island. But it still wasn't known how he had gotten there. By Peel Sound, as McClintock believed? By a channel southwest of Cape Walker, as Lady Franklin continued to hope, wanting to believe her husband had followed his instructions to the letter? Or had he got-ten there by going down Prince Regent Inlet and through Bellot Strait, if indeed Kennedy had been correct about that passage's existence? Nobody knew and so McClintock was effectively as much in the dark as Franklin had been.

But, in a way, McClintock was in a worse position than Franklin. Franklin, whatever he may have expected to find at Victory Point, had been confident of success. McClintock, on the other hand, knew something terrible had happened to his predecessor. After all the confidence, all the expense, and all the preparation, something had gone disastrously wrong and 129 men had perished in horror. Now McClintock planned to follow them. "Ahead lay chances unknown and incalculable," wrote historian Leslie Neatby. "The track of the *Erebus* and the *Terror* had been traversed only once — by those who had never come back."

Some had been buried ... some had not

McClintock steamed south from Beechey Island to his destination, Peel Sound. Five years before, he had planned to sledge down the sound, until his proposal was foiled by Sir Edward Belcher. Now, crossing Barrow Strait, the *Fox* "shot gallantly past Limestone Island" at the mouth of the passage. And there, sure enough, the water lay clear ahead. Where was the multi-year ice frozen to the bottom? Where was the impassable ice of James Clark Ross and Willy Browne? In someone's imagination, apparently. With his crew and himself "in a wild state of excitement — a mingling of anxious hopes and fears", McClintock steered straight down the throat of the passage, success nearly within his grasp. And then, disappointment. Twenty-five miles down Peel Sound, the *Fox* ran into ice. There was still no sign of the multi-year ice; this was melting ice, "much decayed, and of one year's growth only". But it was enough to prevent the tiny *Fox* from proceeding further.

Though frustrated by this obstacle, McClintock knew he couldn't waste time fighting his way through it. He turned around and hurried back up Peel Sound, then down Prince Regent Inlet to the mouth of Bellot Strait. The strait cut through the Boothia-Somerset landmass at its slimmest point: a mere twenty miles long, a scant mile wide at it narrowest. In spite of this, towering granite cliffs measuring 1600 feet high loomed against the sky on either side, the whitewater depths plunging straight down to an astonishing 400 feet only a quarter of a mile from the shore. But here too McClintock was foiled. Six times he braved the narrow, steep-walled strait, each time being driven back by ice, whirlpools, and a powerful current from the west.

In the end, frustrated, the season too late even to return to Peel Sound, McClintock returned to the mouth of Bellot Strait to spend a second winter in the cold and the dark.

Once again, no better proof exists of the navy's purposeful stalling tactics, than the contrasting efficiency with which the non-naval searches were conducted. McClintock set out on February 17, 1859. Only Kennedy and Bellot's moonlit January trek to check for Franklin at Fury Beach could claim an earlier beginning. Taking fifteen dogs pulling two sledges and provisions for twenty-four days, McClintock set off with Petersen, the interpreter, and Alexander Thompson, who had also previously been on Penny's expedition. Following the margin of Bellot Strait to the west coast of Boothia Peninsula, the party sledged south along the shore to the North Magnetic Pole. That is where McClintock hoped to meet with the local Inuit whom James Clark Ross and John Ross had encountered when they had wintered in the area back in 1829. Instead of weighing themselves down with tents, the party built rough igloos.

It was an astonishing picture: an officer of Her Majesty's Royal Navy travelling with dogsleds and building igloos? What had happened to the aversion against "going native"? Apparently, that particular aversion only applied while naval officers were operating under the instructions of the Admiralty, not otherwise.

On March 1st, the expedition had still not located James Clark Ross' cairn marking the Magnetic Pole, their provisions were in a "reduced state", and six of the fifteen dogs were too sick to pull the sledges. Certain they could travel only one more day, and still having failed to encounter any Inuit, McClintock looked behind him. To his astonishment, he found a party of Inuit *following* his party. "Petersen and I immediately buckled on our revolvers and advanced to meet them."[2]

McClintock noticed one Inuk wore a naval button, which McClintock used as an icebreaker to open questions about the lost expedition. Over the next few days more Inuit arrived, having heard that white men were offering to buy relics. McClintock purchased six silver spoons, forks, a silver medal belonging to the assistant surgeon of the *Terror*, a gold chain, more buttons, and knives made from iron and wood that were obviously taken from one of the ships. He noticed one of the native sledges was made from the stout keel of a ship's boat, and he bought a six-and-a-half foot spear that seemed to be made from a boat's gunwale. None of the Inuit had actually seen the lost expedition, but the party was told of a ship crushed in the ice in the direction of Cape Felix at the northern tip of King William Island. Apparently the entire crew had made it to shore safely, but later one Inuk claimed to have seen their bones on an island. Some had been buried, the man told McClintock, some had not.

Having learned all he could, McClintock returned to the *Fox* to wait for the spring to arrive and the real search to begin.

THE UNSPEAKABLY PRECIOUS DOCUMENTS

On April 2nd, the sledge teams set out once again. Once more, McClintock's efforts could not help but raise questions about the sincerity of the naval expeditions which had preceded him. True, the searchers now had a rough idea as to where to look. Rae's informers suggested the mouth of the Great Fish River was a likely spot to find relics and bodies; specifically, five bodies had been mentioned as lying exposed on Montreal Island. On the other hand, McClintock's informers spoke of a ship being crushed in the ice near the northern tip of King William Island. If both stories were true, then Franklin's crew must have abandoned ship in the ice of Victoria Strait and trudged all the way down the west and south coasts of King William Island, then crossed Simpson Strait to the mainland near the Great Fish River. This hardly narrowed down the search area.

As well, there was the question of the second ship. The Inuit McClintock had spoken to only told him of one ship which had been sunk by ice. What had happened to the other one? It had to be out there somewhere, but where?

Franklin was most probably to be found on King William Island, but McClintock wasn't prepared to take the chance that he might be wrong. Though he had neither enough men nor enough dog-drivers, McClintock resolved to divide his small party into three groups [see map 21]. McClintock himself would lead his

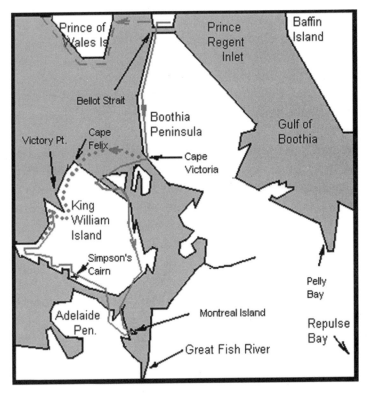

Map 21
McClintock's 3 Sledge Parties

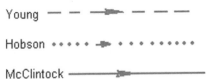

group down to the Great Fish River, then back to King William Island from below. A second group, under the leadership of Lieutenant William Hobson, McClintock's second-in-command, was to cross to King William Island from the north, beginning their search at the north tip of the island and tracing the west coast southward. Finally, a third group, under the command of Allen Young, the *Fox*'s navigator, was instructed to search Prince of Wales Island, already partially searched by the naval sledgers under Ommanney and also by Kennedy and Bellot.

Historians have generally held that McClintock gave Hobson the most promising area to search as a magnanimous gesture. For example,

Leslie Neatby commented, "Thus, with a generosity in strong contrast to the egotism later displayed by Robert Peary in a similar situation, he [McClintock] yielded to his lieutenant the first chance of making the prized discovery of Franklin's record."[3]

In fact, McClintock did nothing of the kind. His instructions from Lady Franklin had been quite clear. In a letter, she had begun by assuring him, "You have kindly invited me to give you 'Instructions,' but I cannot bring myself to feel that it would be right in me in any way to influence your judgment in the conduct of your noble undertaking; and indeed I have no temptation to do so, since it appears to me that your views are almost identical with those which I have independently formed."[4] She might not be prepared to tell him where to look, but she certainly intended to make sure he knew what he was after:

> As to the objects of the expedition and their relative importance, I am sure you know that the rescue of any possible survivor of the 'Erebus' and 'Terror' would be to me, as it would be to you, the noblest results of our efforts.... Next to it in importance is the recovery of the unspeakably precious documents of the expedition, public and private .... I trust it will be in your power to confirm, directly or inferentially, the claims of my husband's expedition to the earliest discovery of the passage.

McClintock's instructions then were to search for survivors (which were unlikely to be found after so many years), retrieve the ship's records, and prove that Franklin's crew, in their last desperate march over the bleak snows, had recognized the Northwest Passage for what it was. McClintock was not being generous by sending Hobson to the northern tip of King William Island; to have done otherwise would have been to betray Lady Franklin's trust. Wherever Franklin's crew had begun their death march, they had completed it in the south, along the south shore of King William Island and the mainland beyond. This was where the final link in the Passage lay and only there could the proof of its discovery be found.

As for the "unspeakably precious" records, McClintock believed that there was one obvious place to search; that was a famous cairn erected on the south shore of King William Island by Thomas Simpson during his explorations with Dease. McClintock felt, "The opportunity afforded by the cairn of depositing in a known position — and that, too, where their own discoveries terminated — some record of their own proceedings, or, it might be, a portion of their scientific journals, would scarcely have been disregarded."[5] Thus Simpson's cairn beckoned like a light in the fog. There the records must be found, and to search there, McClintock trusted no one but himself.

CHAPTER TWENTY-TWO

The Other Shoe Drops

Anything like the sound of a rat
Makes my heart go pit-a-pat!
Robert Browning,
The Pied Piper of Hamelin

THE SECOND SHIP

Initially, the searchers divided into two groups, with Young setting off for Prince of Wales Island, while McClintock and Hobson travelled together. Silk banners fluttered in the chill air, festooning the sledges, McClintock's given to him by Lady Franklin personally and embroidered with her name. The men wore coloured spectacles to protect their eyes, but still found themselves suffering the horrible agonies of snow blindness. Two days later, the party reached the west coast of Boothia Peninsula and on April 20th they ran into the same Inuit from whom they had bought relics back in March.

Once again, McClintock noticed tools fashioned from wood obviously taken from a ship's boat — a snow shovel, a spear handle, a bow. From a young man, he purchased a knife that had indistinct markings "such as ship's cutlasses or swords usually have".[1]

Then, from the same young man, he obtained something else.

The Inuk told McClintock that the knife had been taken from a ship which had been stranded on the shore. On the shore? In March the Inuit had told McClintock the ship sank in Victoria Strait. Now, to his astonishment, he learned that there had been two ships: one had sunk, the other had become stranded in the shallows.

McClintock was amazed and more than a little suspicious. Why had the Inuit purposely kept this second ship secret, when he had expressly asked if there was only one ship when he had spoken to them earlier in the year? What was worse, McClintock was convinced the younger Inuk had only revealed the existence of the second ship by accident, after which the others had no choice but to admit the truth. Speaking of the older man who had first told him of the sunken ship, McClintock commented darkly, "I think he would willingly have kept us in ignorance of the wreck being upon their coasts, and that the young man unwittingly made it known to us."[2]

What reason did the Inuit have for hiding the stranded ship from the searchers? Just as John Rae had met with resistance from the Inuit of Pelly Bay, and Charles Francis Hall would later discover, McClintock found the Inuit strangely determined to hamper his effort to reach the lost expedition. Why?

Even more remarkable, McClintock was told (again, by the young man) that some Inuit had climbed aboard the stranded vessel and discovered the body of a "very large man" with "long teeth".[3] This had happened many years before when the young Inuk was just a boy. A body? But whose? The discovery of this stranded ship now became an important priority in the search.

Another piece of information gleaned from the Inuit seemed unimportant at the time, but McClintock made note of it just the same. Speaking of King William Island, the Inuit told McClintock, "Formerly many natives lived there, now very few remain."[4]

King William Island

The expedition continued southward to Cape Victoria. At this point, Hobson's party departed to begin their search along the west coast of King William Island, while McClintock's sledges headed for the island's east coast. Crossing the hummock-cluttered ice using sledge-sails, McClintock and his men reached a bay on the opposite side in three days, where they camped on the ice. On May 2nd, the party set foot on King William Island for the first time.

King William Island — they had arrived at last. Here, somewhere, somehow, Franklin's expedition had met with terrible disaster. Since that time, no white man had walked these low, snow-clad shores. McClintock and his party were the first. He could not have helped but feel uneasy.

For two days they worked their way south down the coast. The land lay silent and empty around them, with no sign of the island's inhabitants. Anxious to contact the local Inuit, McClintock decided to cross to a small island in Rae Strait. There he came upon a village of twenty snow-huts. Other huts were discovered scattered within a few miles to either side. Yet there was no sign of the village's inhabitants; the place had been deserted, McClintock believed within the past fortnight. Apparently the Inuit had departed so hurriedly, they had left behind an "abundance of blubber", which McClintock now confiscated for fuel. There were also "scraps and bones of seals strewed about" which the dogs happily gorged themselves on. It was clear that the village's inhabitants had discovered the wreck on their shores; wood chips were found scattered around. But where had they gone?

Continuing his journey, McClintock passed through a deep blinding fog for two days, losing his way before coming upon another snow-village on a small islet. This one had also been recently abandoned, and tracks led off to the east toward Boothia Peninsula. McClintock concluded the villages had been winter hunting places, deserted with the approach of spring. But wandering amongst these scattered vacant dwellings, with only the lonely whispering wind and the crunching of his feet in the snow, McClintock might have recalled what he had been told by the Inuit of Boothia Peninsula, that "Formerly many natives lived there, now very few remain."

Now, travelling only at night to protect their spectacled eyes from the sun's burning glare off the snow, they returned to King William Island, then trudged southward down its barren shore. Finally, they came upon an inhabited village of twelve snow-houses and forty Inuit. After so many days spent visiting eerie ghost-villages, it was a relief at last to encounter living beings again. Indeed, the Inuit seemed just as pleased to see the searchers, the children gathering around the small party, poking and prodding them curiously. Again and again the Inuit tapped McClintock on the chest, telling him, "Kammik toomee". We are friends.

Once again, McClintock found in their possession relics of the lost expedition, which he purchased in exchange for needles. McClintock still found the Inuit surprisingly difficult to question, partly because Petersen wasn't entirely comfortable with the dialect, but also because the Inuit were "far more inclined to ask questions than to answer them."[5] Eventually he learned that the stranded ship was to be found five days away on the west side of King William Island. The Inuit told him that their people had pillaged the wreck extensively. They also claimed that the ship had lost her masts. Then they laughed and mentioned something about "fire". McClintock wasn't able to learn more about this fire, but Petersen (still having trouble with the dialect) thought the Inuit were saying they had burned down the masts for the wood.

Once again, McClintock found that none of his informers had actually seen Franklin's crew while the men were still alive, but they had seen the unburied bodies strewn along the shore, from which they concluded that the seamen had "dropped by the way as they went to the Great Fish River."[6] "They did not themselves witness this," wrote McClintock, "but discovered their bodies during the winter following." The most recent visit to the stranded wreck·had been made by a woman and a boy during the winter McClintock had spent trapped in the pack of Baffin Bay.

The searchers resumed their trek southward. Beyond a wide bay, they came upon a lone snow-hut, surrounded by a fabulous clutter of reindeer and walrus meat, blubber and skins, and, of course, more objects fashioned from wood taken from the stranded ship. But this time, the reception accorded to the party was entirely different. It took some time before the hut's owners, a man and a woman, came out to meet the visitors. Their behaviour was puzzling. "They trembled with fear, and could not, or would not, say anything except 'Kammik toomee'": we are friends. They claimed to have purchased the wooden tools from other Inuit, insisting they knew nothing about the one hundred or so white men dead on their shore. It is hard to believe, given that everyone else in the Arctic seemed to know; how could these two be unaware of the grisly remains scattered on their doorstep? One thing was certain: something had frightened them. McClintock found that "their wits seemed paralyzed, and we could get no information."[7]

WHO HAS ANY DOUBT NOW?

Giving the woman a needle as a parting gift of friendship, McClintock continued along the coast, passing through yet another ghost-village.

Then he left King William Island and crossed over to the mouth of the Great Fish River to the south. But, like Anderson, he found little evidence to support the attention that the Inuit stories seemed to give the place. On Montreal Island, Petersen discovered a few Franklin relics obviously gathered by some Inuk in the past and indicated by a "native mark", a large stone placed upright on top of another. The island seemed to be covered with these stone markers, but there was no other evidence of the lost expedition and no sign of a cairn.

Supremely disappointed, the party returned to King William Island on May 24th, reaching the shore near the mouth of the Peffer River and working their way westward. McClintock was headed for Cape Herschel where Thomas Simpson had erected his famous cairn. There McClintock felt certain the expedition's records would have been deposited. It was the only logical place to search. He came upon a different cairn near Gladman Point, apparently very old and untouched for a long time [see map 22]. Eagerly it was taken apart stone by stone, the ground beneath was searched with a pickaxe, but no record was found. Was it just a cairn left by the Inuit? Possibly. But Simpson's cairn still beckoned, so onward the party trudged.

And then, quite suddenly, they came upon their first body.

After all the years of speculation, all the grisly stories gleaned from the Inuit, all the buttons and cutlery and plates, it must still have been a shock. Here was proof, final and irrefutable, that Franklin's expedition had met with disaster in this terrible, empty place.

It was just after midnight and the skeleton lay on a gravel beach where the wind had cleared some of the snow mantle. Amongst the bleached bones, pieces of blue clothing showed through the snow — a uniform composed of a blue jacket with slashed sleeves and braided edging. The loose knot of a handkerchief around the corpse's throat told McClintock that the man had been a steward. The skeleton lay on its front, and McClintock, writing in his journal, recalled what the Inuit had told him: "they fell down and died as they walked." The Inuit hadn't seen the event itself, only the skeletons, just as McClintock did now.

He noticed that the skeleton's limbs and smaller bones had either been "gnawed away by small animals" or "dissevered". It was a curious word to use, and perhaps it was a subtle reference to the thought which must have been constantly on his mind: cannibalism. What horrors might he encounter if he continued along the coast? John Rae had

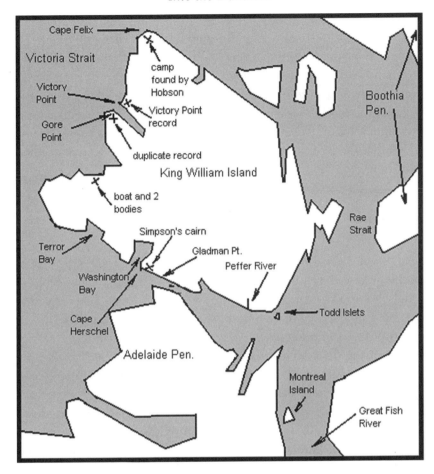

Map 22
McClintock's discoveries on King William Island, 1859

been told of kettles filled with human flesh, bodies cut up. Though McClintock carefully avoided the topic in his journal, it must have haunted him incessantly.

Near the skeleton, McClintock found a clothes brush and a horn pocket comb "in which a few light-brown hairs still remained."[8] For the first time, a written document was found, a small notebook; but, frustratingly, the pages were frozen together. Perhaps it was just as well the party wasn't able to open that book; it could only have further added to their anxiety had they known what it contained.

Later, it would be thawed and found to belong to Henry Peglar, captain of the foretop on the *Terror*. The notebook contained writing in two hands — one belonging to Peglar, the other unidentified to this day. Much of the book was indecipherable, but one sentence stood out as having been written during that final desperate march. It was in the handwriting of the unknown man; weirdly, many of the words were spelled backwards. It read: "Oh Death whare is thy sting, the grave at Comfort Cove for who has any doubt how."[9] As frightening as this final message was, it grows more disturbing still if we consider — given that the writing was barely legible — the final word as reading not "how" but "now".

THE CAIRN

McClintock noted that the Inuit would surely have looted the corpse had they discovered it; this was the first of many observations which would lead him to conclude that the Inuit, inexplicably, had refused to venture into the area in search of the wealth of artifacts which they so clearly knew were there.

After the discovery of the steward's body, the mood could only have deepened. Grimly, the party continued westward, no longer in doubt that they were walking over the same ground which Franklin's lost crewmen had followed to their end. They passed another ghost-village peopled only with silent snow-huts. And then they reached Cape Herschel. It was here that Thomas Simpson had constructed his cairn in 1839, atop a towering height of land 150 feet high and set back a quarter mile from the ice-heaped thrust of the cape. Here, more than any other place, McClintock hoped to find the records that he knew Franklin's crew would have carried with them on their retreat. Eagerly, the party climbed to the cairn, still standing after so many years.

And then McClintock could only stare in disbelief. Someone had been there before him. One side of the cairn had been torn down and the central stones had been pulled out, "as if by persons seeking for something deposited beneath."[10] Now there could be little doubt remaining; something had indeed been left in the cairn and someone had stolen it long before McClintock's arrival. The significance could hardly be missed. The navy had put up remarkably little resistance to Lady Franklin's final voyage; permission had been granted for officers to join; pemmican and powder had been kindly provided. If Jane Franklin had been there to witness the discovery of the looted cairn, she would most certainly have heard the other shoe drop.

CHAPTER TWENTY-THREE

Whodunit?

And to her amazement she discovered
A wicked man in the bathroom cupboard.
Gavin Ewart,
Miss Twye

UNLESS THEY FOUND WHAT THEY SOUGHT

McClintock was adamant. In his published journal, he fretted over the problem like a sledge dog worrying a seal bone, italics abounding. "Close round this point, or by cutting across it as we did, the retreating parties *must* have passed." The chance to leave their records in such an obvious location "would scarcely have been disregarded."[1] The men tore apart the cairn, then attacked the ground beneath with pick-axes, but there was nothing to find. "I cannot divest myself of the belief that *some record was left here* by the retreating crews." McClintock emphasized angrily, "and perhaps some most valuable documents which their slow progress and fast failing strength would have assured them could not be carried further."[2]

But who? Who could have taken it? McClintock's party were supposed to be the only white men to have walked the shores of King William Island since Franklin's crew had died here. In his published journal, McClintock placed the blame on the only people he could: the Inuit. Perhaps, he hypothesized, after the Inuit learned of the last march of Franklin's crew, they had then "lost no time in following up their traces, examining every spot where they halted, every mark they put up or stone displaced."[3] And yet, had not McClintock already noticed that the Inuit had so clearly not looted the steward's body found to the east? Indeed, it would soon become evident that, far from "examining every spot where they halted", the Inuit had confined their looting to the southernmost spots along King William Island and the mainland, and to the stranded ship, wherever that was.

But McClintock continued, "To the eye of the native hunter these marks of a recent cairn are at once apparent: and unless Simpson's cairn ... had been disturbed by Crozier [Franklin's second-in-command], I do not think the Esquimaux would have been at the trouble of pulling it down to plunder the cache; but having commenced to do so, would not have left any of it standing, *unless they found what they sought.*"[4]

The italics are all his and it was a remarkable statement. McClintock was well aware that the Inuit had no use for papers, which they tended to either give to their children to play with or else scatter to the winds. Even if an Inuk had opened Simpson's cairn and discovered records left by Franklin's crews, the discovery could only have encouraged him to continue the dismantling of the cairn in the hopes that something of real value might be found. As McClintock said, the fact that the cairn had been only partially dismantled proved that, whoever had done the deed, had "found what they sought". It is difficult not to see in McClintock's statement a hint of accusation, subtly worded, but there just the same. He was convinced the cairn had contained the records of the Franklin expedition. Someone had deliberately opened that cairn and "found what they sought", then left the remainder of the cairn untouched. Blame the Inuit though he might, his words suggest a different line of reasoning.

THE SUSPECTS

But, if not the Inuit, then who?

The list of suspects was hardly extensive. Ignoring the possibility of a secret expedition, the suspects are confined to the few expeditions known to have visited the area in the years after Franklin's disappearance. There was Captain Kennedy and Bellot, whose original plans would have carried them down the west coast of Somerset Island and Boothia, perhaps even to King William Island. But, as far as anyone knew, Kennedy and Bellot altered their plans at the last minute, instead visiting Prince of Wales Island to the north.

The sledgers under Captain Ommanney had likewise confined their searches to Prince of Wales Island. Then there was Captain Collinson; during his sledge trip, he had visited the east shore of Victoria Island just across the strait from King William Island. Could he have crossed the strait to loot Simpson's cairn at Cape Herschel? It is certainly possible, but though he was a mere fifty miles from Victory Point, this does not mean he was close to Cape Herschel, which would have required a considerable journey to reach from Victoria Island.

In fact, the only searcher to truly come close to Simpson's cairn was Chief Factor Anderson. He had been sent up the Great Fish River to check out Rae's story. In visiting Montreal Island, he would only have had to cross Simpson Strait to find any records left at the famous cairn. But everyone had agreed: the boats carried by the Anderson expedition were incapable of crossing Simpson Strait during that time of the year. Anderson was in the area, but he was unable to reach King William Island even if he had wanted to.

But who else did that leave? No searchers, perhaps, but one obvious suspect remains: John Rae.

Rae had not been in the area searching for Franklin, at least not originally. After wintering at Repulse Bay, Rae had travelled along the coast of the Gulf of Boothia to Pelly Bay, where he met with such strange resistance from the Inuit (and where his interpreter tried to run away). According to Rae, after this, while continuing westward, he encountered In-nook-poo-zhee-jook, the Inuk with the naval cap-band. In-nook-poo-zhee-jook told Rae only that some forty men had died near a river to the west, but the Inuk had not revealed specifically where this place was. It was not until Rae returned to Repulse Bay later in the year that he learned from the Inuit that the place was the Great Fish River and King William Island. By that point, it was too late to go back, so Rae opted instead to set out for home, to deliver word of his find to England. In Rae's words, "I therefore considered it my imperative duty to put the Admiralty in possession as soon as possible of the information."[5] This then was the story told by Rae.

In England, Rae's tale provoked an uproar. As Roderic Owen said, "Too many things smelled too strongly of fish."[6] Rae was the man who travelled like the natives, living off the land, sleeping in igloos. During his first expedition back in 1846, Rae had spent the winter at Repulse Bay without the benefit of a ship or provisions, with only the food that he had caught by dint of his own hunting expertise. True, his accomplishments seemed nothing short of miraculous compared to the efforts of the Royal Navy, but he did it just the same. Apparently travel through the Arctic wasn't the trial for Rae that it was for other men. Why then had he returned to England without checking out the stories first?

And cannibalism? Surely he could have seen those kettles for himself before promulgating such damaging accusations. Wrote Peter Newman in Rae's defence, "One problem was that in his anxiety to document the evidence of the Franklin explorers' demise, Rae did not simultaneously stress the reasons why he had decided against going back north to validate the find."[7] Rae's explanation was that he hadn't known where to look until returning to Repulse Bay, by which point, he was in much the same situation as Anderson would be the next year: facing half-melted waterways with inadequate boats. It was a perfectly reasonable excuse; Rae was an experienced Arctic traveller, not a miracle worker. Even he couldn't have returned to the Great Fish River so late in the season.

On the other hand, Rae couldn't escape the uncomfortable fact that he had already been there earlier in the year. Following his meeting with In-nook-poo-zhee-jook, Rae resumed his explorations as if nothing at all had happened. By his own admission, he crossed the Isthmus of Boothia to the mouth of the Castor and Pollux River squeezed tightly between Boothia and the Great Fish River. This was where Dease and Simpson's explorations had ended and so where Rae's were to begin. From there, he traced the west coast of Boothia northward, proving that King William Island was separated by a strait and also demonstrating conclusively that there was no water passage through Boothia. To his critics back home, this was just too close for comfort. The ever harsh Dr. King fumed, "That he should have stood on the shore of the Castor and Pollux River, his right eye directed to Point Ogle and his left to Montreal Island knowing that the fate of the Franklin expedition was to be read there."[8] But Rae *hadn't* known; that was precisely his point.

But if he *had* known...

IF RAE HAD KNOWN

Therein lies the crux of the issue. Was Rae telling the truth? He claimed In-nook-poo-zhee-jook "had never been there, that he didn't know the place and could not go so far."[9] Yet, by the time Rae had returned to Repulse Bay, it seemed everyone in the Arctic knew where the dead men were to be found, including many Inuit formerly encountered at Pelly Bay. Why should In-nook-poo-zhee-jook have been the only one still in the dark? It was possible that In-nook-poo-zhee-jook, like the Pelly Bay Inuit, was trying to keep Rae from finding the place. On the other hand, Roderic Owen noted that In-nook-poo-zhee-jook "chased after Rae in order to unfold his tale."[10] Would the Inuk have done so if he were anxious to keep the whole thing a secret?

But is there any reason for thinking Rae might have lied? Dr. King certainly thought so. According to King: "The means by which Dr Rae became possessed of the relics of the Franklin expedition will ever be a matter of doubt in my mind."[11] Not only was this an accusation fraught with unpleasant implications, it was libellous. Was King suggesting perhaps that Rae had not obtained the relics from the Inuit, as he claimed? But, if not from the Inuit, how? Obviously there was only one other way: Rae must have visited the place himself, but for some reason refused to admit it.

Why should he refuse to admit it?

If we consider our scenario, a clear picture emerges. We hypothesize: Rae encountered In-nook-poo-zhee-jook and learned of the dead men to be found near the Great Fish River and King William Island. He set out to investigate his discovery, innocent of any purpose other than to find the lost explorers as so many others had tried and failed to do. Upon reaching the Great Fish River, perhaps he discovered relics scattered about, perhaps not. Either way, he then decided to investigate King William Island to the north, easily crossing Simpson Strait, which at that time of the year was still frozen. Perhaps here he discovered more relics. But he too was well aware of Simpson's famous cairn at Cape Herschel and, like McClintock, Rae could have guessed that that was the place to look for any records left by the expedition. He went straight to Cape Herschel and saw that the cairn had indeed been disturbed within the past few years. Eagerly he tore down the south side of the cairn. Inside he found records, books, something. Still, up until this point, Rae had no aim in mind other than to discover the fate of Franklin's lost crew. But then he began to read.

Quickly he understood what it was he had discovered. And he understood the extreme importance the Admiralty would attach to the recovery of the documents he had found. Rae travelled with six other men; he swore them all to secrecy. His story of receiving relics and information on his return to Repulse Bay was no doubt true. After that, he sent his report to the Admiralty while he followed across the ocean.

But why should Rae have lied? Why should he, who had nothing but disdain for the navy, have helped them in their conspiracy?

THE MOTIVE

There was one obvious motive: greed.

From the start, Rae's detractors felt he was far too eager to profit by his discovery. They claimed the reason he hadn't bothered to check out the Inuit stories was because he had been anxious to return home to collect the 10,000 pound reward outstanding for "any Party who shall by virtue of his efforts first succeed in ascertaining" the fate of the lost crews.[12] Rae insisted that he hadn't known about the reward. Historian Peter Newman commented, "Rae quite rightly pointed out that he could have known nothing of such a reward while isolated in Repulse Bay."[13] On the other hand, Pierre Berton remarked, "This is hard to swallow."[14] The original reward of 20,000 pounds for succouring Franklin's crew had been announced in 1848. The second reward had been posted in 1850. "Rae had spent an entire year in England, " continued Berton, "from the spring of 1852 to the spring of 1853, at a time when Franklin fever was at its height .... He visited the Admiralty and pointed out on a map what he considered to be the likeliest spot (southward and westward of Cape Walker) for discovering Franklin's fate .... it passes all comprehension that he didn't know that whoever found the first Franklin relics would be rich for life."[15]

In other words, John Rae lied.

The Admiralty decision to award Rae the 10,000 pounds (8,000 pounds for Rae, 2,000 pounds for his men) was itself a puzzle to many at the time, none more so than Lady Franklin who vehemently fought the decision. The reward hadn't been posted for the discovery of relics; it was to be granted to anyone "ascertaining" the fate of Franklin's expedition. Certainly Rae had done that — if you believed the second-hand accounts of the Inuit. But when before had the Admiralty ever taken the word of the Inuit? The Inuit of Boothia had told James Clark Ross that Boothia was a peninsula; the Admiralty refused to believe it. And then there was Adam Beck's story gleaned from the natives of Greenland. At worst, it was a total fabrication, according to the navy. At best, a mistake.

Noel Wright, in his book *Quest for Franklin*, counted at least five Inuit stories which had been heard one way or another prior to McClintock's voyage. None of them had come to anything. Why should the Admiralty have suddenly decided to take Rae's second-hand stories as proof?

And then there was the cannibalism question. The Admiralty couldn't accept Rae's Inuit testimony as final proof without also accepting his story of cannibalism among some of the most famous names in the navy's history. Indeed, the Admiralty seemed in a remarkable hurry to do so, rushing Rae's grisly report into print while the explorer himself was still on his way to England. At the very least, one might have thought the Admiralty would have wished to speak with Rae in person before handing his report to *The Times*. Of course, if we assume the Admiralty was indeed eager to spread the cannibalism story for precisely the reason that they knew it to be false, we are left to wonder: what secret could possibly justify such a ghastly and damaging lie?

Perhaps final evidence of Rae's covert visit to King William Island may be discerned in his altered plans for exploring the final link in the Northwest Passage. Rae had intended to trace the west coast of Boothia, starting from the Castor and Pollux River and working his way up to Bellot Strait. He was then to trace Bellot Strait to Prince Regent Inlet, after which he would have returned to his home base at Repulse Bay. In the end, he actually completed only a very small portion of this exploration, mapping the Boothia coast from the Castor and Pollux River to Cape Porter, located on the latitude that crossed the middle of King William Island. At Cape Porter, Rae claimed he abandoned the rest of his plans because of a storm. Leslie Neatby wrote, "Perhaps doubting the wisdom of his decision, Rae did not attempt to reach Bellot Strait."[16] It is hard to imagine John Rae, the man who lived like the natives, abandoning the completion of the Northwest Passage because of one storm. On the other hand, it doesn't take much to see that, if Rae had learned of the lost expedition's whereabouts from In-nook-poo-zhee-jook, he would have certainly travelled due west to Cape Porter then mapped the Boothia coast down to the Castor and Pollux River, which was on his way anyhow, before proceeding to King William Island and Simpson's cairn [see map 23]. By the time he had completed his search of the area, it would have been too late in the year for him to resume his explorations of Bellot Strait, and so he was forced to return to Repulse Bay with his explorations only partly complete.

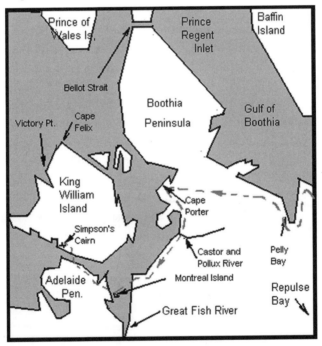

Map 23
John Rae's secret visit to Simpson's Cairn?

INNOCENT OR GUILTY?

Was the 8,000 pounds Rae received really enough to warrant this accusation? Was Rae the one who opened Simpson's cairn and stole whatever had been deposited there? Did he make up the story about cannibalism or did he really believe, based perhaps on evidence he himself had seen, that Franklin's officers had devoured their comrades before they died? Answers to any of these questions must be, of course, conjectural.

As for Simpson's cairn, there can be little doubt that something *was* left at Cape Herschel and that *someone* looted it before McClintock's arrival. John Rae had the means and the opportunity.

As for the motive — the reward money — Peter Newman wrote, "Halfway through his life and at the top of his form, John Rae uncharacteristically opted for retirement. Whether this was the result of physical exhaustion from his adventures or was simply a planned, gradual retreat is a matter of conjecture."[17] The same year as he received his payment in full, at the age of forty-three, the Tarzan of the Barren Grounds decided he was finished with exploration and trekking through the howling wilds, and promptly retired from the service of the Honourable Company of Adventurers to which he had given his life. In Newman's words, Rae "spent the last four decades of his life in self-satisfied hibernation, dividing his time between London and his shooting grounds at Westhill in the Orkneys."[18]

In 1967, Rae's own diary describing his explorations was discovered. On perusing its contents, its readers were surprised to find that the manuscript abruptly broke off in mid-sentence and did not resume. The break occurred in April, 1854, just before Rae would have described his first encounter with In-nook-poo-zhee-jook.

CHAPTER TWENTY-FOUR

Two Bodies and a Note

A shudder in the loins engenders there
The broken wall, the burning roof and tower
And Agamemnon dead.
W.B. Yeats,
Leda and the Swan

THE VICTORY POINT RECORD

"It was with a deep feeling of regret," wrote McClintock, "and much disappointment that I left this spot without finding some certain record of those martyrs to their country's fame. Perhaps in all the wide world there will be few spots more hallowed in the recollection of English seamen than this cairn on Cape Herschel."[1] Yet, McClintock was wrong. It wasn't Cape Herschel that was destined to become a hallowed spot in the Arctic. But, after travelling a mere twelve miles further along the coast, McClintock came upon another cairn and the revelation which would at last see that one spot on King William Island would indeed attain a hallowed status: Victory Point.

McClintock could immediately see that this second cairn was only newly constructed, the dirt still clinging to the stones. Eagerly tearing it apart, he discovered a record inside left by Hobson, who had arrived there from the north only six days before. Hobson's record was amazing: his party, though failing to discover the stranded ship, had found two documents left by Franklin's expedition, one being a partial duplicate of the other.

After separating from McClintock's party in late April, Hobson and his men had crossed the ice to Cape Felix at the north tip of King William Island. Almost immediately, they met with success, discover-

H. M. S.hips *Erebus and Terror*

28 of May 1847 Lat 70°5' N Long 98°23' W

Having wintered in 1846-7 at Beechey Island in Lat 74° 43' 28" N. Long 91°39' 15" W After having ascended Wellington Channel to Lat 77° and returned by the West side of Cornwallis Island.

Sir John Franklin commanding the Expedition.

All well

WHOEVER finds this paper is requested to forward it to the Secretary of the Admiralty, London, *with a note of the time and place at which it was found*: or, if more convenient, to deliver it for that purpose to the British Consul at the nearest Port.

QUINCONQUE trouvera ce papier est prié d'y marquer le tems et lieu ou il l'aura trouvé, et de le faire parvenir au plutot au Secretaire de l'Amirauté Britannique à Londres.

CUALQUIERA que hallare este Papel, se le suplica de enviarlo al Secretario del Almirantazgo, en Londrés, con una nota del tiempo y del lugar en donde se halló.

EEN ieder die dit Papier mogt vinden, wordt hiermede verzogt, om het zelve, ten spoedigste, te willen zenden aan den Heer Minister van de Marine der Nederlanden in 's Gravenhage, of wel aan den Secretaris den Britsche Admiraliteit, te London, en daar by te voegen eene Nota, inhoudende de tyd en de plaats alwaar dit Papier is gevonden geworden.

FINDEREN af dette Papiir ombedes, naar Leilighed gives, at sende samme til Admiralitets Secretairen i London, eller nærmeste Embedsmand i Danmark, Norge, eller Sverrig. Tiden og Størdit hvor dette er fundet ønskes venskabeligt paategnet.

WER diesen Zettel findet, wird hier-durch ersucht denselben an den Secretair des Admiralitets in London einzusenden, mit gefälliger angabe an welchen ort und zu welcher zeit er gefunden worden ist.

Party consisting of 2 Officers and 6 Men left the Ships on Monday 24th May 847

Facsimile of Victory Point Record

ing the remnants of an encampment. This encampment "had apparently been occupied for some time by a party consisting of twelve officers and men." Three small tents were used; they were lying flat when found by Lieutenant Hobson, and beneath them lay bearskin and blankets. Boarding pikes had apparently served as tent poles. Three fireplaces were near the tents.[2] A wealth of relics were found: broken pipes, tobacco, matches, broken china, needles, clothing, and a badge from a shako, but nothing with a name or initials on it.

But it was further on, at Victory Point, that the searchers discovered the prize which so many had sought for so long. Hobson found himself walking amongst a veritable junkyard of cast-away relics, amounting to something like ten tons in weight. There was a huge mountain of clothing piled four feet high. There were hollow brass curtain rods, heavy cooking stoves, button polish, four feet of lightning conductor, a medicine chest still filled with drugs, navigational equipment (a sextant and dip circle), and books, so many books! In the middle of it all was a stone cairn. At the base of the cairn, amongst some fallen stones, Hobson found a metal cylinder for protecting messages. At one time the end had been soldered closed, but Hobson found it broken open.

There were actually two messages, written a year apart on the same piece of paper. The paper itself was a standard Admiralty form given to ships for the purpose of mapping ocean currents, with blanks for the name of the ship and the time and position, to be filled in prior to tossing the paper overboard, secured in a bottle. An area for any comments was then followed by another blank space for the commander's signature. The lower half of the paper was then taken up with messages in six languages requesting the finder of the paper to forward it to the Admiralty in London. Whoever had drawn up the original form letter could never have imagined the important message it was now asked to convey.

The Victory Point record was badly stained with rust from its cylinder and one corner had disintegrated, destroying a small part of the message: the date of the second note. However, historians have had no hesitation quoting this second message, date intact, by basing their conclusion on the message's contents, usually without making note of their inference. The first message had been written in the blank space for further comments provided on the form, with the date, the ships' names and the latitude and longitude marked in the appropriate spots at the top. Between the ships' names and the position, the author had written "Wintered in the Ice in", with a long bracket connecting the three lines. The message thus read:

H.M. Ships Erebus and Terror
Wintered in the Ice in
Lat. 70° . 5' N Long. 98° . 23' W

28 of May 1847
Having wintered in 1846-7 at Beechey Island
in Lat 74° . 43' . 28" N. Long 91° . 39' . 15" W after having
ascended Wellington Channel to Lat 77° — and returning
by the West side of Cornwallis Island.
Sir John Franklin commanding the Expedition. [Commander
crossed out.]
All well.

At the bottom of the paper, beneath the multilingual messages, there was an addition.

Party consisting of 2 officers and 6 men
left the ships on Monday 24th, May 1847.
Gm. Gore, Lieut.
Chas. F. Les Voeux, Mate

This was how things had stood in 1847 after two winters in the Arctic. Unable to fulfil their orders to seek a passage to the southwest of Cape Walker, the ships had indeed gone up Wellington Channel, but then, presumably encountering more ice, they had returned to take up a winter berth at Beechey Island.

Immediately, though, the searchers noticed a strange error in this first message. The graves found at Beechey proved the expedition had wintered there in 1845-1846, not the next year as the message read. Still, the mistake was put down to simple inattention, even though the author had so obviously put so much care into recording all the latitudes and longitudes. The next summer, Franklin must have found Peel Sound open and happily sailed down to King William Island, only to find himself trapped in the implacable ice to the west. Still, as the message said, "All well."

But then there was a second message written a year later (the three last numerals of the year had just missed being torn away with the corner). This message was in the same handwriting as the first (Fitzjames', as it turned out), and it ran first up the left side of the page, then up the right eventually spilling upside down along the top. It was written using a slightly different coloured ink from the ink used the previous year.

[April 25th 1]848 H M Ships Terror and Erebus were deserted on the
22nd April 5 leagues NNW of this [hav]ing been beset since 12th Sept.
1846. The Officers & Crews consisting of 105 souls under the command
[of Cap]tain F.R.M. Crozier landed here – in Lat. 69° . 37'. 42" Long. 98° . 41'
[This] paper was found by Lt. Irving under the cairn supposed to have been
built by Sir James Ross in 1831 – where it had been deposited (four miles
to the northward) by the late Commander Gore in [May crossed out] June
1847. Sir James Ross' pillar has not however been found and the paper
has been transferred to this position which is that in which Sir J Ross pillar
was erected — Sir John Franklin died on the 11th June 1847 and the total
loss by deaths in the Expedition has been to this date 9 officers & 15 men.
F.R.M. Crozier
Captain & Senior Offr James Fitzjames HMS
and start on tomorrow 26th Erebus
for Back's Fish River.

Such a tantalizing record. On the one hand, it answered quite a few questions. On the other hand, it just raised more. It was now known that Sir John Franklin had died a year before the expedition itself was forced to desert the ships. In fact, Franklin had died only two weeks after the first note had been written. Graham Gore had also died some time after the first message that he had signed, since he was referred to as the "late" Commander Gore in the second note.

A total of nine officers and fifteen seamen had perished even before the decision to abandon the ships was made in 1848. Franklin and Gore made two, while the three bodies on Beechey accounted for three more. That left a staggering total of nineteen deaths still unknown. More importantly, there was an astonishingly disproportionate number of officers killed. How to explain this? No one knew. On Arctic voyages the officers were expected to command, not work. It was the men who hauled in the traces and the men who suffered and died from this back-breaking labour. The officers even ate better and so were the last to come down with scurvy. How had they died? The note, infuriatingly, didn't say.

Nor did it tell the searchers the reason the ships had been abandoned. The ships were said to have been beset since September, 1846, indicating the expedition had been trapped in the ice off King William Island for two full winters. At the very least, Franklin had carried provisions enough for three winters in the Arctic. But this was a minimum. In an emergency, he could have stretched that for a fourth year. Still, after three winters in the Arctic, and with Franklin dead, Crozier — who had now assumed command — would have surely begun to make plans for escape. The problem was, why desert the ships in April? Crozier would have been better to have waited a month or two until the warmer weather arrived, thawing the waterways and allowing his men to travel by ship's boat. Everything seemed to point to a strangely hurried escape, which might have been explained if there was any indication the ships had sunk; but the record specifically stated the ships had been "deserted", proving that both were still afloat when the abandonment took place. More and more, the record served only to compound the mystery.

One thing at least seemed clear. Having deserted the ships, Crozier had led his doomed party of 105 men down the west coast of King William Island, headed for "Back's Fish River". Apparently, Crozier had initially almost left the record without that additional information. Only after he had signed his name had Crozier (at least, it was presumed to be his writing since it wasn't in Fitzjames' hand) remembered to add the final crucial report: "and start on tomorrow 26th for Back's Fish River."

Yet, even here was a mystery. What had Crozier thought he was doing? The Great Fish River? It is true that Dr. King had urged that a search party be sent to the mouth of that river to look for signs of Franklin's lost expedition, but not even Dr. King had believed the explorers might try to use that river to escape the Arctic. It was sheer madness. Pierre Berton commented, "The Great Fish River was trial enough for strong, healthy, well-fed voyageurs, as George Back had discovered. For Crozier's men, it would have been an impossibility to navigate, even if they had reached it."[3] All along, everyone had believed that if Franklin's crewmen found themselves trapped in the ice southwest of

Cape Walker (as they had), they would travel, not south, but northeast to the cache at Fury Beach, where they stood at least some chance of being picked up by whalers. Here was yet one more mystery to be explained.

AN ATTACK THAT NEVER CAME

McClintock, having read the copy of the Victory Point record deposited by Hobson, had no time to ponder the many questions it raised. He set out immediately, travelling north up the coast of King William Island, and worked his way over ground already searched by Hobson. He wished to see for himself the relics left at Victory Point by the retreating expedition. But then he came upon another discovery, as amazing in some ways as the Victory Point record itself.

It was a ship's boat mounted on a sledge. A record left at the site told McClintock that Hobson had been over the place already. The boat was large, weighing about 800 pounds, but the keel had been partially trimmed to lighten the load. The sledge upon which the boat sat was a huge ponderous device which added a further 650 pounds to the mass which the seamen had been forced to haul; a total of 1400 pounds, which McClintock called, "a heavy load for seven strong healthy men."[4]

More amazing still was the profusion of relics found inside the boat. Just as Hobson had discovered so many useless items piled around the cairn at Victory Point, here McClintock found piles of clothing, an assortment of winter boots, towels, soap, a sponge, a toothbrush, combs, bayonet scabbards shortened to hold knives, two rolls of sheet-lead, five watches, needles and thread-cases, saws, files, and even five books, including a copy of the "Vicar of Wakefield". And, once again, there were those omnipresent silver forks, spoons, and teaspoons engraved with the initials and crests of the officers of the *Erebus* and *Terror*. Though no meat was found, there was an empty pemmican-can which had held twenty-two pounds, and the searchers found forty pounds of chocolate.

And then there were the bodies. Only two skeletons were found in the boat and, when a search for graves failed to turn any up, it became evident that the two men had been left behind by whoever had helped haul the boat this far. The youngest man was in the bow of the boat, in a "disturbed state" which McClintock attributed to "large and powerful animals, probably wolves."[5] The older man, in a better condition, lay under the after-thwart, his body surrounded by clothes and furs. Leaning upright against the side of the boat were two shotguns, one barrel in each carefully loaded and cocked, in Owen Beattie's words, "as if ready to fend off an attack that never came."[6]

But as strange as all this was, McClintock was even more astonished to find the sledge-mounted boat was pointed toward the north instead of the south. For some reason, this sledge party had been headed back toward Victory Point and the abandoned ships, rather than toward the Great Fish River. The only explanation he could come up with to solve this puzzle was to assume that some of the crewmen, finding the journey south more than they had bargained for, had turned back, finally abandoning even their boat (and two comrades) when their strength was nearly gone. It was an unlikely scenario, but the only one imaginable. If the crewmen hoped to find the ships still beset in the ice on their return, why did they attempt to drag the ship's boat with them? If they thought they would have to cross water, the ships themselves would have either sunk or floated away.

Yet, the evidence was irrefutable. At least some of the crewmen had turned back. Why?

The pieces of the puzzle lay scattered like ice floes in Lancaster Sound, jostling and meeting, then just as suddenly breaking apart again. A picture is hinted at, but never fully resolved. McClintock based his conclusions according to certain seemingly self-evident assumptions. He assumed the ships were abandoned because the expedition was faced with starvation. He assumed they trekked down the west coast of King William Island weakened and racked with scurvy. He assumed their greatest enemy was their own fading strength and gnawing hunger. Thus, he assumed they turned back because they couldn't go any further. It never occurred to the searcher that the crewmen might have turned back because escape had been cut off, that they had been forced to retreat back to the north for the reason that they were trapped, with nowhere else to run but north.

And yet, the evidence was there, though mute and circumstantial. Two bodies lay in the boat, one badly mauled. Two shotguns stood by, loaded and cocked. If they perished of starvation, why did they leave forty pounds of chocolate behind? If their strength was failing, why didn't they jettison all the extra weight? McClintock was amazed to find that the ponderous boat had been partially knocked off its sledge. He proposed the deed had been done by "a violent north-west gale"[7] It was a powerful gale indeed which could lift an 800-pound boat.

And finally, the eeriest clue of all: of the two bodies discovered, McClintock wrote: "No part of the skull of either skeleton was found, with the exception of the lower jaw of each."

CHAPTER TWENTY-FIVE

A Trail of Bones

Still round and round the ghosts of beauty glide,
And haunt the places where their honour died.
Alexander Pope,
Epistles to Several Persons

PUZZLES

Few historical documents have been studied and pondered, dissected
and analyzed, as has been the record found at Victory Point. From
McClintock to the present, historical scholars and armchair explorers
have tried to make sense of the two short messages left by the doomed
expedition, striving to read between the lines, to answer the questions
left infuriatingly unanswered, while seeking to resolve the further puzzles raised by elements of the record itself. Here we propose, not only
to answer those questions, but to do so with a simple solution.

First though, we shall comment on another puzzle, one which
only became evident over many years after later searchers had visited
King William Island.

FROM THE TODD ISLETS TO STARVATION COVE

John Rae's informers told him that five bodies had been seen on
Montreal Island in the mouth of the Great Fish River [see map 24].
In the spring of 1869, Charles Francis Hall explored the south shore
of King William Island over a period of four days, while searching
for Franklin relics. Near the mouth of the Peffer River he discovered

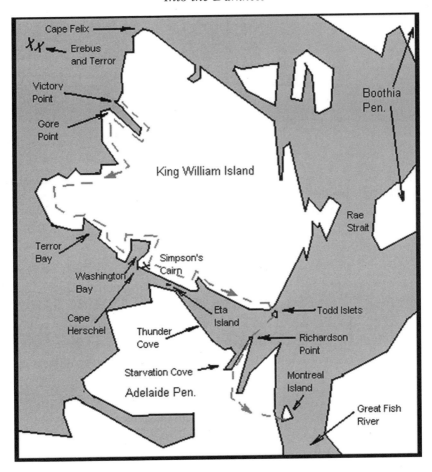

Map 24
Crozier's path to the Great Fish River?

a skeleton that was later identified as Lieutenant Le Vescont of the *Erebus*, based on a gold tooth crown. Several other skeletons were found, including one discovered on the Todd Islets, just off the south coast, where Hall had been told by the Inuit that five skeletons had previously been seen. Hall learned from the Inuit that the largest concentrations of bodies had been located at Terror Bay on the west coast of King William Island, and at Starvation Cove on the mainland just to the west of the Great Fish River, but he didn't visit either of these places.

In 1879, Lieutenant Frederick Schwatka of the 3rd United States Cavalry led an expedition to King William Island. After so many years, little remained of the lost expedition's last march, but Schwatka discovered six graves scattered along the island's west coast. He also learned from the Inuit of the many bodies which had been seen at Terror Bay and of the (possibly) forty corpses which had lain at Starvation Cove on the mainland. One Inuk informant told Schwatka he had seen an upright boat at Starvation Cove — "Outside the boat he saw a number of skulls. He forgot how many but he said there were more than four."[1] It was also said that there had been a box filled with books at Starvation Cove. "Some of the books were taken home for the children to play with, and finally torn and lost, and others lay among the rocks until carried away by the wind and lost or buried beneath the sand." Though Schwatka visited Starvation Cove, he could only find a single skull, for which he gave the place its grim name.

In the end, based on the bodies discovered along the west and south shores of King William Island and at Starvation Cove, a clear vision of that final march emerged. The doomed crewmen had followed the coast down to the south shore, then eastward as far as the Todd Islets before using the islets as a jumping-off place to cross Simpson Strait to the long thrust of Richardson Point on the mainland. Then the men moved south down Richardson Point, ending up at Starvation Cove where most of them died. As for the boat and five bodies reported on Montreal Island, both Hall and Schwatka thought that story had arisen through confusion with the bodies at Starvation Cove further west. Alternatively, it was possible a final party had pushed on to Montreal Island still intent on ascending the Great Fish River, where they perished all the same.

WHERE DID THEY CROSS?

This scenario raises a troubling question. In making the long trek to the Todd Islets, the crewmen had to pass along a length of shore around Eta Island where the gap separating King William Island from the mainland was very narrow, a mere two miles. Chief trader William Gibson felt that Crozier must have been "topographically confused" to have passed this point without making the crossing.[2] It would have been no effort at all to have crossed over along this area of coast, yet instead the crewmen continued steadily eastward, while the mainland gradually grew farther and farther away, fading into the distance. In the end, they chose to make their crossing forty miles farther on, at a place where even the tip of Richardson Point was no more than a dot on the horizon. Their decision makes no sense.

Even more strange, to reach Richardson Point from the Todd Islets, the crewmen had to travel in a diagonal southwest across Simpson Strait, going back to the west once again. Finally, to reach Starvation Cove, the crewmen must have travelled down the *west* coast of the Richardson Point peninsula. Why would they have done so when they were headed for the Great Fish River to the *east* of the peninsula?

To add to the mystery, in August 1936, D.G. Sturrock and L.A. Learmouth — the Hudson's Bay Company post manager at Gjoa Haven, a settlement eventually founded on the southeast corner of King William Island — discovered the remains of three skeletons, a George IV half-crown, and an antique sailor's button at Thunder Cove fifteen miles *to the west* of Starvation Cove. But why would the crewmen have travelled west from Starvation Cove? It made no sense — unless, of course, we assume the retreating crewmen really did cross to the mainland at the narrowing of Simpson Strait near Eta Island. In this case, they reached Starvation Cove while travelling eastward along the mainland headed for the Great Fish River, rather than by way of Richardson Point. But what about all the other bodies scattered along the south shore of King William Island between Eta Island and the Todd Islets?

For the answer, we must return to the Victory Point record.

CHAPTER TWENTY-SIX

The Victory Point Record Explained

He thought he saw a Rattlesnake
That questioned him in Greek,
He looked again and found it was
The Middle of Next Week.
"The one thing I regret," he said,
"Is that it cannot speak!"
Lewis Carroll,
Sylvie and Bruno

THE FIRST MESSAGE

In the midst of the cluttered maelstrom of the Franklin mystery, the Victory Point record serves as a focal point around which all other questions circulate. It was the only message ever discovered whose purpose was to provide later searchers with the information they sought. For that reason, it is all the more remarkable that the record has so thoroughly defied interpretation.

The first message, written either on or before May 28th, 1847, seemed simple and to the point. Its purpose was merely to report the progress made thus far in the expedition. So it did. The *Erebus* and *Terror* had wintered at Beechey Island after ascending Wellington Channel and returning down the opposite side of Cornwallis Island. After that, the two ships reached King William Island, where they became beset in the ice. Sir John Franklin was still in charge of the expedition. All was well.

But then a postscript was added. A party of two officers and six men had left the ships on the 24th of May. This is all we are told of that party. Why they left the ships, the record doesn't say. At the bottom of the page, Lieutenant Graham Gore and Lieutenant Des Voeux signed their names.

This entire 1847 message was found duplicated on a second record discovered by Hobson at Gore Point, with one exception: the date at the top read only May 1847 — the 28 was missing.

Immediately a question arises. Why didn't Franklin sign the record on the space provided for his signature? Historian David C. Woodman noted, "Sir John was known to have signed a similar form which had been tossed overboard on 30 June 1845 (and which was later recovered on the coast of Greenland), and presumably he would normally have signed these documents as well. But he did not."[1] The explanation favoured by historians was that Franklin was even then ill with whatever sickness would take his life in two weeks time. It is certainly plausible, but Franklin would have had to be very sick indeed to be unable to sign his own name.

As well, there was some question regarding the dates. It was presumed the May 28th date at the top of the record referred to the date upon which the paper was placed or was expected to be placed in the cairn on King William Island, rather than the date upon which it was first filled out. But why should it have taken Lieutenant Gore four days (24th to 28th) to travel from the ships to King William Island? Even taking into account hummocky ice, four days was a remarkable delay for such a short trip.

THE SECOND MESSAGE

And then there was the second message. Written one year later, it told an entirely different story, while simultaneously shedding some light on the first message. The ships, we are now told, had been beset since September 12th, 1846. On April 22, 1848, the ships were deserted and the remaining crew of 105 reached the shore near Victory Point. (The actual landing place, now called Crozier's Landing, was actually a couple of miles south of Victory Point.)

The second message refers to Gore as the "late Commander Gore", indicating not only that Gore had died sometime after the original message was left, but that he had been promoted, since he had left England a lieutenant. Once again, historians have been puzzled. Gore promoted? It has generally been agreed that Franklin might have had the authority to promote Gore, but only under very exceptional circumstances. Promotions were the prerogative of the Admiralty and were supposed to be left until the expedition returned home. What could possibly have justified this unusual action?

The most likely explanation, under the circumstances, is that it was already known Gore wasn't going to live long enough to be promoted in England. If Gore had done something exceptional to warrant a promotion, we could easily imagine Franklin deciding to take the unusual step of promoting his officer before Gore's death. But what could Gore have done to warrant such an honour? An act of extreme courage and heroism, surely. Perhaps this heroic act had itself led to his death. In fact, we might wonder if this act and Gore's death were in some way connected to the expedition which he led from the ships.

There may even be evidence for this theory.

In recording when Gore had placed the record in the cairn at Victory Point, Fitzjames initially wrote "May", then crossed it out and wrote "June". Obviously he wasn't certain. This might suggest that when Gore had returned to the ships, he had been in no condition to give an account of his journey and had died soon afterward.

But now there was another problem with the dates. The ships were deserted on April 22nd. According to the addition under Crozier's signature — "and start on tomorrow 26th for Back's Fish River" — tomorrow was the 26th. That meant the second message was written on April the 25th (and, though the date was torn away, historians routinely report it as complete). Why had it taken the crewmen three days to cross the ice to shore? It was the same problem encountered in the first message. Four days for the 1847 party to reach Victory Point, now three days to travel to essentially the same place. It made no sense. During his visit in 1830, James Clark Ross had walked all the way from Cape Felix to Victory Point in only four hours.

A SURVEY PARTY?

Again, we notice that the first message was written in two parts. The first, detailing the expedition's travels up Wellington Channel and back, ended with the "All well" and the confirmation that Franklin was still in command. Clearly, this was supposed to be the whole of the record. But then, the information about a party of two officers and six men leaving the ships was added, suggesting this party's departure was abrupt and unexpected. Why? More importantly, why did Fitzjames feel it was necessary to report this party's leave-taking? It has long been assumed that this was a survey party, perhaps dispatched to Cape Herschel to locate the final link in the Northwest Passage. But surely many such survey parties would have been sent out. When this party returned to the ships in a few days or weeks, the message would become obsolete. What was so special about this party that Fitzjames felt it was necessary to report their absence from the ships?

Is it possible Fitzjames decided to mention the absent party because, even at that time, he had reason to think the rest of the expedition was in danger? If he thought there was some possibility the ships and their crews might soon meet with disaster, he would have decided to leave a message to tell searchers that eight men were still out there, somewhere. Which raises yet another question. Why was the record not recovered when the party returned to the ships? One year later, the second message clearly relates how Lieutenant Irving had retrieved the record from the cairn where Gore had placed it the year before. Yet, once the party was back aboard the ships, the message became obsolete and misleading. Why was it allowed to remain on King William Island? One possible answer is: those eight men never returned to the ships.

But if the party reported in the 1847 message never returned, what happened to them?

ABRUPT ABANDONMENT

Perhaps it is time to reconsider our basic assumptions. The first message leaves far too many unanswered questions. Clearly we are missing a crucial piece to the puzzle. That piece may be this: what happens if we assume Fitzjames was not aboard his ship when he wrote the message? Instead, we may picture Fitzjames as stationed at the encampment near Cape Felix that Hobson discovered in 1859.

Suddenly the entire scenario changes drastically. Franklin did not sign the record because he wasn't at Cape Felix; he was still aboard his ship frozen in the ice of Victoria Strait. The party that left the ships on May 24th did not leave Fitzjames on that date, but rather arrived at his location *after* having left the ships. We no longer need to assume a period of four days (May 24th to 28th) to reach Victory Point from the ships; the party could have reached Cape Felix in one day, then set off down the coast a few days later.

This also would explain why the party's departure apparently took Fitzjames by surprise, so much so that he could only append the information to the bottom of his record. Having just completed his record describing the expedition's travels up Wellington Channel, Fitzjames was surprised when a party arrived from the ships, having been dispatched by Franklin. Fitzjames, being isolated at Cape Felix, hadn't been involved in the decision-making that had led to the party being sent.

But why didn't Fitzjames sign the document which he himself had written (as he *did* sign the 1848 message)? Why did he leave the final signing of the record in the hands of Gore and Des Voeux? Perhaps because the party dispatched from the ships had brought word that Fitzjames was to abandon Cape Felix and return to the ships immediately. Thus, Fitzjames left the two document papers with Gore and Des Voeux, who signed the records sometime before setting off on their journey. Gore deposited the one record at Victory Point and the other at Gore Point.

After that, something happened to the party. We don't know what, but Gore at least returned. He was in a bad condition and died soon after, but not before Franklin rewarded him through the unusual step of promoting him. Was Gore rewarded for some special act of heroism which he reported on his return? Perhaps. But, since he apparently was unable to reveal enough of his journey to allow Fitzjames to judge in which month Gore had deposited the record at Victory Point, it seems doubtful he could have been coherent enough to describe his adventures. On the other hand, the alternative is to suggest that there was something so important about the party's mission that it warranted such a high honour being bestowed.

The evidence did indeed indicate the hurried abandonment of Cape Felix. Hobson found old clothing, a copper cooking stove, three small tents, a bearskin and blankets, boarding pikes, broken china, pipes, tobacco, matches, some shot, an ensign, and smaller items. What's more, there is reason to believe that after Fitzjames deserted Cape Felix no one else returned to the King William Island coast until the abandonment of the ships the next year. In Fitzjames' second message in 1848, he seems almost surprised by the discovery of Gore's record. He wrote, "[This] paper was found by Lt. Irving under the cairn supposed to have been built by Sir James Ross in 1831." He does not say the paper was "recovered" but that it was "found", suggesting the discovery was accidental. Obviously Gore had not been able to tell

Fitzjames where the record had been left, but it is equally obvious that no parties had visited the area since the abandonment the year before or they would have found the record earlier.

Thus we are left with three disturbing conclusions. First, in 1847 a party was hurriedly dispatched from the ships, a party which never returned. Secondly, Fitzjames was then ordered to abandon Cape Felix and return to the ships. And thirdly, for an entire year after this until the desertion of the ships, the expedition refused to venture back to Victory Point.

What happened to cause this abandonment? All we know for certain is that, one year later, the remaining crew of 105 deserted the ships on April 22nd and reached the coast near Victory Point. Franklin was dead and Crozier now had command. When Lieutenant Irving discovered Gore's record in a cairn slightly to the north, Fitzjames updated the document along the margins, noting Franklin's death and the total number of deaths so far. He and Crozier signed the document upside down along the top. Then, belatedly, someone (not Fitzjames) remembered to add the final crucial information: "and start on tomorrow 26th for Back's Fish River."

Beyond that point, the only evidence to be found lay in a trail of bones down the west and south shores of King William Island and the mainland further south. According to the Inuit, five bodies had lain on Montreal Island in the mouth of the Great Fish River. Other bodies had been found at Starvation Cove. The evidence was irrefutable. And yet ...

THE GREAT FISH RIVER?

David Woodman commented, "When the fate of Crozier's men became known, many 'experts', with the advantage of hindsight, found it hard to understand his [Crozier's] reasoning. John Rae, himself the foremost proponent of living off the land, was sure Franklin's men could have survived if only they had marched north."[2] George Back, who first explored the Great Fish River with Dr. King, described that river as "most embarrassing to the navigator, and broken into falls, cascades and rapids to the number of no less than eighty three."[3] What could Crozier have thought he was doing to take on such a Herculean journey? Even if by some miracle he had managed to ascend that epic watercourse with his army of 105, what did he hope to find at the other end?

Fort Reliance on Great Slave Lake.

Deep in the heart of the Canadian wilderness, this tiny Hudson's Bay Company trading post (ambitiously called a "fort") was expected to somehow shelter and feed 105 men? It simply wasn't possible. By trying to make his escape up the Great Fish River to Fort Reliance, Crozier was acting in a manner which can only be described as senseless, made all the more incomprehensible by the fact that a safer refuge lay close at hand. As Berton remarked, "Ironically, a mountain of stores, not to mention several boats, lay at Fury Beach to the northeast."[4]

Logic pointed to Fury Beach. But the evidence of the Victory Point record seemed irrefutable. The men had set off for the Great Fish River. So, what was Crozier thinking?

THE ANSWER

Once again, to find an answer to this question, we must alter our assumptions. We must return to the origin, to the Victory Point record itself. The final part of the record reads:

> [This] paper was found by Lt. Irving under the cairn supposed to have been built by Sir James Ross in 1831 – where it had been deposited (four miles to the northward) by the late Commander Gore in [May crossed out] June 1847. Sir James Ross' pillar has not however been found and the paper has been transferred to this position which is that in which Sir J Ross pillar was erected – Sir John Franklin died on the 11th June 1847 and the total loss by deaths in the Expedition has been to this date 9 officers & 15 men.
> F.R.M. Crozier
> Captain & Senior Offr James Fitzjames HMS
> and start on tomorrow 26th Erebus
> for Back's Fish River.

We can't help but notice something odd about the final addition — "and start on tomorrow 26th for Back's Fish River". It is not a real sentence. Surely, in adding this postscript, the writer might have said: "We start on tomorrow" or "Shall start on tomorrow" Instead, the sentence not only begins with the word "and", but it even starts with a small "a".

Clearly, even though it was added later, it was supposed to be read as the completion of a previous sentence. And yet, it does not fit at the end of the last sentence, which would then read "... the total loss by deaths in the Expedition has been to this date 9 officers & 15 men ... and start on tomorrow, 26th, for Back's Fish River." Indeed, in the entire Victory Point record there is only one sentence that this addendum could be intended to complete. That sentence had been written the year before and, linking the two together, the complete sentence would then read: "Party consisting of 2 officers and 6 men left the ships on Monday 24th, 1847, and start on tomorrow 26th for Back's Fish River."

CHAPTER TWENTY-SEVEN
The Final March

> Into the jaws of Death,
> Into the mouth of Hell.
> > Alfred, Lord Tennyson,
> > *The Charge of the Light Brigade*

ALTERED DATES

It would be difficult to overestimate the significance of this slight alteration in the reading of the Victory Point record. We now see that "tomorrow 26th" means the 26th of May, 1847, not the 26th of April, 1848. Therefore, we no longer know on what date the second message was written, since the April 25th date quoted in most history books was inferred solely from the belief that "tomorrow" was the 26th. We know only that the message was written some time after the ships were abandoned on April 22nd.

As well, we now see that Crozier's last message gives no clue as to where he was headed or what his intentions were. Perhaps more significantly, the earlier message now tells us that the party dispatched so hurriedly from the ships in 1847 was in fact headed, not for Cape Herschel to complete the Northwest Passage, but for the Great Fish River. This in itself is a strange revelation. Why should a party have been sent there?

THREE INKS

But before continuing, we must consider a possible objection to this reconstruction of the Victory Point record.

The ink used to write the 1847 message had a slightly different colour from the ink used to write the 1848 message — including the postscript about the Great Fish River. This would seem to be a fatal flaw in our reconstruction. On the other hand, in our reconstruction we are still assuming the postscript was added sometime after the first message had been written. It is not hard to imagine Gore thawing a new bottle of ink to add the final note about the destination of his party.

But would it match the ink used by Fitzjames one year later?

Certainly the differences in colour were slight; if Gore's ink used to make the addition was closer in colour to the 1848 ink than it was to the 1847 ink, it is easy to see how the document's readers assumed there were only two shades of ink, instead of three. But what we require is final proof that ink was used in the 1847 message that closely matched the ink used one year later.

That proof is to be found in the date.

There were two records found on King William Island, both identical copies of the 1847 message. But the record found at Gore Point lacked the "28" for the May date at the top. The record at Victory Point had the "28" filled in, but the number was written in an ink matching the ink used one year later. Because of this, it was concluded that when Fitzjames recovered the document the next year he remembered the precise date upon which Gore had placed the record at Victory Point and so filled in the space. This seems doubtful. As we have seen, Fitzjames clearly didn't know when Gore had placed the record in its cairn since he initially wrote "May", then crossed that out and wrote, "June". It makes more sense to assume it was Gore who added the 28, shortly before setting out in 1847. This then serves as proof that a third ink had been used which closely matched the ink used one year later.

RECONSTRUCTION

This then is what might have happened.

In 1847, Fitzjames filled out two Admiralty forms while stationed at the camp near Cape Felix. Then, before he could sign his name, Gore arrived leading a party dispatched from the ships. Gore had set out from the ships on the 24th of May, reaching Cape Felix one day later on the 25th. This party was under orders to travel immediately for the Great Fish River. At the same time, Gore also carried orders from Franklin instructing Fitzjames to abandon the camp at Cape Felix and return promptly to the ships. Fitzjames departed immediately, leaving Gore and his party at Cape Felix with the two records. Gore's mission was important and he was in a hurry. He and Des Voeux placed their signatures on the two records, and had lead-sealed one in its metal cylinder before realizing they should include their own destination on the records. Rather than break the seal on the closed cylinder, they decided to append the "and start on tomorrow 26th for Back's Fish River" to the record which had not yet been sealed. To make this addition, they used different ink than Fitzjames had used for the rest of the message. Then Gore noticed that Fitzjames had left the date blank at the top of the form, so Gore filled it in based on a rough guess of when he suspected he would deposit the record somewhere to the south. He gave himself two days, the 28th of May. Then Gore sealed the record in its cylinder and set off on his journey the next day, depositing the more complete record at Victory Point and the other record at Gore Point.

After that, Gore's party continued southward, headed for the Great Fish River. Sometime later, Gore barely made it back to the ships, perhaps able only to reveal that the others were dead. He died himself soon afterward, but not before Franklin promoted him as a reward for his bravery. Franklin himself must have died only days after that. For the next eleven months, the crew remained trapped aboard the ships, frozen in Victoria Strait and unwilling or unable to risk venturing back to the shore so near at hand.

There may have been more deaths. The 1848 message reported nine officers and fifteen men dead. If we subtract Franklin, Gore, the three men at Beechey Island, and the seven other men of Gore's party, we are left with the staggering total of twelve deaths unaccounted for. We also notice the disproportionate number of dead officers. In every way they should have lived a healthier life than the rest of the crew — better food, better living conditions, less work (and work contributed to the onset of scurvy). In fact, we might say the officers had only two functions on this expedition: one was to command the men; the other was to carry out the scientific experiments for which they had been so carefully chosen.

Then, abruptly, the ships were abandoned on April 22nd, 1848. The remaining men trudged across the ice to shore carrying with them a staggering profusion of useless junk. Fitzjames added the new information to the record recovered by Lieutenant Irving, not realizing that the little "and start on tomorrow" addition made by Gore the year before would eventually be the cause of so much confusion.

THE PASSAGE THAT DIDN'T EXIST

But why did they desert the ships so early in the year? Why couldn't Fitzjames take the time to write out a proper record? Why did the belongings salvaged from the ships seem to be chosen without proper thought, almost as if the men had caught up whatever they could and then run for their lives? Four feet of lightning conductor? No less than four cooking stoves? Brass curtain rods? And then there was the four-foot mountain of clothes, and the medicine chest filled with drugs, and the sextant, the shovels, the iron hoops, old canvas, all of it simply left behind. On the one hand, the men clearly had carried more than they needed to sustain them during their march; on the other hand, they had brought so many unimportant items and left so much behind on the ships. Everything seemed to point to a frantic flight, without plan or order. This was not a long-anticipated desertion brought about by the prospect of slow starvation; this was a sudden, unexpected retreat, a desperate rush where every man grabbed what he could, and it must have been provoked by an equally sudden threat. And yet the ships were not sinking.

Now we can at last return to our earlier question.

What was Crozier thinking?

The Victory Point record no longer tells us that he was headed for the Great Fish River. Without that seemingly irrefutable evidence, we have only the physical evidence left behind, and that tells an entirely different story. True, Crozier headed south. True, he was headed in the direction of the Great Fish River (just as the Inuit all assumed, when they discovered the bodies the next year). We have seen that evidence discovered to the west of Starvation Cove shows that men crossed over to the mainland at the narrowest part of Simpson Strait near Eta Island, just as we would expect, still headed for the Great Fish River. But what about the long line of other bodies extending along the south shore of King William Island to the Todd Islets far to the east of Eta Island? If Crozier crossed to the mainland at the narrowing of Simpson Strait, why would he also cross over forty miles farther on at the Todd Islets?

Obviously he wouldn't.

To make sense of the evidence, we must first consider Gore's party dispatched the previous year. Gore had been ordered — quite suddenly, it seemed — to take his seven men to the Great Fish River. Eight men were easily enough to drag a boat. The Inuit reported five bodies and a boat on Montreal Island. They reported more bodies at Starvation Cove. The Inuit also reported a box filled with books at the same place. Slowly a clear picture emerges.

Fitzjames wrote: "All well". Yet, the hasty departure of Gore's party and Fitzjames' sudden recall to the ships suggest that all was not well. Fitzjames left a record of Gore's departure because there was a danger the main expedition might not survive; if that happened, he wanted a relief expedition to know Gore's party was still out there. In other words, Fitzjames' "All well" did not mean the expedition was all well; it meant only that the expedition had been a success. It was a message to the Admiralty reporting that the mission had been accomplished.

And Gore's party? They had been dispatched on the same journey which historians had thought Crozier had chosen in his final doomed march: Gore was to ascend the Great Fish River to Fort Reliance on Great Slave Lake. For an army of 105, it would have been unthinkable, but not for eight well-chosen men — George Back had proven that.

Why was this small party dispatched up the Great Fish River? All was well. The mission had been accomplished. But there was a danger the expedition would not escape to deliver their findings to the Admiralty. Franklin made the only decision he could. He ordered a small party to escape while there was still time, carrying copies of the journals, the precious reports, to those who awaited them in London.

Gore's party never made it up the Great Fish River. They got as far as Montreal Island and there their journey ended. Gore (and perhaps two others) were forced to retreat, leaving five others behind. They tried to carry the records with them, but were forced to abandon them at Starvation Cove. Somehow Gore made it back to the ships with the news that he had failed.

One year later, as Crozier led his crewmen past Eta Island with the mainland only two miles away, he dispatched a splinter party to recover the records left at Starvation Cove [see map 25]. Those men reached the cove but never escaped alive. The Inuit found the bodies and the records still there. Crozier continued eastward along the south shore of King William Island. It was a nightmare trek. Men died all along the way, limbs "dissevered". Whatever they were flee-

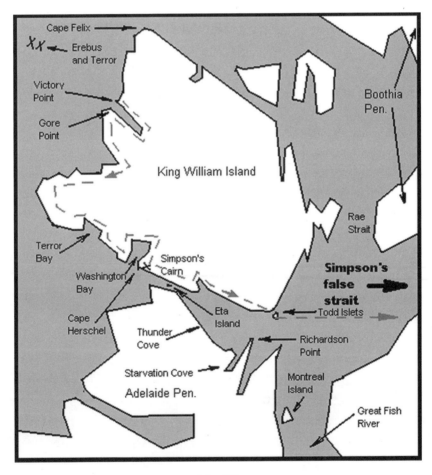

Map 25
Was Crozier searching for a strait that didn't exist?

ing was with them still. They kept going because they had no choice. But where was Crozier headed? Not the Great Fish River, surely? That would have been madness and he knew it. And so he was headed east, due east, to the strait that Thomas Simpson had claimed cut through Boothia to the waters of Prince Regent Inlet. Just as Jane Franklin had predicted, the lost expedition had tried to reach the famous cache at Fury Beach by travelling, not northeast, but south, searching in vain for a water passage that didn't even exist.

Chapter Twenty-Eight
The Second Winter at Beechey Island

> Come you back to Mandalay,
> Where the old Flotilla lay:
> Can't you 'ear their paddles chunkin' from
> Rangoon to Mandalay?
> Rudyard Kipling,
> *Mandalay*

A SECOND WINTER?

So far we have only been concerned with discovering what happened to the Franklin expedition after it became beset to the northwest of King William Island. But, the very first problem raised by the Victory Point record involved events prior to this. The record read:

> *H.M.Ships Erebus and Terror*
> *Wintered in the Ice in*

> *28 of May 1847   Lat. 70° . 5' N Long. 98° . 23' W*
> *Having wintered in 1846-7 at Beechey Island*
> *in Lat 74° . 43' . 28" N. Long 91° . 39' . 15" W after having*
> *ascended Wellington Channel to Lat 77 – and returning*
> *by the West side of Cornwallis Island.*

Yet, the graves on Beechey Island were from the winter of 1845-6, Franklin's first in the Arctic, not 1846-7 as the record claimed. Stranger still, Fitzjames had made the same mistake on the duplicate left at Gore Point. Then in 1848 he had failed to correct the mistake, even when noting that the ships had been beset since September 12, 1846.

Could Fitzjames really have made such an elementary mistake and, more, could he have made the mistake twice?

Obviously, the first question we should ask ourselves is: could the dates be right?

Clearly, Franklin had spent his first winter at Beechey Island; the graves leave no doubt about that. But that doesn't preclude the possibility of a second winter at Beechey Island, spent after ascending Wellington Channel.

Certainly, historians have long been amazed at how much was apparently accomplished in Franklin's first summer in the Arctic. David Woodman commented that, "[The Victory Point record] would tell of a surprisingly successful first year of effort."[1] McClintock remarked, "Seldom has such an amount of success been accorded to an Arctic navigator in a single season."[2] Success indeed. Franklin entered the Arctic in August. Freeze-up usually came in early September. His orders were to seek a passage to the southwest of Cape Walker, therefore he must have travelled down Lancaster Sound, through Barrow Strait, and then tried to get past Cape Walker only to be stopped by ice. After that, he would have certainly tried Peel Sound — even though it was believed to be a bay, there was still the possibility it formed a water passage pointing south. Foiled again, only then would he have tried Wellington Channel. Amazingly, he had travelled up the channel all the way to a latitude of 77 degrees, before finally turning back and returning down the west side of Cornwallis Island.

All this added up to an epic voyage for so short a time. It would be more reasonable to imagine Franklin sailing up Wellington Channel after spending a first winter at Beechey Island.

On the other hand, there are two very obvious objections to placing Franklin at Beechey Island during the second winter of 1846-7. The first Victory Point message was written at the end of May, 1847, at which time the ships were clearly stuck in the ice off King William Island. Still, although Fitzjames wrote "H.M.Ships Erebus and Terror Wintered in the Ice in.", this may not mean they had spent the winter there; he may simply have been stating the condition of the ships — meaning "*at present* wintered in the ice" off King William Island.

But this is of little help. Even if we imagine, by some miracle, the ships had spent the winter at Beechey Island, then been freed from the ice (before May!) and sailed down to King William Island only to become stuck again, we must contend with the second objection. In the 1848 message, Fitzjames helpfully noted that the ships had been deserted after having been "beset since 12th Sept. 1846."

Had Fitzjames made a mistake with the Beechey Island dates, after all? Are there any other reasons, apart from Franklin's remarkably successful first year, to suggest Franklin had visited Beechey Island twice?

Certainly such an assumption clears up the mystery of the cairn made out of 700 Goldner meat cans that searchers discovered on Beechey Island. There seemed to be far too many cans for a single winter at Beechey Island. It was for this reason that the cairn of cans was seen by some people as evidence that the expedition's meat had gone bad, forcing Franklin to discard much of it at Beechey Island; this led to a shortage of provisions which in turn led to starvation and cannibalism two years later. The 700 cans are not a mystery, though, if Franklin spent, not one winter, but two on the island.

ADAM BECK'S OTHER TALE

But the most intriguing proof of all may have come from the most controversial source of all: Adam Beck. Beck, an Inuit, had been John Ross' interpreter during Ross' search for Franklin aboard the *Felix* in 1850. It was Beck who interviewed the Greenland Inuit and claimed to have gleaned from them a story of two ships that were attacked and burned by natives, their crews massacred. Though Beck insisted he was telling the truth, no one believed him except John Ross. Only a single day was spent checking out Beck's story, before rejecting it as either a fabrication or a mistake based on the *North Star*, which had spent the winter on the Greenland coast. Beck was branded a liar, and when Charles Francis Hall encountered him years later, Beck had become a ruined man.

Later that same summer, while the searchers combed Beechey Island after uncovering their first evidence of Franklin's voyage, Adam Beck made another discovery. He claimed to have found an elmwood post in the snow, with a slot cut in one end by a saw. Wedged in the slot, there had been a tin plate on which something was written in white on a black background. But Beck claimed (in his deposition) to have accidentally lost the tin plate when he slipped down a snowy hill, "not soft snow, by which it might be buried, but hard ice which, he said, he could not climb to recover it."[3] Thus he was able to produce the post, but not the plate. John Ross again stood by his interpreter, insisting that he had been watching Beck through a telescope when Beck made the find, and that Ross too had seen the tin plate, though not the writing.

What makes Beck's story so remarkable is his claim that on the tin was the inscription: "September 3 1846". He made this claim nine years before the Victory Point record was discovered, when all the evidence (namely the graves) indicated Franklin had left Beechey Island long before that date. We can't help but notice the coincidence of the two dates: Adam Beck's and the date given by Fitzjames on the Victory Point record. Fitzjames said the ships were first beset in the ice on September 12, 1846; Beck's sign placed the expedition on Beechey Island only nine days before this. Taken together, the two dates clearly indicate that Franklin, knowing the 1846 season was almost over, returned to his berth on Beechey Island on September 3, having found the way south blocked by ice for the second year in a row, and having already explored Wellington Channel. Nine days later, the ships were stuck fast. This is what Beck's find would seem to be telling us.

Of course, once again, everyone called Adam Beck a liar.

CHAPTER TWENTY-NINE
The Passage from Beechey Island

"Well, sometimes I've believed as many as
six impossible things before breakfast."
Lewis Carroll,
Through the Looking-glass

A VOYAGE IN ICE?

If Franklin spent his second winter at Beechey Island, how did he get into the ice off King William Island in the spring? More importantly, Fitzjames made it clear that the ships had been beset in the ice all winter, since September. How could the ships become beset in the ice off Beechey Island, yet end up beset in the ice off King William Island, without becoming "unbeset" somewhere in the middle?

One solution to this puzzle was proposed by Parker Snow, Lady Franklin's civilian champion, who had tried so hard to keep Captain Forsyth from giving up the search in 1850. Snow got his idea from the incredible winter voyage of the first American expedition, when those two ships had been pushed up Wellington Channel, then back down to Barrow Strait, east through Lancaster Sound and south down Baffin Bay, all while stuck in a huge ice-pan.

Snow proposed, "Let us suppose that on September 12th, 1846, the *Erebus* and *Terror* were beset and had to winter (their second winter) at the outer part of Beechey Island. They are in the pack, as the Americans were, only more clear of the drift. They remained there till, say April, when they are forced out of the place, carried away to the westward and then driven down Melville Sound to King William Island before May."[1]

It was an ingenious solution, bolstered by the evidence of the American expedition's drift — but objections could certainly be raised. The Americans had shown that the ice drift carried ships out into Baffin Bay by way of Lancaster Sound, not west toward Peel Sound. The spectacular ice stream flowing down from the Beaufort Sea also travelled east before flowing south down to King William Island. To have reached either Peel Sound or the ice stream, Franklin's ships would have to have somehow drifted west through the very spot where the Americans had drifted east. Even more damaging is the fact that in 1875 Sir Allen Young (who had searched Prince of Wales Island while McClintock visited King William Island) tried to journey through the Northwest Passage (Franklin's, not McClure's) aboard the *Pandora*. Again, he found Peel Sound almost totally clear of ice, except at the bottom near Bellot Strait, where he was forced to turn back before a field of ice which was slowly drifting *north* up the sound. A century later, photographer Mike Beedell and Jeff MacInnis (the son of Canadian explorer Joe MacInnis) travelled through the Northwest Passage using a tiny 450-pound Hobie catamaran. In Peel Sound they worked their way north, sometimes sailing, sometimes scrambling over the ice, and sometimes riding the floes, all with a wind at their backs from the south. Could Franklin's ships have drifted westward where the Americans had drifted eastward, then south down Peel Sound where the ice flowed north?

THE INCREDIBLE OMISSION

As if all this weren't puzzling enough, the Victory Point record itself adds still more to the mystery. Astonishingly, nowhere in the 1847 message does Fitzjames indicate what route the ships used to reach King William Island. It was an incredible omission, and one that has never been explained. The record gave a detailed report of the voyage up Wellington Channel, even including the highest latitude reached, and the route by which the ships returned. Yet, none of this was important to what was ostensibly the purpose of the voyage: the completion of the Northwest Passage. Franklin broke no records by reaching 77 degrees latitude; Edward Parry had attained a north latitude of 82 degrees in 1827. The journey was interesting, certainly, but it was no more than a side trip. What mattered was knowing how the ships had gotten as far as they had. How had they reached King William Island? Southwest of Cape Walker? Peel Sound? Or through one of the hypothetical straits thought to link Prince Regent Inlet to the water west of Boothia?

How could Fitzjames have failed to recognize how important that information would be? Because of this omission, even today historians remain uncertain about how the expedition arrived at King William Island.

If Franklin did use Peel Sound, as most believe, whether under his own steam or adrift in an ice pan, shouldn't Fitzjames have recorded the vital discovery that Peel Sound was not a bay but a sound? When Franklin set out from England, Cape Walker was thought to be the northwest corner of Somerset, which was why he was ordered to seek a passage only beyond that point. Shouldn't the Victory Point record have noted that Cape Walker was actually the northern tip of Prince of Wales Island, that there was a passage — *the* Passage — between Somerset and Prince of Wales Island, and that Franklin had violated his orders by travelling, not southwest of Cape Walker, but southeast?

For all these reasons, Fitzjames' omission makes positively no sense — no sense that is, unless Fitzjames *did not know how he had reached King William Island.*

THE RESOLUTE AND THE OCTAVIUS

It is a remarkable hypothesis, but let us consider it closely. In the Victory Point record, Fitzjames carefully described the explorations up Wellington Channel and down the west side of Cornwallis Island but nothing else. It is as if that was all that had yet been discovered. We are given the latitude and longitude of the expedition's wintering stop at Beechey Island, but there is no hint of geographical knowledge extending further south. It is almost as if the voyage to King William Island never happened. Or, more properly, it is as if the expedition went from Beechey Island to King William Island without passing through the country between.

Is this possible? Certainly not that we know of. And yet...

We can't help but think of the case of the *Resolute*, Captain Kellett's ship. When Edward Belcher ordered Kellett to abandon the

Resolute, the vessel was still locked fast in the ice deep inside Viscount Melville Sound. The very next year, the *Resolute* was found floating in Baffin Bay, her hatches still sealed and her rigging frozen. Without a crew, somehow the *Resolute* found her way through the heavy ice and the labyrinth of shoals found in Viscount Melville Sound, which she had been unable to navigator *with* a crew two years before. (The steam powered *Intrepid* pulled her off the shoals.) Somehow she had sailed through Barrow Strait and Lancaster Sound, then out into Baffin Bay, all without being sunk by the heaving, grinding icepacks along the way. On boarding her, the salvagers found unspilled glasses of wine still set out on a table. If it had not happened, we would say it was impossible.

Then there is the even stranger case of the *Octavius*. Nearly a century before, in November 1762, this British vessel entered the Arctic from the west with a crew of twenty-eight. North of Point Barrow, Alaska, she became trapped in the relentless ice and, unable to get free, vanished into the Arctic. She was presumed lost with all hands. Then on August 17, 1775, the *Octavius* was found again by the *Herald*. The lost ship was drifting with the twenty-eight-man crew still aboard her, all frozen to death. She had reappeared off the coast of Greenland fully *thirteen years* after her disappearance on the opposite side of the Arctic. Thirteen years. How could any ship, let alone a ship built in the 1700s, have remained afloat in the Arctic ice for thirteen years? How could the *Octavius* have crossed the Arctic without a crew, somehow navigating the Northwest Passage, which the navy's far more powerful vessels later failed to traverse?

THE REST IS MERE CONJECTURE

If an answer is to be sought to this mystery, it is to be sought at only one place: Beechey Island. Here the Franklin expedition spent its first winter in the Arctic. We have already glimpsed a hint of strange happenings during that first winter; the three deaths, the two grim Biblical passages on the headstones: "Thus saith the Lord of Hosts: Consider your ways."; "Choose ye this day whom ye will serve."

Then, if we are correct, the expedition returned to Beechey Island for a second winter. There were no deaths this time, but somehow, early in the spring, the members of the expedition found themselves locked in the ice off King William Island with no idea how they had got there.

The later searchers commented on the evidence of a remarkably hasty departure from Beechey Island. But for us, one detail more than any other seems imbued with a disturbing significance. This is the pair of cashmere gloves discovered carefully set out on a rock, a pebble in each palm to keep them from blowing away. Those gloves had been set down for only a short time, but their owner had never returned to claim them.

However, perhaps the eeriest event to occur at Beechey Island concerns none other than Jane Franklin's champion from across the English Channel, Joseph-René Bellot. As we have already seen, Bellot took part in the Canadian expedition under Captain Kennedy. Though no sign of Franklin was discovered, Bellot was not one to give up easily. On his return, he set about trying to convince his own government to organize a French expedition to take up the search. In the end, his zeal wasn't shared by his compatriots and he was turned down. Lady Franklin offered Bellot a ship of his own, the steamer *Isabel*, and Kennedy even offered to serve under his former subordinate. In the end, the *Isabel* left without Bellot, which was just as well since it got only as far as Valparaiso before the crew mutinied on Kennedy.

Instead, Bellot returned to the Arctic in a last-minute posting aboard the transport *Phoenix*, sent out to re-provision Belcher's expedition. In charge of the *Phoenix* was Captain Edward Inglefield, who we have previously met exhuming the body of John Hartnell. It was to be Bellot's final expedition and one which would cost him his life.

His death sent shockwaves back across the Atlantic; Jane Franklin was especially distressed by his loss, and she later saw that a memorial plaque was placed on Beechey Island beside her husband's. As to what actually happened, historians have been remarkably varied in their recountings. Stephen Leacock, in *Adventurers of the Far North* (part of the famous *Chronicles of Canada* series), played it safe by simply noting, "The gallant Bellot, attempting to carry dispatches over the ice, sealed his devotion with his life."[2] Noel Wright wrote that Bellot, "appears to have been swept off an ice-floe by the force of the wind."[3] Pierre Berton stated, "Without warning, a great fissure fifteen feet wide opened up under him. He was gone in an instant."[4] And Peter Newman claimed Bellot "drowned en route to Lancaster Sound."[5]

The reason for these many interpretations lies in the truly mysterious circumstances of his death. When the *Phoenix* reached Beechey Island, Bellot promptly offered to carry dispatches up Wellington

Channel to Belcher's ships, *Assistance* and *Pioneer*. He set off on August 12th with a sledge, a gutta-purcha (a type of latex) boat, and three companions, including one who would later serve as quartermaster on the *Fox*. The party travelled on the ice for two days, until Bellot decided it would be safer if they returned to the shore. But suddenly, a lead opened up and Bellot and two of his four companions found themselves trapped on a drifting, hummocky ice floe. The three castaways proceeded to erect a tent, and settled down for the night.

In the morning, the men were still adrift and thoroughly frightened they might not get back alive. Bellot, to encourage his companions, assured them, "If God protects us, not a hair of our heads will fall to the ground."[6] Then he left the tent to see how far they had drifted. Four minutes later, one of the other men followed Bellot out. To the man's astonishment, Bellot was nowhere to be seen. The two men searched the ice floe, but the French officer was never found.

It was concluded that he had somehow been blown into the water. And yet, no cry for help had been heard, nor a splash. On a small ice floe, surrounded by water, Joseph-René Bellot simply vanished. As one searcher said, "The rest is mere conjecture."[7]

PART IV
In Whose Land Ye Dwell

And always keep a hold of Nurse
For fear of finding something worse.
    Hillaire Belloc,
    Jim

CHAPTER THIRTY
Mock Suns and Other Northern Lights

You common people of the skies,
What are you when the moon shall rise?
Sir Henry Wotton,
On his Mistress, the Queen of Bohemia

THE AGE OF REASON

"Ever since the old [John] Ross' disastrous sighting of the 'Croker Mountains'," observed Roderic Owen, "it had been a curious chance that observations made in this one corner of the Arctic should continue to produce false conclusions."[1] And observations there were, of many shapes and sizes, colours and lights.

Perhaps nowhere on the face of the planet was there a geographic region more prone to the production of inexplicable sightings (and less prone to the asking of questions) than the eastern Arctic. Whether it be the sighting of solid land where there should be no land, or hissing lights in the Hyborean sky, Arctic explorers took it all in stride, coolly jotting it all down with an astonishing equanimity which might leave modern readers shaking their heads in wonder. The explanation for this remarkable resilience in the face of bizarre phenomena can be summed up in one word: dioptrics.

The nineteenth century was the age of reason. In an astonishingly short time, it seemed, science had succeeded in unravelling mysteries that had existed since the dawn of civilization. The scientists of the Renaissance — Galileo, Kepler, Newton, Hooke — had all looked upwards and outwards to the heavens, charting the elliptical paths of the planets, or gazed inward, fashioning new mathematical techniques and the laws of physics. But the worthies of the nineteenth century turned their attention to the earth itself, seeking to explain the miracles sitting under their very noses.

It was the era of museum collections, when science largely involved going out and shooting whatever you could find, preferably several hundred of them, just to be certain. Fossils were no longer "sports of nature", whimsically placed in the ground by God to fool gullible humans; they were the evidence of past worlds, fantastic but now well within the realm of scientific understanding. Charles Lyell published his landmark *Principles of Geology*; Charles Darwin unleased *The Origin of Species*. The term "Natural History" itself implied progress and scientific achievement, dominion over the earth; it rang with the sort of state-of-the-art high-tech importance which a later age would accord to terms like "quantum mechanics" and "bioengineering".

And yet, it was a curious irony that the century which ushered in our own era of scientific reason, also begat the first wave of seances and spirit mediums. Still, here too, science took it all in stride. Scientists studied the famous Fox sisters as they might a pair of finches on the Galapagos Islands, soberly listening to the sound of spirits rapping out their messages from the grave (never guessing the one sister was merely cracking the knuckle of her toe). Even ghosts, they felt, could be fit into a niche somewhere in the grand edifice of Natural History — along with the newly discovered gorilla, perhaps.

In this climate of progress, inevitable and unrelenting, it should hardly surprise us that visitors to the Arctic realms so easily accepted all that they found there. Dioptrics was the key: the study of light refraction. No explorer entered the Arctic ice without first hearing of the astonishing way warm air layers or suspended ice particles could bend and warp light, creating an infinite variety of mirages and illusions, phantom mountain ranges and lights in the sky. The explorers were assured before even setting out from England: if they witnessed ships suspended in the air, it was just the refracted image of some unseen whaler hidden over the horizon. It might not look like a whaler, but that was because the image might be squeezed, upside down, or otherwise distorted. Other shapes seen hovering over the chill waters were likewise ascribed to the distorted images of mountaintops or icebergs, again hidden over the horizon.

None of this is to dispute the reality of light refraction; images are indeed refracted through layers of air. But the problem with the science of dioptrics was that it was too successful at explaining away just about anything without any way of proving that the explanation itself was valid in any particular case. Those nineteenth century explorers might have watched a B-52 bomber passing low over the Arctic floes and calmly recorded the observation as yet one more curious "refractive phenomenon".

If we were to try to categorize those things seen by the northern explorers, we might divide them into two main groupings. The first group might be titled: "phantom geographical features". More properly, these were the fata morgana.

THE FATA MORGANA

Into this category falls all those strange islands, land barriers, and mountain ranges seen and sworn to by experienced explorers, yet which had mysteriously vanished by the time the next expedition happened along. John Ross had seen his "Croker Mountains"; Kennedy and Bellot had seen land across the bottom of Peel Sound. In 1909, Robert Peary, on his way to the North Pole, sighted "Crocker Land" north of Ellesmere Island. He swore it was a mountainous island, "not a small island but something that filled the horizon — clear and unmistakably icy peaks rising against the northern sky."[2] But unmistakable or not, in 1913, another expedition found neither hide nor hoar of Peary's island. There was President's Land, Petermann Land, Keenan Land, and King Oscar Land, which all vanished when later expeditions happened through. Were these mere tricks of the light?

Yet the situation may not have been so simple. As Barry Lopez commented, "Expeditions sent out later to verify these new lands sometimes saw the same fata morgana, further confusing the issue."[3] Of course, some might say a mirage seen years later by another expedition somewhat violated the meaning of the term.

The elusive Isle of Buss, for example, appeared on maps for more than two centuries. It was first reported by the seamen of the *Emmanuel,* during Martin Frobisher's third expedition to Baffin Island in 1578. The Hudson's Bay Company laid claim to Buss Island in 1673, even though Henry Hudson had been unable to locate the place during his voyage to Hudson Bay in 1609. On the other hand, Zachariah Gilliam, captain of the *Nonsuch*, had spotted the mysterious island five years before the Hudson's Bay Company laid their claim, so the Honourable Company's application to ownership wasn't entirely without foundation. But finally, in 1791, Charles Duncan, working for the Hudson's Bay Company, determinedly searched the area where Buss Island was supposed to lie and concluded, "it is my firm opinion that no such island is now above water if ever it was."[4] And yet, two different expeditions had verified its existence.

AERIAL PHENOMENA

The second category of things seen in the Arctic might be titled: "Aerial phenomena". This in turn could be subdivided into luminous and non-luminous. The non-luminous variety could take on bizarre shapes, frequently altering form before the eyes of the clinical observer. For example, Dr. Kane, with the American Franklin search in 1850, made a remarkable observation while sailing off the Greenland coast. He wrote, "There is a black globe floating in the air about 3 degrees north of the sun ... Is it a bird or a balloon? ... on a sudden, it changes shape ... It is a grand piano ... you had hardly named it before it was an anvil ... it made itself duplicate (a pair of colossal dumbbells. A moment! and it is a black globe again."[5]

Charles Francis Hall made a curious observation while sailing in Baffin Bay en route to search for Franklin relics: "Looking to windward I saw the top of a distant berg; then all at once I saw a snow-white spot, not larger than a pin's head, appeared in the clouds hanging directly over the berg. In a few seconds it enlarged to the size of an Egyptian pyramid inverted .... this resplendently white pyramid seemed to descend and kiss the sea, then as often ascended again to its celestial throne."[6]

Sometimes, the descriptions returned by the Arctic explorers were so weird as to appear positively otherworldly. For example, Hall observed (on the same voyage), "Strange sights tonight. Looking through my marine glass to the north-east, ... I was astonished at the view before me. Mountains, islands, icebergs, and the sea were in one vast confusion. From the sun northerly to the south-west, wherever I turned my glass, confusion worse than things confounded met my sight. A little reflection, however, brought me to a realization of the fact. The extraordinary appearance of everything at and beyond the horizon was from 'refraction', so called."[7]

Similarly, Thomas Simpson, during the overland journey that discovered Simpson Strait below King William Island, encountered a weird phenomenon at Methye Lake. "While crossing the lake," wrote Simpson, "I witnessed an extraordinary effect of the mirage caused by the rays of the evening sun. It covered the land to the west with a mist-like veil and the ice even close around us appeared to dance with a strange undulating motion." Simpson's experience is oddly reminiscent of an observation made by Edward Parry during his miracle voyage back in 1819. Parry was puzzled to note, "a strong rippling on the surface of the water, and as we could discover nothing like shoal water, or unevenness in the bottom, we concluded that it must have been occasioned by some particular set, or meeting, of the tides in this place."[8] The two ships were passing in the vicinity of Beechey Island at the time.

Northern Lights?

But of far more interest than undulating ice and hovering black globes were the observations of luminous phenomena reported by those who first ventured into the land of the midnight sun. Yet, here too, the explorers were unfazed by whatever they chanced to see. This was hardly surprising, for, while refraction took care of explaining away bobbing pyramids and floating ships, every traveller entering the north was told to *expect* to see strange lights in the sky; this was the land of the Aurora Borealis, after all — the Northern Lights.

The Northern Lights often appear as an undulating screen of light, pale green and pink, with some crimson sometimes seen along the bottom edge. If seen from directly below, the lights can appear thin and snake-like. The effect rarely occurs lower in the atmosphere than one hundred miles up. Like refraction, there is no doubt that the Northern Lights are a reality; even Canadians in more southern climes can witness the rippling curtains of light on the northern horizon. The difficulty arises from the fact that these lights can manifest in such varied forms and colours that they too could easily have served as a convenient explanation for sightings that were something else.

Adding to the possible confusion between the Northern Lights and other stranger phenomena is the fact that these lights (or, more specifically, the sunspot activity which causes them) are known to cause radio interference, cause problems for electronic navigation equipment and even induce currents in power lines. Even compasses have been reported to swing erratically during the appearance of the Lights. For example, Captain G.F. Lyon, during his failed attempt to reach Repulse Bay in the *Griper* in 1824, recorded: "At this hour [9:00], Mr. Kendall observed, that during the prevalence of an unusually brilliant Aurora, the larboard binnacle compass would remain stationary at no particular point."[9]

It does not take much to see that attempting to distinguish between the Aurora Borealis and any other lights seen in the night skies would have been a difficult task when it came to interviewing the nineteenth century Inuit, who frequently spoke in a dialect foreign to the interpreter or, when no interpreter was available, used pantomime. This becomes important because the Inuit's "Lights" had some remarkable differences from the Northern Lights we know of. The Inuit, for example, claimed the lights they saw in the sky made a distinctive hissing sound, like a sheet flapping in the breeze. The Aurora Borealis, on the other hand, makes no sound whatsoever. Even stranger, the Inuit claimed the lights they saw would approach closer if whistled to. Needless to say, the Aurora Borealis does not.

The description of a hissing sound takes on an added interest in conjunction with an observation made by a member of Thomas Simpson's expedition while at Cape Alexander in March, 1839. He observed "a semi-elliptical figure apparently very near the earth, in rapid motion, and tinged with red, purple and green. The half-ellipse seemed to descend and ascend accompanied by an audible sound resembling the rustling of silk. This lasted about ten minutes when the whole phenomenon suddenly rose upwards and its splendour was gone."[11] As Roderic Owen humorously commented, "It was a pity that no one yet had invented the term 'flying saucer'."

During the *Fox's* enforced winter in the ice of Baffin Bay in 1857, McClintock related how his quartermaster, William Harvey (formerly one of Bellot's four companions on his final journey), was "a regular magnet" to the younger seamen serving on the voyage. Harvey would spend hours recounting stories about his experiences in the Arctic, "its bears, its icebergs, and still more terrific 'auroras, roaring and flashing about the ship enough to frighten a fellow'!"[11]

George Back, too, had a strange story told to him. At Fort Chipewyan, during the winter of 1821, Back made friends with the local Northwest Company fur traders. One man told this story.

> He was travelling in a canoe in the English River, and had landed near the Kettle Fall, when the coruscations of the Aurora Borealis were so vivid and low that the voyageurs fell on their faces, and began praying and crying, fearing they should be killed; he himself threw away his gun and knife that they might not attract the flashes, for they were within two feet of the earth, flitting along with incredible swiftness, and moving parallel to its surface. They continued for upwards of five minutes, as near as he could judge, and made a loud rustling noise, like the waving of a flag in a strong breeze. After they had ceased, the sky became clear, with little wind.[12]

JOHN BROWN'S BODY

Apart from the question of what was and what was not the Aurora, the Arctic explorers saw many other unusual lights for which they again invoked that catch-all explanation: refraction. During McClintock's winter spent frozen in the pack of Baffin Bay, one of the men fell down a hatch-way and died of internal injuries two days later. The man's body was placed on a sledge and dragged out to where a hole had been cut in the ice. After a solemn funeral, the body was dropped down through the hole, burying him at sea. McClintock wrote: "What a scene it was! I shall never forget it. The lonely 'Fox' almost buried in snow, completely isolated from the habitable world, her colours half-mast high, and bell tolling mournfully; our little procession slowly marching over the rough surface of the frozen sea, guided by lanterns and direction posts, amid the dark and dreary depth of Arctic winter; the deathlike stillness, the intense cold, and the threatening aspect of a murky, overcast sky."[13] And then overhead, "one of those strange lunar phenomena which are but seldom seen even here." McClintock observed "mock moons or paraselenae to the number of six." He noted that "The misty atmosphere lent a very ghastly hue to this singular display, which lasted for rather more than an hour."

On May 29, 1860, Charles Francis Hall set out from New London, Connecticut aboard the barque, *George Henry* (coincidentally, the same ship which had salvaged the *Resolute*). His intention was to seek Franklin relics on King William Island. Though he would eventually manage to spend four days searching the island, that year he only got as far as the entrance to Frobisher Bay on Baffin Island, where he spent the winter in Cyrus W. Field Bay, named for one of the promoters of his venture.

In March, two of the seamen, John Brown and James Bruce, began showing signs of scurvy, so they were sent to spend some time at the nearby Inuit settlement in Frobisher Bay, in the hopes the fresh meat would cure them. On March 15, two Inuit men were dispatched from the ship to the settlement with dogs and a sledge, to trade for meat. Brown and Bruce felt better enough to decide to return to Field Bay with the Inuit and, after a day's delay, the party set out. On the way back, the group ran into hummocky ice, making it difficult to pull the fully laden sledge. The Inuit decided to unload some of the weight, to be left as a cache for retrieval later. But Brown was impatient to get back to the ships. Insisting he knew the way, he decided to go on ahead. The Inuit tried to dissuade him, but he was adamant. A dog was unleashed from the sledge to accompany him on his journey.

Having cached the provisions, the three men continued on to the ship. Because the party had seen Brown's tracks out on the ice of Field Bay, they assumed their concerns had been unfounded. In the morning, they casually asked one of the other men what time Brown had reached the ship. To their horror, they were told he hadn't arrived at all. Hall was immediately informed and he told the captain what had happened. A search was organized and twenty men set out onto the ice of Field Bay.

But Hall noticed something odd. He wrote, "By reference to my journal ... of last night, I see that I there noted the following phenomenon, viz., 'Showers of snow while the heavens are clear. Stars shining brightly.' At midnight, the time of my last visit to the deck, I wrote this, though a previous record had been made of the same phenomenon taking place as early as 9 P.M. 'Twelve, midnight, stars still shining; all clear over the whole expanse, yet snowing!'"[14] He was puzzled. It had been snowing in the night and yet he had been able to see stars shining brightly in the sky.

Throughout the day and into the next evening the search continued. Gradually the twenty searchers dwindled, as more and more returned to the ship. Hall pushed on, determined to save Brown if he could. Brown's tracks were visible in the snow, but, though initially heading straight for the ship, they had unaccountably veered away. Now they led directly out to sea, then back toward the shore, then this way and that. Hall thought Brown must have surely seen the mountains along the shore, by which he could have oriented himself, but no. Brown was going in circles. "They come in rapid succession. Round and round the bewildered, terror-stricken, and almost frozen one makes his way."

Though Hall did not yet know it, the sledge dog, which Brown had taken with him, had returned to the Inuit settlement — alone. Inexplicably, the dog's trace or leash had been cut away close to the harness with a knife.

Finally, in the night, Hall came upon Brown's body, frozen in the snow. Hall noted that, "The place where we found him also exhibited unmistakable signs of a terrible struggle." But there was only one set of tracks leading to the body. Hall concluded the struggle had been made by Brown as he died, fighting to rise again. Wrote Hall, "He died facing the heavens, the left hand by his side, the right extended, and his eyes directed upwards, as if the last objects mirrored by them were the stars looking down upon him in his death struggles."[15]

Four days before, Hall had casually observed, "Parhelia, or mock suns, seen at Field Bay, March 14, 1861."[16]

CHAPTER THIRTY-ONE

Inuit Tales and the Angikuni Connection

But oh, beamish nephew, beware of the day
If your Snark be a Boojun! For then
You will softly and suddenly vanish away,
And never be met with again!
Lewis Carroll,
The Hunting of the Snark

CHARLES FRANCIS HALL

It might be assumed that the story of the Franklin search reached its belated climax with McClintock's discovery of the bodies on King William Island and the recovery of the Victory Point record. But, in fact, the most astonishing clues in the puzzle were yet to be found. Those clues would not be unearthed for several more years and, when they were, it was through the dogged determination of the most unlikely of searchers: Charles Francis Hall.

Unlike the majority of searchers, Hall was an American. A former blacksmith, now the owner of a small newspaper in Cincinnati, Ohio, Hall had absolutely no experience in the Arctic, nor of exploration. But what he lacked in experience, he more than made up for with a truly staggering bull-headed persistence. When he first set out on his adventure to recover Franklin relics and, if possible, to find survivors, one observer wrote, "In New York his expedition has been characterized as hare-brained."[1] But hare-brained or not, experienced or not, Hall not only followed through with his Quixotic quest, but proved himself to be second only to John Rae when it came to survival in the Arctic lands.

Unlike Rae, Hall wasn't quite able to look after himself, but he spent considerably longer periods of time cut off from civilization than Rae ever had, living like the Inuit and, more importantly, living *with* the Inuit.

Hall began his mad quest in 1860, only one year after McClintock's visit to King William Island, yet it would not be until 1869 that Hall would finally set foot on the famous island. During the intervening years he was doomed to meet setback after setback. Yet, when Hall finally reached King William Island after a nine-year delay, his search was limited to only four days and the few bones he found served little more than to confirm what was already known. It was the irony of his quest that Hall's major contributions to the Franklin puzzle were obtained, not from the island, but from the Inuit with whom he spent those many frustrating years.

From the Inuit, Hall heard amazing stories, some of which merely embellished upon what others had learned, but most adding entirely new aspects to the mystery. Like McClintock, Hall heard about the stranded ship pillaged by the Inuit, and learned details about the strange body found aboard her. He now concluded that McClintock had been mistaken: the ship had been stranded on the west coast of the Adelaide Peninsula south of King William Island, rather than on the west coast of the island itself. Hall was told about a tent at Terror Bay on King William Island where many bodies had been seen, the tent littered with bones. He learned about the other bodies found at Starvation Cove and the box with books seen with them. The Inuit plied him with grisly details of bodies apparently cut up with a saw, many with their hands missing, some with holes in their heads. Of all these tales though, two assumed greater importance than the rest. One was the story of a brief meeting between four Inuit families and Crozier's doomed crewmen while in the midst of their final march. This was to be the only eyewitness account ever obtained of that last desperate trek. The second story was even more remarkable.

Hall learned there had been survivors.

THE GIANT CORPSE

It was during one attempt to reach King William Island in 1866 that Hall encountered the Inuit of Pelly Bay. Unlike John Rae before him, Hall found the local Inuit were willing to tell their stories about the two ships seen off the King William Island coast and the many men who had perished on the island. He purchased various relics found in their possession: Crozier's spoon, a barometer case, a pair of scissors. But then, the Inuit began spinning tales of a frightening tribe said to live on King William Island. Hall thought it was just superstition, but his Inuit companions took the matter seriously enough that they refused to travel any farther. In disgust, Hall was forced to turn back.

Finally, in March 1869, Hall began his long delayed journey to King William Island. On the west coast of Boothia Peninsula across from King William Island, Hall entered an Inuit village, where he purchased more Franklin relics and heard yet more stories. The Inuit told him about the ship stranded near Adelaide Peninsula, obviously the same ship that McClintock had heard about but had been unable to find. There had been a body found aboard the ship, Hall heard, again confirming what McClintock had already been told. But now the Inuit gave further details.

McClintock had merely heard that the dead body was of a "very large" man. Hall was told that the corpse had been large indeed, requiring five men to lift it. Stranger still, the corpse was said to have had very long teeth, as long as an Inuk's fingers. The Inuit had left the body on the ship. Unfortunately, they had accidentally knocked a hole in the hull, causing the ship to sink. The Inuit also spoke about a tent found at Terror Bay on the island's west shore. The tent had been filled with bodies and bones. An Inuk named Teeketa said he had seen "A great many skulls — the flesh all off, nothing except sinews attached to them, the appearance as though foxes and wolves had gnawed the flesh off the bones." Even stranger, "Some bones had been severed with a saw. Some skulls had holes in them."[2]

Though Hall had planned to spend the entire summer searching King William Island, his Inuit companions inexplicably refused to remain on the island for more than four days. During that time, Hall discovered the skeletal remains of a few bodies along the south shore, but little else. And yet, for all the lack of physical evidence, Hall had amassed an impressive collection of Inuit accounts, some of them eyewitness and some of them second-hand. The details of the stories gleaned from the Inuit over the course of those many years may, in some ways, be more important in terms of solving the Franklin mystery than were the countless spoons and watches obtained by other searchers. More important, that is, *if they were true.*

ENCOUNTER AT WASHINGTON BAY

Historians have shown little hesitation in outright rejecting many of the stories told to Hall. Pierre Berton wrote, "The natives had a habit of telling white men what they wanted to hear. Hall, in his turn, was prepared to believe what he wanted to believe."[3] Roderic Owen, in referring to the story about survivors, commented, "The Kabloonas [white men] of course, were at liberty to believe what they chose of any of this nonsense."[4] Somewhat more charitably, William Gibson warned, "The accounts he [Hall] reported to have obtained from the Hudson Bay Eskimos ... must be approached with the greatest caution, for many of them would seem to be purely imaginative and without any actual basis whatsoever."[5] Gibson added, "Surely many of the incongruous accounts Hall attributed to the Eskimos of Hudson Bay were not the sober narrations for which the race is noteworthy, but rather the manifestations of a shaman's seance."

On the other hand, David C. Woodman devoted an entire book, *Unravelling the Franklin Mystery*, to an analysis of the Inuit stories, both those told to Hall and to others. Woodman stated, "In researching the Franklin saga, I proceeded from the assumption that all Inuit stories concerning white men should have a discoverable factual basis."[6]

The story of the encounter between the lost expedition and the Inuit on King William Island is one that historians have accepted as a true accounting of events. Hall heard the story first in 1869 from two Inuit named Teeketa and Ow-wer, who claimed to be actual eyewitnesses to the meeting.

The Inuit told Hall that several families had been sealing on the west shore of King William Island, near Washington Bay and slightly north of Cape Herschel. They spotted a white object in the distance, which gradually resolved itself into a sail mounted on a boat atop a sledge and a large party of white men. The Inuit went to meet the white men where a crack in the ice separated them. Two white men walked up to the crack and tried to communicate with the Inuit using only pantomime. Hall wrote, "The 1st man [thought to be Crozier] then showed that he had an oo-loo when he stooped down beside the ice crack which divided the white men from the Innuits & began cutting the ice with a peculiar kind of circling motion with the oo-loo (Civilization mincing-knife or Innuit women's knife) ... At the same time, or rather right after this man had made these 'chippings' or 'scratchings' ... on the ice, he put his hand to his mouth and lowered it all the way down to his neck and breast, as if to say he wanted something to eat."[7]

Much has been made of this scene. Pierre Berton stated, "The starving men had pleaded for seal meat, and the natives had given them some."[8] But the description hardly proves that Crozier was "pleading" for seal meat. He would have been remiss in failing to garner fresh meat when the opportunity presented itself, as it did now. Clearly the Inuit did not think Crozier was in a desperate situation for want of food; Teeketa and Ow-wer told Hall the Inuit left Crozier because "the Innuits were in a hurry — did not know the men were starving."[9]

After crossing over at a narrowing in the crack, Crozier — called "Aglooka" by the Inuit who knew him from his earlier expedition to Repulse Bay — continued with the pantomime. "Aglooka pointed with his hand to the southward & eastward & at the same time repeating the word I-wil-ik [Repulse Bay]. The Innuits could not understand whether he wanted them to show him the way there or that he was going there."[10]

This comment was something of a problem in light of the Victory Point record which seemed to say that Crozier was headed to the Great Fish River. But with our new reading of the Victory Point record, we can see that Crozier was indeed headed toward the southeast and the strait he thought led through Boothia to Prince Regent Inlet. It is possible Crozier did not know the Inuit word for Fury Beach, but did know I-wil-ik, having been there with Edward Parry, and so used the name to indicate his direction of travel — *toward* Repulse Bay, rather than *to* Repulse Bay.

Now Crozier pointed to the north, back the way he had come. He "spoke the word oo-me-en, making them understand there were 2 ships in that direction; which had, as they supposed, been crushed in the ice."[11] Or had they? We have already seen that the ships were still afloat when they were abandoned; the Victory Point record says they were "deserted" without any mention of their sinking; nor is it reasonable to believe that both ships might have sunk at the same time. Finally, there was the ample evidence that one of the ships had remained afloat for months before finally stranding farther south on the coast of the Adelaide Peninsula. But, if Crozier was not telling the Inuit that his ships had sunk, what was he trying to describe?

His pantomime was remembered by the Inuit and recorded by Hall. "As Aglooka pointed to the north, drawing in his hand & arm from that direction he slowly moved his body in a falling direction and all at once dropped his head sideways into his hand, at the same time making a kind of combination of whirring, buzzing & wind blowing noise."[12]

The Inuit interpreted this as the sound of a ship being crushed by the ice. On the other hand, if we were to speculate, we might alternately interpret Crozier's head dropping into his hand as symbolizing something falling or crashing onto the ice. As for the odd noise, we might notice the similarity between Crozier's "whirring, buzzing & wind blowing" and the strange sound which Thomas Simpson's companion had heard accompanying the flying light seen near Cape Anderson (and which George Back's Northwest Company storyteller also described).

A point which should be made: Washington Bay was south of Terror Bay. At Terror Bay the Inuit told Hall they later discovered a tent filled with bodies and evidence of cannibalism in the form of severed limbs and skulls with holes in them. Thus, whatever happened at Terror Bay had already transpired by the time the Inuit met the white men at Washington Bay. And yet, the Inuit saw no indication that Crozier's men were starving to the point of cannibalism. Though Crozier asked for and accepted seal meat from the Inuit, the transaction was carried out more as an orderly re-provisioning than a desperate grab for food. Crozier himself, after first indicating his desire for seal meat, showed no signs of starvation.

Hall was told, "Aglooka [ate] a very small piece" of seal meat given to him by the Inuit.[13]

On the other hand, the Inuit at first felt that something was upsetting the white men. They told Hall, "trouble thought to be among the men; but not so. They were putting up the tent and stopped, staring at the Innuits. When [Aglooka] spoke to them then, they all resumed their work."[14] The next morning, the Inuit resumed their journey leaving the white men behind.

Ten years later, the U.S. Army Lieutenant Frederick Schwatka learned still more details of this encounter from an old Inuit woman named Ahlangyah, Too-shoo-art-thariu's wife, who had also been a witness. Instead of the one-day meeting described to Hall, she recalled the encounter taking place over five days. Her description of the men was especially unusual. She told Schwatka that "Some of the white men were very thin, and their mouths were dry and hard and black."[15]

The Washington Bay encounter is important in affording a glimpse, however brief, of Crozier's doomed party while in the very middle of their last trek. Several details stand out. First, Crozier clearly indicated he was headed in the direction of Repulse Bay, further supporting our new reading of the Victory Point record. Second, though the Inuit later believed the white men perished of starvation — a view which historians have accepted — during the Washington Bay encounter, the Inuit saw nothing to make them think the men were starving even though the meeting itself took place after the men had already left Terror Bay and its grisly tent behind. The Inuit were no strangers to starvation and they would surely have recognized its signs if those signs had been in evidence. Third, with so much to indicate that the ships did not sink until long after they had been abandoned, Crozier's strange pantomime becomes mysterious indeed. If he wasn't trying to imitate the sinking ships, what was he trying to imitate? And finally, there is Ahlangyah's description of "some of the white men", thin with dry, hard, and black lips. One symptom of scurvy is black gums, but the victim's gums become quite soft, not hard, the teeth becoming extremely loose. So, what was Ahlangyah describing?

SURVIVORS

It was Too-shoo-art-thariu who first met Crozier across the crack in the ice. Back in 1864, Hall had been told another story about this same Inuk. This story had come from Too-shoo-art-thariu's cousins, and was later confirmed by information gleaned in 1869. Hall was told that Too-shoo-art-thariu had met with Crozier and three other men while on the ice off the west coast of Boothia Peninsula. The cousins explained that "Crozier's face looked bad — his eyes all sunk in — looked so bad that their cousin could not bear to look at his face." Too-shoo-art-thariu quickly gave Crozier a piece of seal meat. But, strangely, "Did not give any to the other three, for they were fat and had been eating the flesh of their companions."[16] More elaborately, Hall was told, "The cousin soon learned that the three fat men had been living on human flesh, on the flesh of their companions who all deserted the two ships that were fast in mountains of ice; while Crozier was the only man that would not eat human flesh, and for this reason he was almost dead of starvation."[17]

This part of the story seems odd indeed. Even if the other three men had survived through cannibalism, would they really have been "fat"? More to the point, how did Too-shoo-art-thariu know they had eaten their dead crewmates? Are we to imagine that Crozier, considering himself a member of a race in every way superior to the Inuit, would have calmly told the Inuk (using pantomime yet!) that his men had been devouring their bunkmates? But, if Crozier had not said so, why did Too-shoo-art-thariu think they had been?

The cousins continued their story: "The cousin took Crozier and his men along with him, and fed them and took good care of them all winter."[18] One of Crozier's three men died but not from starvation — the cousins were specific on this point("from a sickness". During the summer, Crozier used his gun to hunt birds. Then, after the winter, Crozier and his two remaining men set out in the company of another Inuk headed for the Great Fish River. But before leaving, Crozier gave Too-shoo-art-thariu a sword as a gift.

Unlike the encounter on Washington Bay, this story of survivors has been fiercely rejected by most historians (except Woodman). Hall was bothered because he suspected it was just an altered version of the Washington Bay meeting. Certainly the principle players — Crozier and Too-shoo-art-thariu — were the same. Another similarity was the piece of seal meat given to Crozier. But in 1869, Hall heard the same story. He was told "the cousin had not heard whether Crozier and the two men and Neitchille Inuit had ever come back or not. The Inuits never think they are dead — do not believe they are."[19] Hall wrote, "Tookoolitoo had just made the sympathetic remark('What a pity it is that Aglooka [Crozier] and the two men who started together from Neitchille [Boothia Peninsula] for the purpose of getting to the Koblun-as [white man's] country had never arrived.' ... Seegar sprang from his seat, quick as a flash, and looking staringly at Tookoolitoo, exclaimed with great force and surprise, 'What! Ag-loo-ka not get back! Why the Kin-na-pa-toos (Innuits who belong to Chesterfield Inlet), told me several years ago that Ag-loo-ka and one man with him arrived among their people.'"

To add further credibility to the story, in 1881 Captain Adams in command of the whaler *Arctic* was searching for whales in Prince Regent Inlet when he encountered an Inuk with a remarkably similar story. Captain Adams reported, "The native stated that when he was a young man in his father's hut three men came over the land towards Repulse Bay and that one of them was a great captain. The other two lived some little time in his father's hut, and he showed Captain Adams the spot on the chart where they were buried. The Esquimaux, continuing his narrative, said that seventeen persons started from two vessels which had been lost far to the westward but only three were able to survive the journey to his father's hut."

Too-shoo-art-thariu's cousins spoke of four men (including Crozier) one of whom died. Captain Adams' informer only apparently remembered three men. On the other hand, it could be the confusion arose because of the one death; thus, "only three were able to survive the journey" because one did not survive, but died soon after of "a sickness". Certainly Adams' Inuk informer obviously felt there had been a death or deaths involved, since he indicated "where they were buried."

Captain Adams himself was quite convinced that the story concerned the lost expedition. "From all the information furnished by the Esquimaux Captain Adams has no doubt that the vessels referred to were those of the Franklin expedition and that the great captain mentioned was no other than Lieutenant Crozier." Based on the age of his informer, Captain Adams guessed that the incident had occurred thirty-five years before. Following up on this lead, Captain Adams claimed to have recovered papers found at Repulse Bay, which he promptly forwarded to the Admiralty. What happened to these papers is not known. Woodman noted, "As nothing further was heard of these 'few papers', it must be assumed they held little of interest."[20]

Apart from corroborating testimony, there is another reason for believing the Inuit tale of survivors. Hall was told that the party of white men carried with them a strange air-filled boat. Hall immediately recognized the description as that of the Halkett's "air-boat", an early form of dingy. Though he did not know, Hall was certain Franklin's expedition must have carried a Halkett boat, else how could the Inuit have described it so certainly? As it turned out, the Franklin expedition had indeed taken along a Halkett boat; theirs was the first Arctic expedition to do so. (As with so much else, the Admiralty had spared no expense.)

But, while this went a long way toward validating the story, it wasn't definitive proof. Unfortunately, John Rae had carried along a Halkett boat during his visit to Repulse Bay only the year after Franklin set sail. Anderson had also brought a Halkett boat during his trip to the mouth of the Great Fish River to verify Rae's claims in 1855. Neither Rae nor Anderson had made much use of their inflatable boats, but the fact that they had brought them into the area at all served to muddy the water. On the other hand, Hall was told the white men gave Too-shoo-art-thariu a sword as a parting gift. As a naval officer, Crozier might very well have carried along a sword. But Rae and Anderson worked for the Hudson's Bay Company and so would not have had a sword to give. In 1857, Chief Factor Roderick MacFarlane was given a naval sword and scabbard by an elderly Inuk who claimed it was a Franklin relic. Was this the sword which Crozier gave to Too-shoo-art-thariu?

Woodman considered the possibility that the story was merely a compilation of remembrances of several different expeditions into the Arctic: George Back's, John Rae's in 1846 and 1854, Anderson's, and even John Ross/James Clark Ross' voyage of the *Victory*. He concluded that, "By picking and choosing among the various expeditions and accepting slight discrepancies, we can explain how the story might have come about. But, as always, there is another explanation. The story, although wrongly attributed to Too-shoo-art-thariu, may have been strictly and literally true, and it might be a remembrance of the survivors of the *Erebus* and *Terror*."[21]

The important question should be: is there any reason for doubting the story? In fact, there is not. The story itself is perfectly plausible. We know the lost expedition met with disaster in the area and we now know Crozier was indeed headed for Boothia Peninsula instead of the Great Fish River. Crozier had access to a Halkett boat and he would have carried a dress sword. Because of his former visit to Repulse Bay, the Inuit knew who he was. While we could concoct a complicated scenario by which the Inuit somehow muddled together every expedition to happen through the area since the *Victory's* visit in 1829, it seems simpler to assume that the Inuit knew what they were talking about.

In that case, we have in our possession an astonishing picture. Out of the death and horror of King William Island staggered Crozier and three other survivors. They alone of the 129 crew members had lived through the ordeal. Though one of the men perished of a sickness, the other three spent the winter in an Inuit home. During the long, dark winter months, Crozier tried to tell his host what had happened but was not entirely successful. But, as we have seen, Too-shoo-art-thariu thought the men had "all deserted the two ships that were fast in mountains of ice."[22] Again, this serves to confirm that the ships had not yet sunk when they were deserted in Victoria Strait. Crozier's strange pantomime at Washington Bay remains as mysterious as ever. If not the sinking ships, what was he trying to mimic by dropping his head into his hand and making that strange "whirring" noise?

Indians?

Stranger still, Crozier told Too-shoo-art-thariu that "before the other men from the two ships had died, they had battled with Indians (Etkerlins)."[23] This was a particularly odd story, for the reason that there are no "Indians" in the Arctic. It has been suggested that this part of the story was a confused remembrance of a brief skirmish between George Back's expedition and some Inuit; but, these were not Indians either. But how else to explain this odd story of Indians in the Arctic?

One possibility would be to assume it was Crozier who used the word (Etkerlins) in describing what had happened. Further, he may have done so because the tribe with which he had fought was not Inuit, but had no name he could use. Thus, he told Too-shoo-art-thariu that his men had battled Indians only to let his host know that they had not battled Inuit, but something *else for which there was no name.*

It is of course a remarkable suggestion, and yet, the fact of the story remains. Crozier claimed to have battled Indians on King William Island where there are no Indians. How else can we explain this except to suppose that Crozier was trying to distinguish between the Inuit and a people for which there was no name he could use — for the reason that they were previously unknown?

THE HARDWOOD BOX

After spending a winter with Too-shoo-art-thariu, Crozier and the two surviving men set out in the company of another Inuk guide. This time they really were headed for the Great Fish River, taking along a kayak to travel down the waterway. What happened to them after that? As we have seen, Tookoolitoo's friend Seegar told Hall that the Inuit of Chesterfield Inlet had seen Crozier and one other man in their area. If true, this indicates that one of Crozier's companions died during the journey. Beyond this we have no testimony to guide us. Crozier vanishes somewhere to the south.

Yet, in 1948, a possible clue to Crozier's fate was discovered by author Farley Mowat at Lake Angikuni in central Keewatin, "near a famous junction where the Eskimo trade routes between Churchill and the Arctic coasts converge."[24] Here Mowat happened upon "a very ancient cairn, not of normal Eskimo construction, and containing fragments of a hardwood box with dove-tailed corners." Mowat knew of no explorers who had been in the area and so concluded that "the possibility remains that this mute monument was built by Crozier, before he vanished utterly."

Woodman, too, was unable to discover any explorer who had visited Lake Angikuni, who might have built the ancient cairn. He did however find something else of interest. The geologist, J.W.Tyrrell, had passed through the area in 1893. Though there is no evidence Tyrrell visited Lake Angikuni, he did stop at nearby Selwyn Lake. Here the explorer discovered a grave "at the head of which stood a plain wooden cross." Tyrrell suggested, "It was, doubtless, the grave of some Christian Indian who had been taught by the priests at Fond-du-lac."[25] Could this instead have been the grave either of Crozier or of his one remaining companion? Did Crozier build the cairn at Lake Angikuni, perhaps shortly before he died? If so, what was in the hardwood box?

THE VANISHING VILLAGE

There is an intriguing postscript to this story. For, aside from being possibly the southernmost point to which we have traced Crozier after his flight from King William Island, Lake Angikuni is also the location of an Arctic mystery which is second only to the Franklin expedition itself in terms of questions, and first in terms of controversy. The story told about Lake Angikuni comes with a "buyer beware" warning. John Robert Colombo, in his *Mysterious Canada*, commented, "It never dies, despite the fact that it has been debunked time and time again."[26] And yet, this "Angikuni connection" is simply too intriguing to dismiss without due consideration.

On November 28, 1930, Emmett E. Kelleher, a special news correspondent at The Pas, Manitoba, sent a chilling story out to various newspapers across Canada and the U.S. The article appeared the following day and immediately created a sensation. According to Kelleher, the story had been told to him by a trapper named Joe Labelle. Kelleher wrote: "Far up in the heart of one of the most lonely places on earth — in the Lake Angikuni country, 500 miles southwest of the port of Churchill, on Hudson Bay — a whole tribe of Eskimos has vanished. Somewhere, somehow, the endless desolation of Canada's northern Barren Lands has swallowed up 25 men, women and children. It is one of the most puzzling mysteries that has ever come down out of the Arctic."[27]

Kelleher went on to describe how a trapper named Joe Labelle first happened upon an abandoned Inuit village of cariboo-skin tents. The inhabitants had left behind all their possessions, including their clothes and rifles. Labelle found some starving dogs, all skin and bone. He estimated that the village had held twenty-five people, but the rust on a rifle told him they had been gone at least twelve months. "There was no sign of violence, no sign of trouble. The place was simply empty." As he wandered through the ghost village, Labelle grew more and more uneasy, recalling (according to Kelleher) "the Eskimos' 'evil spirit' Tornark, who has an ugly man's face with two long tusks sticking up from each side of the nose."

Colombo characterized the whole thing as "Joe Labelle's tall tale" and "Kelleher's journalistic hoax", insisting that "within two months of its publication the RCMP had debunked the tale." After Kelleher's story appeared, public interest encouraged the local RCMP to look into the matter. The conclusion of Sergeant J. Nelson of The Pas was that the whole thing was a hoax of some kind. Joe Labelle was a real trapper, but there was no proof he had worked near Lake Angikuni. Nor had anyone else reported an abandoned village. A key part of Sergeant Nelson's argument centred on the photograph of the "vanishing village of the dead" which had been used to illustrate the story. This photograph, showing four cariboo-skin tents sitting apparently eerily forsaken, was actually a picture taken by a local RCMP officer, which Kelleher had borrowed. And yet this proved very little. It should hardly surprise us that, since Joe Labelle hadn't carried a camera with him, Kelleher decided the story would get better distribution with an accompanying illustration.

In the end, only Joe Labelle and Emmett Kelleher knew whether the story was true or not. Yet, in the present context, we can't help but find an eerie significance to the tale, not seen by those who read Kelleher's strange story at the time. The original story was told without any connection to the lost Franklin expedition. Now we have found possible evidence tracing Crozier and one man to Lake Angikuni. One body was buried at nearby Selwyn Lake. A cairn was left at Lake Angikuni with a box placed inside. And then what? Did Crozier die on the shore of Lake Angikuni? Might he have died and been buried by the ancestors of the Inuit who later vanished from Labelle's village? What happened to the twenty-five Inuit who had lived in the village? Labelle said, "The whole thing looked as if it had been left just that way by people who intended to come back. But they hadn't come back."

All this is mere idle speculation. And yet, there was one detail to Labelle's story that only now, to us, seems strangely suggestive.

Labelle told Kelleher, "And then I found one of the most puzzling things of all. It was an Eskimo grave, with a cairn built of stones. For some reason the grave had been opened. The stones had been pulled off of one side and there was nothing inside the cairn at all. I had no way of telling when it had been opened, or what had been done with the body it had once contained. I couldn't figure out why it had been desecrated."

CHAPTER THIRTY-TWO
The Tunnit

By the pricking of my thumbs,
Something wicked this way comes.
William Shakespeare,
Macbeth

LIKE A MAN

Among the Inuit, it was said that before their ancestors came to the Arctic the land of the midnight sun was home to a race called the Tunnit (or Tunit, or Tunrit). Theirs was a gentle race made up of giants, who the Inuit drove away in a furious prolonged confrontation. So common and compelling are these stories that anthropologists have little doubt but that the Tunnit did exist. The only question is: who were they?

Anthropologists theorize that the Tunnit legends are a remembrance of the meeting between the Dorset culture and the Thule culture that replaced it 1000 years ago. The Thule culture directly preceded the present Inuit culture now inhabiting the Arctic, and the Thule are believed to have been ancestors to the Inuit. The Dorset, on the other hand, are thought to have been a separate race and culture which arose from the Paleo-Eskimos who first entered the Arctic from Siberia approximately 4000 years ago.

In spite of the remarkable preservative properties of the dry, cold Arctic, very little evidence remains of the Dorset culture to allow us to piece together a picture of their society. As a result, there is considerable disagreement in the literature. For example, Robert McGee wrote, in *Ancient Canada*, "Many of the technological items that were used by the later Inuit occupants of the area, which we generally consider necessary to the Arctic hunting way of life, seem to have been unknown to these early immigrants. For example, they do not seem to have used boats ... nor is there any evidence that they used the domed snow house that provided winter protection to the later Inuit."[1] But Farley Mowat, in *Westviking*, stated, "[The Dorset] used skin-covered boats. They may have built snow-houses."[2]

The Arctic environment offered precious few materials for the fashioning of the sort of artifacts which might be found by modern archaeologists. Their summer houses have been found scattered across the eastern Arctic and as far north as Ellesmere Island, but as for what the Dorset actually looked like, we have little to go on.

For some time it was believed that the Dorset were actually a very small race, but this theory has fallen out of favour. "The idea," wrote Farley Mowat, "which has been proposed and maintained by recent authors, that the Dorsets were a pygmy race, seems to have originated in part from the small size and delicate nature of their artifacts."[3] The few bones which have been recovered do not suggest that the Dorset were much larger (if at all) than the Inuit. And yet, the Tunnit, who are said to represent the Dorset in the stories of the Inuit, were clearly described as a race of giants. Are these legends merely an exaggerated remembrance of a race which, in reality, could only have been at most slightly larger than the Inuit?

Stranger still, the Vikings also apparently encountered this giant race. As Farley Mowat wrote, "This is found in the Floamanna Saga in connection with the story of Thorgisl Orrabeinsfostri, who was shipwrecked far to the north of the Greenland settlements, apparently on Baffin Island, about 997. Thorgisl met natives who are described as giants."[4] We might suppose that the Inuit thought the Dorset were "giants", but it becomes harder to imagine the Vikings thinking the same thing. But, if not the Dorset, then who were these giant Tunnit?

Throughout the eastern Arctic are found large, crudely constructed statues made up of heavy stones. These stone figures are sometimes ten feet tall, and shaped to look human when seen against the horizon. In Inuktituut, the language of the Inuit, these stone statues are called the "Inukshuit", meaning "like a man". No one knows who constructed these statues, nor when. Their purpose likewise remains a mystery. Nonetheless, theories abound. Anthropologists hypothesize that the statues were intended to frighten caribou into corridors where they could be more easily hunted. Alternately, it is speculated that the Inukshuit served the same purpose as the later, simpler cairns, acting as landmarks to guide the Arctic peoples in their yearly migrations over the barren, white islands. The Thule, ancestral to the Inuit, are thought to be the most likely candidate to be Inukshuit-builders.

The Inuit, though, had a different story to tell. To them, the Inukshuit had been built at the time of the great conflict between the Tunnit and the Inuit's Thule ancestors. The great stone statues were said to commemorate that battle, perhaps serving to represent the giants who were defeated. On the other hand, John Robert Colombo noted, "It is the opinion of the contemporary Inuit that they [the Inukshuit] were constructed in the distant past by the Tunit."[5] These stone constructions are tantalizing in their lonely silence, dotting the Arctic landscape in vast numbers, undeniable in their solid reality. Their secret is closely guarded — are they meant to represent a race of giants, a race "like a man", but not being a man? Or were they constructed by that giant race itself?

But the Inuit had other things to tell about the people who had come before. The Inuit ethnographer Peter Freuchen spent many years living among the Arctic people, recording their stories and trying to understand them in a way which few had done before. His only equal in this area was said to be Knud Rasmussen, the great Danish-Inuit explorer and ethnologist. In his *Peter Freuchen's Book of the Eskimos*, he recorded this story about the people who had preceded the Inuit: "The first people were much stronger than people are now. Thus, they could with their magic make their houses fly, and a snow shovel could move by itself and shovel snow. People lived on earth, and when they wanted new nourishment they just sat in their houses and let them fly to new places. But one day a man complained over the noise the houses made when they flew through the air. And his words were powerful, and houses lost their ability to fly at that moment. And since then houses have been stationary." Freuchen was also told: "At that time new snow would burn like fire, and often fire fell down from the sky."[6]

SKULLS WITH HOLES

The Tunnit (or Tunrit) are closely linked with King William Island. According to Paul Fenimore Cooper, in *Island of the Lost*, "A thousand years or so ago — according to legend — a race of giants, the Tunrit came to the island ... These Tunrit were a strange people, big and sturdy, yet stupid and easygoing ... Their strength was great. One of them could single-handedly pick up a bear and throw it over his shoulder or pull a walrus from the sea .... Often when in a rage, they struck their harpoons so forcibly against the rocks as to make a shower of stone splinters."[7] But King William Island, it seemed, wasn't big enough for Inuit and Tunrit together. "It was the Tunrit's amiability and stupidity that proved their downfall," Cooper continued. "At first they let the Eskimos live on the island side by side with them in peace. But quarrels soon arose, and before long the newcomers [Inuit] took to hunting the giants down like game." Most remarkable is the manner in which the Inuit were said to have dispatched those Tunnit whom they caught. According to Cooper, "These doomed ones were tracked until caught asleep; then the Eskimos quickly killed them by drilling holes in their foreheads."

This story of holes in Tunnit foreheads seems oddly similar to another claim made by Cooper: that the Tunnit themselves were in the habit of making holes in heads, but for another reason. "They had a certain skill in the treatment of the sick (wrote Cooper); when one of them had a bad headache, a hole was drilled in his head, and relief gained by letting blood and matter ooze out."[8] The practice of relieving pressure around the brain by drilling a hole in the skull is called "trepanning". It is not especially unlikely that an Arctic race might have used this method on occasion to treat the sick. On the other hand, in conjunction with the story about Inuit killing Tunnit by drilling head-holes, we might ask ourselves whether both stories aren't perhaps distorted memories of something else again.

All of this takes on a strange significance when we recall that Charles Francis Hall was told about skulls with holes on King William Island. In the tent at Terror Bay, the floor apparently had been littered with bodies and bones. Teeketa told Hall: "A great many skulls ... Some bones had been severed with a saw. Some skulls with holes in them."[9] Another Inuk related how he had discovered a second boat slightly westward of the one discovered by Hobson and McClintock. Near this boat, there had also stood a tent with bones. "The Innuit say there was and is now a pile of skulls with other bones on the outside of where the tent was — the skulls having holes in them by which they say the brains must have been taken out to prolong the lives of the living." Hall continued, "As this is told me ... everyone in igloo sad — and silence only now and then broken by low weird voices."[10] McClintock himself did not find skulls with holes but, on the other hand, he was unable to find the skulls for the two bodies discovered in the boat. They were unaccountably missing.

Roderic Owen suggested: "Posterity might have appreciated it more had he [Hall] brought back some of the bones — such as skulls with holes in them."[11] Unfortunately, McClintock and Hobson found only the three bodies during their visit to King William Island, and Hall's four-day search produced only a few more. Later searchers such as Schwatka and Gibson added more skeletons to the tally, although at times it is likely the searchers were merely rediscovering the bones previously discovered by those who had searched before. In all those years, no one reported any holes drilled in a bleached skull.

But then in 1987, Jeff MacInnis and Mike Beedell did indeed discover such a grisly artifact during their traversing of the Northwest Passage by catamaran. The skull however was found, not on King William Island, but on the west coast of Boothia Peninsula across the water from Cape Felix. MacInnis wrote, "I was quietly reading a book in the lee of a boulder when Mike startled me by thrusting a human skull at me. On an exploratory hike, he'd found old fire pits containing charred bone fragments and the skull, which was of considerable age and in which a hole had been smashed on one side."[12] Unfortunately, MacInnis felt a skull taken along on their perilous journey could only be harmful — superstitiously-speaking — and so the skull was left behind. But a photograph of the skull was taken by Beedell and included in MacInnis' book, *Polar Passage*, with the caption: "A haunting reminder of past tragedies in the harsh Arctic. This is most likely the skull from an early explorer. The hole on the side is probably the result of a cannibalism bludgeoning."

The discovery of a skull on Boothia Peninsula across from Cape Felix is itself odd. How did it get there? All evidence clearly indicates that Crozier's crewmen, after abandoning the ships and reaching land at Victory Point, headed south. Eventually, their path turned east, headed — we have surmised — for the nonexistent strait said to run through Boothia. The skull discovered by MacInnis and Beedell was found across the water on the Boothia coast and slightly north of the northern tip of King William Island. We could hypothesize that some survivors managed to cross the water to Boothia Peninsula. After discovering that a strait did not exist to the east but a water passage *did* reach up the coast to the north, they could have worked their way up through Rae Strait. But there is another possibility.

McClintock was puzzled when he realized the boat he had discovered was pointing north instead of south. From this, he (and many later historians) concluded that a party of men had tried to return to the ships. On the other hand, everything about that last trek — the useless items carried along, the too-brief note left at Victory Point, the departure made so early in the year — all point to a frantic abandonment of the vessels. The Inuit even told Hall that they found food on board the stranded ship near Adelaide Peninsula. Would Crozier have left food behind aboard ships that might have been crushed in his absence? Further, the crew continued to carry the useless items on their final march, indicating that they remained in a hurry, too concerned about other things to discard what wasn't needed. So much seems to suggest that the crew was not just abandoning their ships, but fleeing from them.

We have already noted another interpretation of the northward pointing boat: the possibility that some of the crewmen were headed back because their path had been cut off to the south — that they were now in retreat. In this case, they would not have returned to the ships; this was where their flight had begun. Instead, they would have tried again to reach Fury Beach, this time by travelling to the north tip of King William Island and across to the Boothia Peninsula [see map 26].

Remarkably, an Inuk named Seepunger had told Hall that three skeletons were to be found at Cape Felix. This, of course, did not fit in with any reconstruction, including a return to the ships. No bodies should have been left at Cape Felix, since it was far north of Victory Point, the starting place for the final march. But then in 1949, Inspector H. Larsen of the RCMP discovered "a human skull

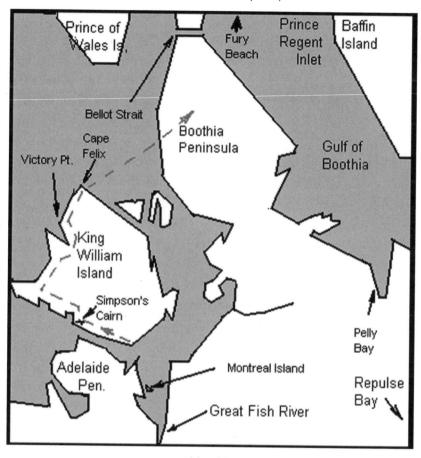

Map 26
Crozier's retreat to Cape Felix and Boothia Peninsula

embedded in moss between some rocks on a ridge about a half mile from the sea" at Cape Felix.[13] Because Crozier's men should not have passed that way, it was presumed the skull had come from an earlier burial made from the ships before their abandonment. Yet, in conjunction with the skull-with-the-hole discovered on the Boothia coast, the skull at Cape Felix suggests that some men did indeed retreat that way. Perhaps Crozier was in charge of this party and encountered Too-shoo-art-thariu sometime after reaching the Boothia coast. If so, then the skull-with-the-hole would indicate that whatever danger dogged them in their flight followed them even after they had reached the opposite shore.

THE GIANT WITH LONG TEETH

Apart from the stories of skulls with holes, Hall also heard details about the ship said to have been stranded somewhere near the Adelaide Peninsula, to the southwest of King William Island. It was McClintock who had first learned about this stranded ship, when he encountered the Inuit on the west coast of Boothia. He had been convinced that the Inuit had only revealed the wreck's existence by accident. Why they should have wanted to keep it a secret he couldn't know. But, once the cat was out of the bag, more details emerged and he heard about the body said to have been found aboard the vessel.

At that time, McClintock had only learned that the body was of a man, "that he must have been a very large man, and had long teeth."[14] Now, ten years later, Hall also heard about the ship and the dead body. He was told: "A native of the island first saw the ship when sealing; it was far off seaward, beset in the ice. He concluded to make his way to it, though at first he felt afraid; got aboard, but saw no-one, although from every appearance somebody had been living there."[15] Though we don't know what was meant by "from every appearance", this comment would likewise seem to suggest that the ship had been hastily abandoned when the crew deserted and headed for Victory Point; they had left so quickly that it still looked as if "somebody had been living there."

What's more, there was food on the ship. Hall reported, "On my asking if they saw anything to eat on board, the reply was that there was meat and tood-noo in cans, the meat fat and like pemmican."[16] It is impossible to imagine Crozier abandoning provisions aboard a vessel almost certain to be crushed in the ice, unless he had no choice — unless the abandonment had been so sudden and so unexpected that there simply wasn't time to gather up all the food.

After the first Inuk had visited the stranded ship, he set off to bring a party of friends to see what he had discovered. They soon returned and entered the vessel, where they found a body. McClintock had been told that it was a "very large" man, with long teeth. Hall was also told about the long teeth. As for how large this man had been: "They found there a dead man, whose body was very large and heavy, his teeth very long. It took five men to lift this giant kob-lu-na [white man]. He was left where they found him."[17] Hall also recorded: "Another native at this interview told nearly the same story of the ship and of the man found on board, adding that he was found dead on the floor, his clothes all on."[18]

In general, historians have simply assumed that this "giant kob-lu-na" who required five men to lift him was merely a figment of the Inuit imagination; there had been a body perhaps, but it had been of normal size, conceivably one of the crew hypothesized to have returned to the ship. Others, though, have found the story too specific to pass off as imagination. But what could it have been? Certainly not a member of Franklin's crew — not if it really took five men to lift the body.

Noel Wright suggested that the Inuit had stumbled upon a ship's figurehead. It was his theory that the ship discovered by the Inuit wasn't one of Franklin's, but was in fact McClure's *Investigator*, having been carried by the ice stream down to Adelaide Peninsula after its abandonment in 1853. He noted that neither the *Erebus* nor the *Terror* had figureheads, but the *Investigator* did. As for the long teeth: "They must have been enormous for their size to have astonished the Eskimos, whose own teeth are by no means small. I have told how McClure's famous ship was put afloat as the *Resolution*, and, although the builder's records no longer exist, I suggest that any shipwright who had to produce a figure head exemplifying 'resolution' would have carved a face showing the teeth firmly clenched."[19]

This was surely a clever theory, and one with which W.G. McKenzie agreed. On the other hand, a dissenting opinion was expressed by L.A. Learmouth who wrote, "As for the big, heavy man with long teeth ... Mr McKenzie agrees with Admiral Noel Wright apparently that it possibly could have been the ship's figurehead rather than a true man. This though one of the Eskimos in question, In-nook-poo-zhee-jook, an intelligent and much travelled man, 'had seen Ross and party on the *Victory*, and Rae in 1854' and would not likely mistake a ship's wooden figurehead for a kablunak."[20] Learmouth went on to recall Hall's report that the body had been found "his clothes all on", further weighing against the figurehead theory. Learmouth believed the Inuit had simply found the corpse of one of Franklin's crew.

Other theories advanced to explain the giant corpse were that it was the body of Franklin himself preserved in rock salt for the voyage back to England, or alternately, some sort of coffin. In the end, though, any explanation founders against the same treacherous shoals: surely the Inuit knew a corpse when they saw one? But, for any corpse to require five men to lift it, it must have been truly giant indeed.

Of course, it is obvious where this is headed. The Inuit told legends from the distant past involving a race of giants, the Tunnit, who inhabited the Arctic and, specifically, King William Island. In one way or another, the legends speak of holes being drilled into foreheads. Some of the skulls left by the doomed members of the Franklin expedition were said to have had holes in them, a claim which is supported by the Boothia skull. The Tunnit were said to be giants, while it has been proven that the Dorset were not. A giant corpse was found on board the stranded ship. Aside from being remarkable for its tremendous size, the corpse was also remembered for its long teeth. We have no direct evidence that the Tunnit had long teeth. There may, however, be indirect evidence.

SHAMAN'S TEETH

If the Tunnit really did fight the ancestors of the Inuit a thousand years ago, and if they were not the Dorset, then both the Dorset and the Thule must have come in contact with this giant race. And, while Arctic cultures tend to leave few artifacts behind, the Dorset were remarkable for the quantity and quality of the carvings they have bequeathed to later ages. Yet, many archaeologists have found the Dorset carvings strangely frightening. Barry Lopez, in *Arctic Dreams*, noted that "the observation that Dorset art is unsettling, while the art that preceded and followed it is not, is common among archaeologists dealing with this period."[21] In one case, Lopez related how "an archaeologist working at a Dorset site in the high Arctic uncovered a cariboo scapula that left him shaken. Both surfaces of this flat bone were incised with scores of small human faces with gaping mouths ... 'I was frightened out of my wits by it,' he told me."[22]

This penchant for crowding agonized faces onto the surface of a single artifact is particularly unnerving. Some wands made of antler have up to sixty faces, "human and semi-human", twisted and deformed, all seeming to rise from the surface as if seething up out of a liquid or out of a fog.[23] What were the Dorset trying to say by such nightmarish images? What was the inspiration for these carvings?

And what about teeth? According to author Robert McGee, "Sets of ivory animal teeth, designed to be held in the mouth, must have been used in other ceremonies, in which the shaman transformed himself into an animal." But what animal? A bear? Is it possible the Dorset shamans were trying to imitate something else they had seen, something even more frightening than the polar bear? A life-size wooden Dorset mask was found at Button Point, Bylot Island, in the high Arctic. It is presumed to have been worn by a shaman during a ceremony. Yet, there is something very odd about this shaman's mask. It is astonishingly life-like, with none of the exaggerated features found, for example, in the Iroquois false-face masks. Yet, there is no denying that this mask also seems frightening and menacing, with eyes fiercely narrowed. But the most striking feature of this mask is the teeth. They are large and clearly emphasized, being prominently displayed in a toothy, gritted snarl. Here was no depiction of a polar bear; there is no doubt this mask was meant to represent something human or semi-human. Was this the face of the Tunnit?

What was the giant corpse found on the stranded ship? Who made the holes in the skulls found on King William Island? Were these the marks of cannibalism, or something else? As a final point, we might recall that when Owen Beattie exhumed the body of Thomas Hartnell, he discovered the corpse had already been autopsied. Though Beattie reported no mysterious holes in Hartnell's head, drilled or otherwise, X-rays were unable to penetrate Hartnell's head for the reason that his brain had frozen solid: he had "a solid block of ice in his head."[24] It was not until it came time to X-ray William Braine that this discovery took on a more mysterious colouring. The X-rays easily penetrated Braine's head, proving that his brain had not frozen. As one of the team remarked, "I really don't have any explanation for that because they were both buried under similar circumstances."[25]

CHAPTER THIRTY-THREE
The Last Resource

If I were a cassowary
On the plains of Timbuctoo,
I would eat a missionary,
Cassock, band, and hymn-book too.
                    Bishop Samuel Wilberforce

A GHOULISH FASCINATION

How did they die?

Surely, when all is said and done, this is the most basic question — the one which holds the interest of the public. We can't get away from the fact that it is a decidedly ghoulish fascination that draws people to ponder the fate of the lost Franklin expedition. For one thing, there were so many men who died — 129 of them. That staggering body count alone raises the Franklin expedition out of the mundane realm of the commonplace tragedy and elevates it to the grim heights attained by such later disasters as the *Titanic* and the Halifax explosion.

Then there is the comically mythic juxtaposition of those oh-so-*British* members of the Royal Navy, utterly confident in their power to conquer whatever the world could throw at them, ending their lives, in Peter Newman's words, "stumbling across frozen drifts and rocks ... commendably correct in hauling along their swank silver tea services and crystal decanters of port."[1] And then, perhaps more than any other reason, there is the dark taint of cannibalism that lurks forever behind the scenes like the phantom of the opera peering from the flies.

SEVERED HANDS

When John Rae first reported the Inuit stories of cannibalism in 1854, the news was received with scathing Victorian reproach. It seemed impossible to imagine "the flower of the trained adventurous spirit of the English Navy" (in Charles Dickens' purple phrase) feeding like ghouls on their fallen comrades, no matter what the desperation of their plight.[2] This blinkered response alone lends to the story a certain cruel satisfaction, a sense of just desserts. Newman, again, best exemplified this view when he observed that John Rae "had tampered with the Victorian dream; by denying Franklin his essential heroic mystery he deprived the British of a martyr."[3]

And yet, as we have seen, there was reason enough to be surprised by both Rae's and the Admiralty's haste in making public such a damaging story, based as it was on second-hand information. Not even the Inuit ever claimed to have witnessed this cannibalism. They found the bodies and drew their own conclusions. But in more recent histories, belief in cannibalism among the Franklin survivors has taken on a sort of necessary certainty. It is the final perfect indignity, the crowning finish to a story which long ago ceased to be history and became instead a morality tale.

In contrast to the disbelief with which the cannibalism stories were originally received, modern writers have gradually grown more and more lurid in their imaginings of that terrible ordeal. Owen Beattie noted that in most recorded instances of cannibalism "The brain is either pulled through the base of the skull or eaten after the face is cut off. The need by members of Franklin's dying crew for a portable food supply was the reason for the only exceptions to this pattern."[4] Beattie's grisly image was quickly picked up by Peter Newman: "Beattie theorized that the skulls were carried along as a portable food supply: the panicked survivors must have supped on the brains of their fallen comrades."[5] And yet, the only eyewitness report we have — that of the encounter at Washington Bay — makes no mention of skulls carried along as a portable food supply. We may assume that the Inuit would have noted this detail, if present.

And yet, the evidence for cannibalism is not wholly confined to the Inuit stories. We have already noted the skull with the hole discovered on the west coast of Boothia Peninsula. Owen Beattie visited King

William Island in 1981 and 1982, when he recovered bones left by the lost expedition. Particularly, the skeleton of one man found at Gladman Point "now began to reveal more ominous secrets."[6] The skull was in pieces and Beattie noted "fracture lines also indicated that the skull had been forcibly broken." Grooves made by a knife were discovered on one femur, and the absence of other bones apart from the limbs and the skull was seen as further evidence "that the body had been intentionally dismembered."

In 1992 and 1993, a Canadian expedition under Barry Ranford and Anne Keeleyside visited what was probably the second boat location, which Hall had been told about by the Inuit. Like Beattie, Keeleyside employed modern forensic science to analyze and study the 400 bones recovered. And, again, marks were discovered which indicated knives had been used on the bodies. Keeleyside concluded, "With the number of marks I see and their distribution, the evidence strongly suggests cannibalism. I can't think what else could have caused those marks."[7] But there are reasons to doubt this interpretation.

Beattie observed, "Cannibalism seems to follow a pattern in instances of starvation: once the decision is made, the initial sections removed from the body are the meatier areas like the buttocks, thighs, lower legs, and arms. Recognizably human parts, such as hands and feet, are not eaten first."[8] And yet, Hall heard many stories about bodies with the hands missing. One woman told him: "One man's body when found by the Innuits, flesh all on and not mutilated except the hands sawed off at the wrists."[9] Another Inuk, speaking about the bodies at Starvation Cove, related: "Inside of the boat under a 'tent' covering it from end to end were many dead white men in bed; that under blankets. Some with hands sawed off at wrists."[10] Barry Ranford, in an *Equinox* article about the 1993 expedition to King William Island, quoted Beattie's passage about hands, then observed, "It is a telling measure of the crew's desperate state that among [Anne Keeleyside's] inventory are cut finger bones."[11] Of course, this doesn't preclude the possibility that the crewmen, for some unknown reason, failed to follow the expected pattern and, in some cases, actually devoured the hands of their comrades before any other part. But it does raise questions.

PEMMICAN AND CHOCOLATE

Moreover, the question of cannibalism is intrinsically linked with another issue: starvation. The expedition's survivors would only have resorted to "the last resource", if indeed they had run out of other foods. When the bodies were found on King William Island and the Victory Point record proved how the ships had been deserted so early in the year, starvation seemed the only explanation. And yet, there was a problem.

The Franklin expedition had entered the Arctic with at least three years worth of provisions. This could have been stretched to four years if necessary. By the time the ships were abandoned, barely three years had passed. While Crozier should certainly have been concerned, he should not yet have been desperate. Thus, efforts were made to explain what had gone wrong. The 700 cans left at Beechey Island were held up as proof that the food had spoiled. We have suggested that the large number of cans was the result of two winters spent at Beechey Island, rather than one. But, even apart from this, there is more direct evidence that the crew was not starving during that final march. When McClintock discovered the two bodies in a boat, he also noted forty pounds of chocolate, plus an empty pemmican-can which had contained twenty-two pounds of meat. Though the pemmican-can was empty, it must have contained meat up to that point in the trek; yet the boat was headed back to the north, indicating it had almost certainly been deserted sometime late in the march, when the crewmen were retreating back the way they had come — presumably after the atrocities at Terror Bay (to the south) had already occurred. As for the chocolate — while sweets would hardly have kept them alive, the crew would surely have eaten this before resorting to human flesh.

Then there was the claim made by the Inuit that food had been found on board the stranded ship. Hall had also been told that food had been found with the bodies on the Todd Islets, the farthest point reached by the expedition. Pooyetta assured Hall that a two-pound can of meat had been discovered: "The can was opened by the Innuits and found to contain meat and much toodnoo with it. No bad smell to it. The contents eaten by the Innuits — the meat and fat very sweet and good."[12]

Finally, there is the evidence of the encounter at Washington Bay when, as the Inuit assured Hall, they had seen nothing to make them think the men were starving. These same points were made by Woodman, who noted that "evidence shows that they [the crewmen] did not lack food in early 1848, and full tins of meat were found along their retreat .... The natives also invariably stated that the men did not die from starvation but because they were 'sick'."[13] Added to this is yet another piece of evidence which has never been remarked upon.

Everyone from Hall to Berton has had something to say about the Inuit who supposedly left the men to starve at Washington Bay. Hall was horrified to think the Inuit could be so heartless (refusing to believe their claim that they hadn't known the men were starving), while Berton properly pointed out that the Inuit had their own lives to worry about in a land where game was scarce. What has not been wondered at is how remarkably complacent Crozier apparently was when, according to the Inuit, he watched his meal ticket slowly wander off down the coast. Crozier's men were heavily armed; the Inuit were not. Surely, faced with starvation, having already "supped on the brains" of fallen crewmen, Crozier would have tried to force the Inuit to hunt some seal for his starving crew. Instead, the entire encounter was civil, with Crozier receiving some seal meat from the Inuit, then calmly watching them as they left the next day. Crozier was said to have repeated the Inuit word for "seal" as the natives departed; a final desperate plea for sustenance. Yet, his behaviour suggests he was simply thanking the Inuit for the seal meat they had already given, rather than begging for more. The simple fact is, Crozier had the firepower; he didn't need to beg.

BODIES UNDER BLANKETS

The questions we have raised are vitally important. For, if the crew was not starving during that final march, they would not have resorted to cannibalism. But, if they did not cut up and eat their dead, how do we explain all the other evidence which says they did? What caused the knife marks on their bones? Why had hands been cut off, limbs dissevered, flesh cut away?

We can't help but think of the body of John Hartnell buried on Beechey Island. In the descriptions of the Inuit, there is sometimes the subtle feel of an autopsy room. The handless bodies at Starvation Cove were neatly covered with a blanket. One woman told Gilder (with

Schwatka) about the bodies found at Terror Bay: "There were dead bodies in the tent, and outside were some covered with sand .... One of the bodies had the flesh on, but this one's stomach was gone."[14] Is it possible, what the Inuit took to be evidence of cannibalism was really evidence of something else? Could it be, the bodies of the dead crewmen were mutilated for a purpose other than food? As unlikely as this may seem, how else can we explain what was found, given all the evidence which shows that the crewmen were not starving during that final trek?

CHAPTER THIRTY-FOUR
Of a Sickness

For the Angel of Death spread his wings
on the blast,
And breathed in the face of the foe
as he pass'd.

Lord Byron,
Destruction of Sennacherib

LEAD POISONING?

But to return to our initial question: how did they die?

Even after so many years, the standard answer to this question remains remarkably vague. From the beginning, starvation was presumed to be the prime culprit. But, given the problems with that hypothesis, scurvy was also invoked as a possible cause of death.

Then, in 1981 and 1982, Owen Beattie recovered bones from King William Island and made a startling discovery. The bones showed extremely elevated levels of lead. Encouraged by this unexpected evidence, Beattie went on to exhume the three bodies buried on Beechey Island. These too showed high levels of lead. From this discovery arose the theory that lead poisoning from improperly soldered meat cans had contributed in some way to the Franklin tragedy and to the death of the crewmen both on Beechey Island during that first winter, and on King William Island two years later.

Beattie's lead findings were the first real new evidence to be unearthed since the recovery of the Victory Point record itself. Yet, his theory has had remarkably little impact. There are several reasons for this. For one thing, the effects of lead poisoning are poorly understood and are dependent on so many factors — such as the period over which the lead accumulated in the individual — that we can only make vague guesses as to what effect the lead poisoning might have had on the crews of the *Erebus* and *Terror*. Moreover, Beattie made it clear he was not suggesting the lead poisoning itself had killed the crewmen, but rather that it might have weakened their systems, making them more susceptible to other diseases. The autopsy report concluded that "the significance of the elevated lead levels in determining the course of the expedition remains uncertain."[1]

Given the conflict between the indisputable evidence of lead poisoning and the difficult to define nature of its effects, it isn't surprising that lead poisoning has taken on something of the nature of a wild card in reconstructions. Barry Ranford wrote, "The almost inescapable conclusion is that when they left the ships, they would have been malnourished, weak, racked with scurvy, suffering from varying degrees of lead poisoning, and otherwise terribly dispirited."[2] On the other hand, David Woodman was less convinced, concluding, "Although lead poisoning may have been an overall contributing factor to the debility of Franklin's men, we must agree with the autopsy report's opinion that the 'findings do not illuminate the events that led to the loss of the remaining members of the expedition in 1847 and 1848.'"[3]

Apart from its ability to render victims more susceptible to other diseases, there is another reason the lead poisoning has provoked such interest. "It is the effects on the mind," observed Beattie, "that may have been of greatest importance in isolating the impact of lead on the expedition."[4] Beattie noted that along with colic, weakness, fatigue, and loss of appetite, lead poisoning can also cause "disturbances of the central and peripheral nervous systems, producing neurotic and erratic behaviour and paralysis of the limbs." David Chettle, the director of medical physics and health physics at McMaster University, (as quoted by Ranford) argued that the rapid build up of lead in the human body "'could give rise to the classic neurological and behavioral symptoms of lead poisoning', including anorexia, fatigue, irritability and irrationality."[5]

And yet, what precise behavioural effects there might have been remains irritatingly vague. Was the crew quite literally insane by the time they abandoned the ships? Or were they just a little less on the ball than they should have been? Beattie hardly helped the matter by observing, "Only clear minds in control of situations can hope to make correct decisions."[6] The Franklin tragedy wasn't a drunk driving accident. If we are to blame the disaster on the neurological effects of lead poisoning, we require something more concrete than that the officers lacked "clear minds".

Perhaps more importantly, what evidence we have gives every indication that Fitzjames' mind at least was perfectly clear as he sat down to write out his final message at Victory Point. If he had suffered three years of brain damage, could he have so precisely recorded so much information, from the date of Franklin's death the year before to the longitude and latitude of his present position, the number of men dead (divided into officers and men) and the number still remaining? Nor does his handwriting give any hint of neurological damage. We are even able to compare his handwriting in 1848 with his handwriting the year before — there is no evidence of any deterioration during the intervening months.

While there can be no denying the evidence of high levels of lead poisoning, we simply have no way of knowing whether or not the lead had an appreciable effect on the health or behaviour of the crewmen.

SCURVY?

But what about scurvy?

Almost certainly many, if not most, of the crew suffered from its dreadful effects. But men suffering from scurvy is not the same thing as the entire crew of 129 dying of the disease. Scurvy was a common problem during the Arctic expeditions and men did on occasion die from it; but never had scurvy spread so thoroughly as to immobilize an entire crew.

The disease was not really a disease as we think of the term; it was the result of a lack of vitamin C from fresh meat. Its most obvious symptoms were black and bleeding gums, loose teeth, swelling joints and internal bleeding. All expeditions suffered its effects except John Ross' *Victory*, where the disease was prevented through the fresh meat procured by the Inuit. Bones recovered from King William Island showed evidence of scurvy, but this is only to be expected. Whether the men actually died of the disease is another matter entirely.

Hall was told by the Inuit that the men died of a "sickness", and this sickness was presumed to be scurvy. But surely the Inuit would have known scurvy when they saw it. When Jacques Cartier's men suffered from scurvy, the Iroquois taught him how to make a concoction of herbs to cure the disease.. The Inuit had encountered Arctic expeditions before; from time to time they must have seen examples of its effects.

We must also consider the descriptions of the men given by the Inuit. Some of the men at Washington Bay were said to have had hard, dry, and black lips. Was this a description of the soft, black gums characteristic of scurvy?

When Too-shoo-art-thariu encountered Crozier and the three survivors near Boothia Peninsula, the three men were said to be "fat" because they had been eating human flesh, while Crozier was thin because he had not. But how did Too-shoo-art-thariu know the men had eaten their comrades; are we really to imagine Crozier would have told him this? More importantly, even if the men had resorted to cannibalism, could they really have grown "fat" on human flesh? Is it possible Too-shoo-art-thariu only thought the men had been feeding on human flesh because of something he saw, an aspect of the men's appearance that convinced him they were cannibals, but which the Inuit, who were horrified by cannibalism, could not bring themselves to detail for Hall?

Could it be that the men had fresh blood on their mouths from their bleeding gums — blood which Too-shoo-art-thariu took to be the blood of the flesh they had eaten? In the same way, the hard, dry, and black lips seen on some of the men at Washington Bay could have been dried blood. Scurvy causes such oral bleeding, but so too does another sort of disease, one which the Inuit could not have been familiar with — which they could only have characterized as "a sickness".

Radiation sickness can result in a drop in the number of blood platelets, without which blood won't clot properly and hemorraging results, primarily from the intestines and the mouth. This is the third stage of radiation sickness, the first being a period of vomiting, fever, and intense thirst, the second being a latency period when the patient appears to have gotten better. This third stage may only be reached weeks after initial exposure to a high dose of radiation, following which the patient will either recover or die. Of course, given the choice between scurvy and radiation sickness to explain oral bleeding among the Franklin crewmembers, scurvy seems the more likely alternative. But the Inuit told Hall that Crozier's three companions were "fat". Another symptom of radiation sickness is gastro-intestinal distension —

a distended abdomen. Could this be why Too-shoo-art-thariu thought the men were "fat"(because their stomachs were distended?

Other symptoms characteristic of radiation poisoning are lung fibrosis, a susceptibility to disease (caused by a loss of white blood cells — an important part of the immune response), and a rapid loss of hair. Evidence for any of these would be difficult to recover after all these years. Yet, we might recall that "adhesions" or scarring around the lungs of all three men buried on Beechey Island led to the tentative theory that their deaths had been caused by pneumonia. Other evidence had suggested their immune systems had been weakened, making them susceptible to other diseases.

Finally, as for the question of hair loss, we can never know for certain, but, as with so much about the Franklin mystery, the devil is in the details. One detail in particular stands out, not proof in and of itself, but quietly suggestive, as if hinting at a terrible, long hidden truth. Beside the corpse of Steward Peglar, which McClintock first discovered on King William Island, there was a clothes brush and a horn pocket comb in which, after ten years of exposure to the Arctic gales, "a few light-brown hairs still remained."[7]

Chapter Thirty-Five
The Shaman Light

I have reached these lands but newly
From an ultimate dim Thule –
From a wild weird clime that lieth, sublime,
Out of Space – out of Time.
Edgar Allan Poe,
Dreamland

A BATTLE?

"One of the enduring myths of the Franklin expedition," observed David Woodman, "is that the survivors of the *Erebus* and *Terror* may have fallen in battle with natives."[1] No sooner had John Rae returned with his story of cannibalism than reflexive accusations were levelled at the Inuit. Charles Dickens, renowned champion of the underdog of England, labelled the Inuit as "covetous, treacherous and cruel" and accused them of killing, though not eating, Franklin's crew.[2] Others quickly picked up the cry and, as Peter Newman observed, "In the popular press, the spectre of an Arctic tribe of man-eaters proved irresistible."[3]

The discoveries made on King William Island did little to prove or disprove this theory. What evidence was found, then and later, proved only that the bodies of the crewmen had been mutilated. Whether the mutilations were the result of cannibalism or something far stranger, whether the damage was done after death or before, these questions could not be answered.

But a strong argument against an Inuit massacre lies in the observation made by McClintock that there was no evidence the natives had even discovered some of the corpses. In the barren, treeless Arctic, the vast profusion of relics left at Victory Point and other sites represented a veritable Eldorado of metals, wood, and items capable of being altered to serve other purposes. The quantity of items found in the possession of the natives showed how quick they were to make use of whatever they could find (except, apparently, books and papers). Hall learned that the occasional Inuk had visited sites such as Terror Bay, Starvation Cove, and the Todd Islets. Yet, the fact that so much remained to be found, even years later, suggested that the Inuit had avoided the area of the crewmen's retreat like the proverbial plague. Later searchers learned that the northwest coast of the island had always been avoided by the Inuit of King William Island long before the Franklin expedition met with disaster there. Any attempt to lay the blame on the Inuit must also explain why the natives seemed so reluctant to make off with the spoils of the massacre.

Ironically, though, it was the Inuit stories themselves that furnished the most damning evidence against them. It was the Inuit who related the grisly stories about mutilated bodies. It was Too-shoo-art-thariu's cousins who told how Crozier, during his winter spent on Boothia Peninsula before vanishing forever down the Great Fish River, spoke of a battle with "Indians". But even before John Rae raised the spectre of violent death, the possibility of a massacre had been bandied about as a result of another Inuit story. This was the story which John Ross' Inuit translator, Adam Beck, claimed to have learned from the Greenland natives in 1850. As we have seen, Adam Beck's story was dismissed after only one day's search at Wolstenholme Island on the Greenland coast. In spite of the remarkably specific details of the story, Beck's tale was cast aside with astonishing alacrity, purely because nothing was found to support it at Wolstenholme Island.

The rationale behind this decision was strangely varied. Some insisted the story must have been a muddled remembrance of the *North Star*'s winter stay at Wolstenholme Island the year before — this though little of Beck's story fitted the *North Star* except that it was a navy vessel. Conflictingly, the searchers also labelled Beck a liar, insisting that he had manufactured the whole thing. Captain Austin, in charge of the naval flotilla, damned Beck as a "man in whom no faith could be placed" and called him "about the worst description of a civilized savage I ever saw."[4] Yet, John Ross stood by his interpreter at some personal cost and Charles Francis Hall met Beck ten years later when he concluded Beck had told the truth.

Still, as Woodman observed, "This calumny was to dog Adam Beck for the remainder of his life and into the history books."[5]

Part of the problem with Beck's story lies in its geographic origins. Once proof was found that the expedition had met its end on King William Island, the testimony of natives across Baffin Bay on the west coast of Greenland could not help but seem suspect. Yet, information could travel over vast distances in the Arctic. Nor did a story have to be passed linearly from tribe to tribe. A single Inuk in Prince Regent Inlet could have boarded a whaler which then dropped him off on the Greenland coast; once there, he might have related stories to the local natives. Indeed, Beck might have spoken to such a displaced Inuk without realizing it. Thus, it is entirely within the realm of plausibility that the Greenland Inuit might have had word of the fate of Franklin's expedition. The problem comes when we try to interpret Adam Beck's story.

ADAM BECK'S STORY

The story told to Beck was this:

"When [the natives] came to the ships and asked them [the men on the ships] said they had been here four winters. Tolloit also wintered upon our land. In 1846 two ships with three masts went from our land to Omanek; they arrived safely but the men are dead. Two ships encompassed by ice; otherwise they could not do. Their provisions were consumed. The men went to them; it is said they are dead. Tolloit is also dead."[6] Beck's informers also assured him that "the ships were not whalers, and that epaulettes were worn by some of the white men." Some of the crew were said to have drowned, while others spent "some time in huts and tents apart from the natives" and were "subsequently killed by the natives with darts and arrows." The two ships had broken up in the ice and been "burnt by a fierce and numerous tribe of natives."[7]

The story of the ships being burnt takes on a special interest, given that McClintock encountered Inuit on the east coast of King William Island who told him Franklin's ships had burned in some way. McClintock had been unable to clarify the story and assumed the Inuit had burned down the masts of the stranded ship for wood.

Just as with the story of four survivors, some historians have argued that Adam Beck's tale can be explained as a muddling together of a multitude of separate events, provided we are prepared to include in the list the sinking of a whaler and the burning of another which had taken place in 1835. Apart from the difficulty of explaining Adam Beck's mistake in thinking the story referred to a recent event, neither of these other ships were navy, and so their officers would not have worn epaulettes. Indeed, once again, it seems far easier to assume that the Inuit (and Adam Beck) knew what they were talking about, rather than mixing and matching various events over the past decades.

Certainly, most of the details to Beck's story were corroborated by other sources. The story of the burning ships may have been told to McClintock. The battle with natives had been related to Too-shoo-art-thariu by Crozier. The Franklin ships had become beset in the ice and one had sunk, according to the Inuit. The expedition's provisions would have been nearly exhausted and the men did indeed spend time in tents on King William Island.

In the end, if we assume the story really did refer to Franklin's expedition, we are left with three questions. First, Adam Beck claimed the two ships "went from our land to Omanek." Omanek, as Adam Beck well knew, was the Inuit name for Wolstenholme Island, slightly north of Cape York where he heard the story. Why would the Inuit have said the ships went to Omanek if they meant the ships had travelled to King William Island (called Kikertak)? Secondly, we must ask, who was "Tolloit"? This individual is oddly referred to since Tolloit seems to be separated from the two ships: "Tolloit also wintered upon our land." Thirdly, the people on the ships had apparently told the Inuit that they had been there "four winters". But the Franklin expedition had been in the Arctic only three winters by the time the ships were abandoned. In fact, only John Ross' expedition back in 1829 had spent four winters in the Arctic.

The claim that the ships "went from our land to Omanek" is not as much of a stumbling block as it might appear. Beck knew there was a place near by with that name, which is why he took the searchers there. But it is possible he merely heard some name that sounded similar to Omanek and instantly assumed it was a reference to the near by Omanek.

Certainly, this theory has been considered before. Unfortunately, as David Woodman demonstrated in his book *Unravelling the Franklin Mystery*, there are quite a few places in the Arctic with names sounding like Omanek. In fact, Franklin's expedition had transferred provisions from their tender at "Umanak" (Disko Bay) on the Greenland coast prior to crossing Baffin Bay. John Ross' *Victory* had wintered at "Omanaq" (Lord Mayor Bay) on the east coast of Boothia Peninsula in 1829. There was an island named "Omanaq" near Montreal Island in the mouth of the Great Fish River. It was near here that George Back had fought with some Inuit during his explorations. In the 1960s Canadian Armed Forces helicopters landed on Taylor Island off the west coast of King William Island, there to search from Franklin relics on the basis of Inuit stories that a massacre had occurred on the island. One Inuit name for Taylor Island was "Ommanak". (No traces of the expedition were discovered.) Worse, Woodman observed that there were so many islands with the name "Omanatluk" (meaning "heart-shaped ones") that "it seems to have been almost impossible for a European expedition to travel anywhere in the Arctic without becoming associated with one of them."[8]

It may be there is no way to determine which place Beck's story referred to. But it is also possible we are looking at the problem the wrong way. There is something decidedly odd about Beck's tale. We are told the ships "went from our land to Omanek". Thus, we assume the disaster took place on "Omanek", somewhere away from "our land" (ie. Greenland). Yet, we are also told, "Tolloit *also* wintered upon our land." This would suggest the disaster took place "upon our land" since Tolloit "also" wintered there. Both interpretations cannot be correct. Either the ships met with disaster on "Omanek" or on "our land", but not both.

Suppose, though, we assume "our land" did not mean Greenland or Cape York or anything so specific. Suppose it merely meant "the Arctic"("our land" being the land of the Inuit. Then Beck's story takes on an entirely different meaning. The ships travelled from the Arctic to someplace else. Tolloit came from someplace else and wintered in the Arctic. The ships "arrived safely" at this other place, but somehow the men died anyway. The name of this other place sounded to Adam Beck like "Omanek". But if the place referred to was not Omanek, what was it?

There is an Inuit word, "Qaumaneq". There is no accurate way to translate it for the reason that it is a spiritual term. Barry Lopez, in his *Arctic Dreams*, translated "Qaumaneq" as "Shaman light". It would seem to be a difficult concept to grasp, at once a mystical location somehow separate from the Arctic and a magic power possessed by shamans which allows them to "see" this place. In Lopez's words: The angakoq, or Inuit shaman "has *qaumaneq*, the shaman light, the luminous fire, the inexplicable searchlight that enables him to see in the dark, literally and metaphorically."[9] Speaking of the Inuit's attitude to their land, Lopez observed that "the evidence for a landscape in the Arctic larger than the one science reports, more extensive than that recorded on the United States Coast and Geodetic Survey quadrangle maps, is undeniable. It is the country the shamans shined their *qau-maneq*, their shaman light, into."[10]

Given this new reading, Beck's story takes on a far stranger meaning. Beck wasn't being told the ships had gone from Greenland to King William Island, but rather from the Arctic to Qaumaneq, the shaman light.

Beck was also informed that they arrived safely, but the men died just the same. This could refer to the men who were killed by "natives" and those who drowned. Yet, it seems to refer specifically to the journey itself, rather than the battle afterwards. We have already considered the evidence which suggests some of the men may have died of radiation sickness. Could it be that the trip to the shaman light (and back again) was a success, but that men died from its after-effects — from radiation sickness? Could Fitzjames' "All well" in the 1847 record have been a message to the Admiralty that the mission had been a success and "Qaumaneq" had been reached?

This line of reasoning quickly offers a solution to the second question raised by the Adam Beck story. Who was Tolloit who "also wintered upon our land"? The men, Beck learned, were dead. But he was told: "Tolloit is also dead." Recalling the giant corpse with long teeth found by the Inuit aboard the stranded ship, we might wonder if "Tolloit" was merely Beck's mistaken hearing of the word "Tunnit"?

CHAPTER THIRTY-SIX
Rehearsal for Murder

It is the little rift within the lute,
That by and by will make the music mute,
And ever widening slowly silence all.
Alfred, Lord Tennyson,
The Idylls of the King

FOUR EXPEDITIONS

As we have seen, the third question raised by the Adam Beck story concerns the length of time the massacred expedition had supposedly spent in the Arctic. Beck learned that the men aboard the ships had apparently told the Inuit "they had been here four winters". But the Franklin expedition had spent only three winters in the Arctic.

Four winters would have been an exceptionally long period of time for any expedition to have wintered in the ice. In fact, only John Ross' *Victory* could claim to have wintered for so long. In the case of the *Victory*, the stay was unintentional, arising from Ross' poor choice of harbour. In the end, he was forced to abandon the *Victory* and escape by hitching a ride on a whaler. But, again, there is little else to suggest Beck's tale referred to Ross' expedition. Ross used only one ship, there was no hostile encounter between his crew and the Inuit, no fire, and no one died.

Perhaps, more important, Beck's informers said, "When [the natives] came to the ships and asked them [the men on the ships] said they had been here four winters." Beck's story seems to imply the ships had already spent four winters in the Arctic by the time the Inuit encountered them for the first time. Yet, Ross only encountered the Inuit during the first two seasons. After that, there was no further meeting with the local inhabitants of Boothia Peninsula.

Again, perhaps we need a new perspective on the problem. Perhaps the testimony of the Greenland natives should not be taken so literally. We are assuming the four winters were sequential, during a single prolonged expedition. But what if we suppose the Inuit meant only that, when they encountered Franklin's crew, the white men claimed to have been to that place (King William Island) four times, rather than for four winters? In other words, three expeditions had been there before and Franklin's was the fourth.

This reading leads us into uncharted but possibly fruitful waters. Who were the three expeditions prior to Franklin's? We know James Clark Ross sledged overland to Victory Point in 1830 during his uncle's expedition in the *Victory*. We have also theorized that the Admiralty first learned of Victory Point and what was to be found there during Edward Parry's voyage of the *Fury*, when that ship so mysteriously vanished without a trace. Thus we have three expeditions to King William Island — Edward Parry's, James Clark Ross', and Franklin's.

So, who was the fourth?

In 1839, Thomas Simpson reached the south shore of King William Island. It was Simpson who erected the famous cairn which McClintock later found looted. Simpson's visit took place nine years after James Clark Ross'. Unlike Ross, Simpson was acting under the employ of the Hudson's Bay Company, of which his older cousin George Simpson was governor. If we are correct in our new reading of the Adam Beck story, Thomas Simpson's expedition must be the third of the four.

There is no evidence that Simpson travelled anywhere farther north than Cape Herschel on King William Island. Certainly there is no proof he visited Victory Point prior to Franklin's disastrous visit. On the other hand, Thomas Simpson's death only months after his expedition to the island has itself become a much pondered and disturbing mystery nearly as puzzling and sinister as the Franklin mystery it preceded by five years. Pierre Berton observed, "Since that day, Thomas Simpson's death has been a matter of mystery and controversy."[1] Peter Newman noted that "the circumstances remain unexplained."[2]

MURDER?

Thomas Simpson was not, in the modern vernacular, a happy camper. Simpson was egotistical, quick to find fault in others, and altogether too vocal in his criticisms. Writing to his brother Alexander, Simpson called his partner-in-exploration, Peter Warren Dease, "a worthy, indolent, illiterate soul" who "moves just as I give the impulse."[3] Of his cousin and employer, George Simpson, Thomas had harsh things to say, calling him "a severe and most repulsive master", believing that the governor was bending a little too far over backward to avoid charges of nepotism.[4]

In 1836, George Simpson instructed his young cousin to travel down the Mackenzie River to the Arctic sea, there to seek the Northwest Passage in accordance with the requirement placed in the original Hudson's Bay Company charter. With Peter Dease and a group of paddling voyageurs, Simpson reached the icy sea, where he left the exhausted Dease behind and travelled on in the company of five voyageurs. With some further assistance from Inuit in boats, Simpson managed to reach Point Barrow on the Alaska coast, thereby linking up with the area of previous explorations. Simpson and Dease returned to winter at Fort Confidence on Great Bear Lake.

The next summer, in 1838, they set off down the Coppermine River, this time intending to explore eastward along the roof of the continent. Reaching the Arctic waters at Coronation Gulf, they sighted Victoria Land across the water to the north and saw clear water to the east. But the party was exhausted and they were forced to turn back. The next year, they tried again.

This time Simpson and Dease managed to push eastward, first through Coronation Gulf, then through Dease Strait, then out into Queen Maud Gulf at the southern reaches of Victoria Strait. They were now just south and west of King William Island, which they thought was joined to Boothia. They planned to follow the King William Island coast up to James Clark Ross' farthest travels at Victory Point. But, before they could do so, they discovered the strait running due east beneath King William Island and decided instead to follow this, which Simpson named Simpson Strait [see map 27].

They explored the strait to the mouth of the Great Fish River, then continued forty miles further east to the Castor and Pollux River. Then

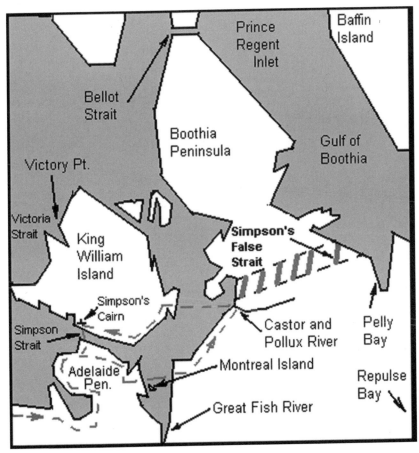

Map 27
Thomas Simpson visits King William Island, 1839

Simpson crossed over to King William Island to the north, completely missing the strait that separated it from Boothia. He explored the south shore, erected his cairn at Cape Herschel, then returned home after briefly visiting Victoria Island.

No sooner had he returned than he applied to the Hudson's Bay Company to carry out one final expedition. He planned to travel down the Great Fish River to the Arctic sea directly south of King William Island. It was his contention that Simpson Strait continued east through Boothia, forming a passage out into the Gulf of Boothia at the bottom of Prince Regent Inlet. If true, then this waterway would form the final link in the Northwest Passage. He wished to prove the existence of this passage.

But why had he failed to seek this strait in 1839 when, at the Castor and Pollux River, the passage's western entrance would only have been a few miles away? Why had he wasted time exploring the south coast of King William Island with success so nearly in his grasp?

His decision to turn back is difficult to explain, unless we presume the supposed strait was merely an excuse to return to King William Island — in which case we must assume that he knew no such strait existed, having already explored slightly east of the Castor and Pollux River. If true, the irony is black indeed. For, as we have seen, Crozier was almost certainly trying to reach Simpson's mythical strait when he abandoned the ships and marched his crew to their graves.

Simpson dispatched his request to London, even offering to spend a fortune of his own money, five hundred pounds, on the venture. He waited for a reply. In London, the Hudson's Bay Company approved Simpson's plan, but it took too long for word to reach him back in Canada. Frustrated by the delay, Simpson resolved to travel to London to plead his case in person. On the way, while travelling through Dakota Sioux territory in the company of four "mixed-bloods", Simpson camped near the Turtle River.

There were only two witnesses to what happened next. James Bruce and Antoine Legros, Jr. were engaged setting up a tent when they heard a gun shot. Turning, they saw Simpson shoot Legros' father, Antoine Legros, Sr., with a shotgun. Another man, John Bird, had already been shot by the other barrel of the gun and lay on the ground dead. Simpson assured Bruce and Legros, Jr. he wouldn't hurt them and that he had acted in self-defence "that the laws of England would clear him".[5] The two men left Simpson with the bodies and went to get help. Returning some time later with more men, they heard a shot from the camp. Afraid Simpson was firing at them, they delayed before entering the camp. When they finally did, they found Simpson dead, shot in the head with a shotgun.

As the explorer, Vilhjalmur Stefansson, noted in his *Unsolved Mysteries of the Arctic*, "Suicide was the official verdict. The popular view from the start, or soon thereafter, was either that the manner of death was unknown or that Thomas Simpson had been murdered."[6]

THE THEORIES

In a striking parallel to the lackadaisical Franklin search, the Simpson mystery extended to the strangely non-existent investigation itself. One writer commenting at the time found, "No properly constituted authority ever investigated the charges, nor did any court ever decide upon them. It was possible to have made a thorough and exhaustive examination into all circumstances, but this was never done."[7] Of the two witnesses, only Bruce was asked to give a deposition. Inexplicably, Legros, Jr. was not. The same writer further argued, "There were very apparent ways of settling whether Simpson had shot himself, but we are not told that any of these were adopted."

Two theories eventually developed to explain the case. The first was constructed largely on the unsteady foundation of Douglas MacKay's conclusion that Thomas Simpson was insane and suicidal. MacKay worked for the Hudson's Bay Company and wrote a history of the Honourable Company. His proof of Simpson's insanity relied entirely on Simpson's tendency toward outspoken criticism and self-aggrandizement. Stefansson, however, demonstrated that there was no proof to support MacKay's theory. "Thomas had a low opinion of George [Simpson]," observed Stefansson, "and expressed it in some of his letters. This has been called a sign of mental unbalance. We can make at least the rebuttal that if disapproval of Governor George was proof of unsound mind, then there must have been an epidemic of this mental affliction in the Fur Empire during his reign."[8]

The second theory, to which most historians are inclined, supposed that Simpson's known animosity toward "mixed-bloods" somehow precipitated the twin murder at Turtle River, with Simpson then being killed in revenge by the other members of his party (or else killing himself when he realized what would happen when the others returned).

Yet this too was a theory based on flimsy evidence indeed. There was no denying Simpson was racist. He once stated, "To the extravagant and profligate habits of the half-breed families I have an insuperable aversion."[9] But, racism was epidemic at the time, especially amongst the members of the Hudson's Bay Company. The fact that Simpson had been travelling with "half-breeds" as his only companions when he died hardly supported the theory that his "aversion" alone was excuse enough for murder. (Besides which, Simpson had called Dease "indolent" and George Simpson "repulsive" — by comparison his comment about "profligate" seems about on par.)

Apart from the madness theory and the racism theory, one other explanation was advanced, but it was soundly rejected and remains so to this day. This was the theory put forward by Thomas' brother Alexander. During his winters spent on Great Bear Lake between treks to the Arctic sea, Thomas kept in contact with his brother through letters. It was Alexander's belief that his brother had been murdered for papers held in his possession — papers which revealed the secret of the Northwest Passage.

THE SECRET

About this theory, Stefansson wrote, "We have admitted that his [Alexander's] opinions were somewhat prejudiced; so we ignore him and pass on to what others have to say."[10] Pierre Berton's comments were similarly expressed. "What secret?" Berton asked doubtfully. "The passage was not a gold mine to be pounced upon in the dark of the night and looted."[11] "In any case," Berton added, "[Thomas] Simpson's theories were wrong." Wrong, if we assume the "secret" was the supposed strait through Boothia; not so wrong, if we suppose the "secret" related to Victory Point and what was to be found there.

Certainly, *something* was stolen from Simpson's papers. Simpson had written a narrative of his explorations, which he had with him before he died. This narrative, along with other papers, was handed over to an American officer after Simpson's death but did not reach England until October, 1841, the next year. Even stranger, the papers were not given over to Alexander until 1844, four years after his brother's death. On receiving those papers, Alexander wrote to George Simpson in a red rage. "I hesitate not to assert," he fumed, "that the depositories of my brother were rifled of valuable papers."[12] More alarming still, Thomas' diary had also unaccountably vanished.

Stefansson asked, "Who abstracted the papers? Who had opportunity?" He considered the possibility that George Simpson had done the deed, but, not surprisingly, had difficulty coming up with a motive. "We have, as said, no evidence to support the idea that Sir George, in his long career, ever plotted with anyone to kill anyone," Stefansson equivocated. "We have no evidence, either, to prove that he did not go that far in a passionate loyalty to the Company which, unless it be murder, seems to have had no limit."[13] Yet, Stefansson admitted that *if* Alexander Simpson was right and Thomas had been killed for the "secret to the Northwest Passage", then Thomas' narrative "might be supposed to contain the secret."[14]

This narrative was given to George Simpson in May 1841, while at Lake Superior. But Alexander was in England at the time. He was astonished to learn that "temporary suppression of the manuscript had been arranged." with the vague promise that it would be included in a "compilation" at some later date. Alexander fought to have the manuscript released and published on its own, under his brother's name. He was successful and the narrative was sent to England in October, by which time Alexander had left for Polynesia. Colonel Edward Sabine took over the job of revising Simpson's narrative. To Alexander, Sabine reported, "On perusal, I found the work in a state of such complete preparation, that the alterations which I saw any occasion to make were very few indeed." Continuing, he observed, "it impressed me with an additionally high respect for your brother's memory, that he should have drawn up the narrative of the expedition on the spot, in such a complete manner that it might well have been printed *verbatim*."[15]

Now we must ask ourselves a question. Thomas Simpson had a big mouth. He did not hesitate to express his disapproval of those he found wanting, often in such uncompromisingly harsh language that Douglas MacKay even came to the conclusion that Simpson was insane. Does Sabine's description of Simpson's manuscript really sound like the unedited narrative penned by such a man? Could anything Simpson might have written really have been published "verbatim"? The suicide theory gained its support from Simpson's vicious slurs on those he worked for and with, but the same evidence serves to prove that someone did indeed rewrite his narrative before sending it on to England.

Thus, less than five years before the Franklin expedition passed quietly and alone into the pack ice of Lancaster Sound, we find all the same elements of conspiracy and duplicity, delay and misdirection, which would mark the Franklin search like a Shakespearean tragedy. The mystery of Thomas Simpson's death played out like a rushed rehearsal for the grander drama waiting in the wings. Only in scale was the Franklin conspiracy different. But for both, the result was the same.

Thomas Simpson's death proved the secret of Victory Point could be kept. The loss of the Franklin expedition and the subsequent conspiracy showed just how far the Admiralty would go to keep it.

But there is one vital difference between these two mysteries. When Franklin and his crew vanished into the Arctic, whatever incriminating records they may have left behind were recovered and suppressed by the navy searchers. The Admiralty tried to do the same to Thomas Simpson. Nevertheless, his testimony may yet have slipped through the covetous fingers of those who sought to silence it, reaching out to us from beyond the grave like the steady rapping of a ghost at the Fox sisters' seance.

A deposition was taken from James Bruce, one of the two witnesses to the tragedy at Turtle River. In this deposition, Bruce testified that Simpson, having shot the other two men, then turned to Bruce and Legros, Jr. "Simpson called out to [Bruce], and ask him if he was aware of any intention to kill him [Simpson], to which [Bruce] replied, that he had never heard of such intention on the part of anyone. [Simpson] then told [Bruce] that his life was perfectly safe; and he further told [Bruce] that he had shot Bird and Legros [Sr.] because they had intended to murder him, on that night for his papers."[16]

EPILOGUE
Proof

Truth will come to light; murder cannot be hid long.
William Shakespeare,
The Merchant of Venice

This is how it always begins.

It begins with two stout bomb-ketches, HMS *Erebus* and HMS *Terror*, their decks heaped with provisions, fastened to an iceberg in Baffin Bay, awaiting the opening of a passage through the ice to the west. That was how the two whalers, *Prince of Wales* and *Enterprise*, left the Franklin expedition, as Captain Dannett continued on his way, blissfully unaware that he had just entered the history books as the last white man to see those 129 souls alive. This is how it always begins.

As for how it ends — like the strange disappearance of Joseph-René Bellot, "all else is conjecture."

This book is all about conjecture, about theorizing and wondering, asking questions and seeking answers, no matter how unusual, no matter where they might lead. Those answers, at times, seemed strange and unlikely, to be sure. Some might even be said to have been horrific. Occasionally, as with our rereading of the Victory Point record, the answers seemed self-evident and clear-cut. At other points, our theorizing acted only like a gust of wind briefly thinning an obscuring fog. In the end, we may find ourselves in the same situation as John Ross during that first voyage back in 1818 when, for ten precious minutes, the mist began to clear in Lancaster Sound and, through the dancing veils and hazy Arctic light, in the distance he could just barely make out ... what? Perhaps even he never knew. Like Ross, we can only squint and ask ourselves: is it there or not? Do we really see what we think we see or is it a fata morgana, a trick of the light — refraction?

In telling our story, we have managed not only to suggest an ending to the fate of Franklin, but we have also steadily pushed back its beginning, back through the mysterious death of Thomas Simpson, back through James Clark Ross' visit to Victory Point, back through the disappearance of the *Fury*, and finally back even to John Ross' first voyage and that moment of half-sight and revelation in Lancaster Sound, twenty-seven years before the *Erebus* and *Terror* weighed anchor. Indeed, it could be said we have even located traces of an even earlier beginning one thousand years ago, when the natives of the Arctic fought a terrible battle with a race of giants with flying houses — traces found only in Inuit legends and stone Inukshuit and a shaman's mask with bared teeth.

And yet, it may still be that everything we have conjectured is false. Perhaps there was no conspiracy, only fantastic bungling. Perhaps the Franklin expedition really was seeking the Northwest Passage, became permanently beset in the ice off King William Island, and abandoned the ships when they ran out of food. Perhaps they did resort to cannibalism and perhaps it was the Inuit who looted Simpson's cairn at Cape Herschel. Perhaps the story of four survivors was just a muddled compilation of several other events, and Crozier never got off that island alive.

Perhaps Adam Beck was a liar.

We might accept this "standard reconstruction", recognizing that it has the advantage of not requiring belief in things which are unbelievable. But, by accepting it we are left with a labyrinth of unanswered and seemingly unanswerable questions. Indeed, enough questions, we might say, to fill a book.

We might instead try to pick and choose from the story recounted here, believing some parts while rejecting others. But, if we believe in a conspiracy but not in the "shaman light", we are hard pressed to find a motive for the duplicity and deception. If we believe Thomas Simpson was killed for the "secret to the Northwest Passage", how do we explain what that secret was? If we believe the mutilated bodies were the result of cannibalism, how do we make sense of the evidence proving the crew still had food when they died? How to account for the boat with the two headless bodies found pointed back to the north as if in retreat, two loaded shotguns set against its side? How do we explain the weird autopsy conducted on John Hartnell, his organs replaced in a mixed mass, his ribs returned upside down? If we do not believe Franklin's mission was to reach Victory Point, how are we to explain Captain Coppin's inexplicable foreknowledge? Ghosts?

In the end, if we do not believe the unbelievable, we are forced into the restless posture of Franklin historians to date: we can only make note of the questions and shrug. One thing only we know for certain: something terrible happened on barren, ice-battered King William Island when Franklin's crew arrived there, and that something was not confined to the white men.

In 1923, Knud Rasmussen was told by the Inuit of a "year of horror" which came to the island.[1] McClintock had been told "formerly many natives lived there, now very few remain." Substantial evidence later showed that the Inuit, while never entirely abandoning the island, had indeed largely deserted it just after Franklin's visit. The Inuit told Hall that they had believed Franklin's crew was to blame for the Inuit's "trouble". Woodman observed that the Inuit "did not elaborate on the nature of the Inuit 'trouble'" but he surmised that the white men had brought on a famine through overhunting. "Although periodic famine was almost routine among the Inuit," commented Woodman, "this must have been a very severe occurrence."

Today, the northwest coast of King William Island remains frozen in time, barely touched since that April day in 1848, when 105 men landed on the shore at Victory Point. One small community lives on the island at Gjoa Haven, pressed against the southeast coast, as far from the site of the disaster as geography allows. In the 1950s, a Distant Early Warning Station was built at Gladman Point on the south shore. It was constructed as part of the DEW line, a string of radar stations stretching across the Arctic, designed originally to detect Soviet missiles launched over the Canadian north and headed for the United States. Innumerable expeditions have scoured the island over the many years, each one finding fewer and fewer relics to take home. Some were searching for answers to medical questions: How did they die? Was there cannibalism? Was there lead poisoning? Others sought more basic treasures: Franklin's grave, for example. But the most sought-after prize was surely the same prize which Lady Franklin had ordered McClintock to bring home if he could — the expedition's "unspeakably precious" journals and records. Of course, for those who sought these documents, the interest was largely and simply because they were there. What could those documents tell us that we did not already know?

But now, we may wonder if there wasn't considerably more to be found in those records — proof of our story. Perhaps the expedition's records contained the detailed results of a fantastically complex and bizarrely dangerous experiment not to be equalled until the coming of the Manhattan Project in another age. The Franklin expedition's officers were chosen according to their scientific expertise, few having any experience in Arctic waters. And, from the start, the Admiralty had meant to keep the results of the mission to itself. Lieutenant James Fairholme, a junior officer aboard *Erebus*, wrote home to his family just before the ships set sail from Greenland. In that letter, he told how "Soon after leaving the Orkney's, Sir John sent for us all into his cabin and read to us such portions of his orders as were not private, particularly as to observing everything, and collecting specimens, also his authority from the Admiralty for claiming all them, all our logs, journals and everything connected with the expedition."[2]

The truth is, whatever those records contained, they are almost certainly gone for good. Time was on the Admiralty's side and time, in the end, was what it got. If records were left at Starvation Cove, the weather destroyed them — this was what the Inuit claimed. If documents were buried in Simpson's cairn at Cape Herschel, they were looted long before McClintock arrived on the scene. It is possible, as some believed, that the expedition's journals were buried underground somewhere along the path of that final march. But, though the Arctic cold preserves many things, paper is not one of them. The records could still be out there, but it isn't likely.

Where does that leave our story? Without hope of proof, without predictive value, all our conjecture can be no more than a fairy tale, a scary story told by the lambent light of a midnight campfire. And so we offer hope in two forms. First, somewhere beneath the jostling ice in Queen Maud Gulf lies the sunken wreck of the stranded ship pillaged by the Inuit. Whether she is the *Erebus* or the *Terror*, we cannot know, but in her hold is a steam engine and in a cabin is the body of a giant. The *Breadalbane* was found to be almost perfectly preserved beneath the waters of Barrow Strait, two of her three masts still standing. The three bodies on Beechey Island looked almost alive. Someday, someone may find that sunken wreck, and find too the body. If our story is more than a story, *then* we will know.

As for the second proof, we can't say where it might be found, but we know what to look for. The paper records of the expedition are not likely to have survived the passage of so many years, but evidence may exist in a more durable form — specifically, silver or silver-covered copper plates. For the Franklin expedition, no expense had been spared. Among its library of 3000 books, its two steam engines, its two hand-organs, its Halkett boat, its telescopes and barometers and sextants, cookstoves and cutlery, dress swords and shoe polish, tin tureens and backgammon board, two dogs, a cat and a monkey — among all the amenities and necessities, a miraculous device was also included. This device had been perfected only a few years before by a man named Daguerre, and Sir John Franklin's expedition was the first to carry one into the Arctic. It was a large wooden box with a hole in the front, capable of creating "daguerreotypes".

Today we would call it a camera.

EXPEDITIONS

1818   **John Ross**, aboard the *Isabella*, sails in search of the Northwest Passage, with William Edward Parry accompanying in the *Alexander*. Ross enters Lancaster Sound, but turns back "as if some mischief was behind him."

1819   **William Edward Parry** commands his own expedition, his first of three. He nearly makes it through the Northwest Passage, but is stopped by the ice stream in Viscount Melville Sound.

1821-1823 **Parry** makes a second attempt at the Passage aboard the ships *Fury* and *Hecla*. He enters the Arctic farther south and is stopped by ice in Fury and Hecla Strait.

1824-1825 **Parry's** third attempt at the Passage, again in the *Fury* and the *Hecla*, results in the *Fury* being abandoned at Fury Beach on the east coast of Somerset Island, along with a cache of supplies. In later years, there is no sign of the *Fury*.

1829-1833 **John Ross** undertakes his second (this time private) expedition in search of the Passage. Aboard the *Victory*, he is trapped on the coast of Boothia Peninsula for three years, then escapes to the supply cache at Fury Beach, where he spends a fourth year before being rescued by whalers. His nephew, James Clark Ross, accompanies him and sledges to Victory Point on King William Island.

1833   **Richard King** and **George Back** travel overland to explore the Great Fish River.

1836-1837   **George Back**, in command of the *Terror*, enters the Arctic through Hudson's Strait. In Repulse Bay, the *Terror* is battered by ice and barely makes it back across the ocean, grounding on the Irish coast with only hours to spare.

1837-1839   **Thomas Simpson** and **Peter Warren Dease** are sent overland by the Hudson's Bay Company to map the southern Passage. Thomas Simpson visits the south shore of King William Island where he builds a cairn. He subsequently dies under mysterious circumstances.

1845-?   **Sir John Franklin** commands 128 men in the *Erebus* and the *Terror* in a final push to complete the Northwest Passage. The ships are equipped with the most up to date technology, including desalinators, internal heating and screw propellers driven by steam engines. No expense is spared, but the expedition meets with disaster.

1846-1847   **Dr. John Rae** is dispatched by the Hudson's Bay Company to map the east coast of Boothia and to determine if there is a passage through it. He finds no sign of a passage and concludes, rightly, that Boothia is a peninsula.

1848-1849   **James Clark Ross** commands the *Investigator* and the *Enterprise* in the first search for the lost Franklin expedition. He searches Somerset Island using man-hauled sledges and visits Fury Beach, but no sign of the expedition is found. Francis Leopold McClintock commands the sledge-teams.

1848-1851   **Dr. John Rae** takes part in a naval expedition led by **John Richardson** travelling overland in search of Franklin. Rae reaches the east coast of Victoria Island across the water from Victory Point but is unable to cross.

1850-1851   **William Penny**, a whaling captain, is hired by Jane Franklin to command the *Lady Franklin* and the *Sophia* in the search for her husband. When the Navy offers to pay expenses, she hands the expedition over to them. Penny accuses the naval searchers of "suppressing" records left by Franklin.

1850   **Charles Codrington Forsyth** is hired by Lady Jane Franklin to command the *Prince Albert* and to search for Franklin on Somerset Island and Boothia Peninsula. A civilian, **Parker Snow**, goes along as the ship's doctor. Forsyth returns to England because of heavy ice with vague news of the discovery of Franklin's camp on Beechey Island.

1850-1851   **Horatio T. Austin** commands a four-ship naval flotilla which discovers Franklin's camp on Beechey Island. The *Assistance* is commanded by **Ommanney** who visits Cape Walker but finds no record left there by Franklin.

1850-1851   **John Ross** commands a private expedition aboard the *Felix* (with the tender *Mary*) claiming he thinks Franklin is to be found in the ice stream in Viscount Melville Sound. His Inuit interpreter, **Adam Beck**, hears a story about naval ships attacked and burned on the Greenland coast, but no evidence is found to support the story.

1850-1851   **Elisha Kent Kane** is surgeon aboard the *Advance*, one of two American ships (the other being the *Rescue*) sent in search of Franklin. Trapped in an ice pan for eight months and twenty-four days, the ships are carried from Wellington Channel through Lancaster Sound and out into Baffin Bay.

1850-1854   **Robert McClure**, in command of the *Investigator*, enters the Arctic from the west hoping to complete the Northwest

Passage, but is stopped by the ice stream near Banks Land and is forced to complete the Passage on foot. He is rescued by **Henry Kellett** in the *Resolute*.

1850-1855   **Richard Collinson** enters the Arctic from the west aboard the *Enterprise*. He reaches the east coast of Victoria Island across the water from Victory Point where he discovers three cairns. Against the advice of his officers, he ignores evidence that Franklin has met with disaster in the area.

1851-1852   **William Kennedy**, a former Canadian fur-trader, and **Joseph-René Bellot**, a French Lieutenant, reach Prince Regent Inlet aboard Lady Franklin's *Prince Albert*. They search Somerset Island and Prince of Wales Island, going over the same ground as Ommanney's naval searchers.

1852-1854   **Sir Edward Belcher** commands a five-ship naval flotilla to search Wellington Channel and Melville Island. The *Resolute* is commanded by **Henry Kellett** and is caught by ice in Viscount Melville Sound. Belcher, also caught by ice, orders four ships abandoned and returns to England, leaving Collinson who is still somewhere in the southern Arctic.

1853-1855   **Elisha Kent Kane** commands the second American expedition which searches Smith Sound.

1853-1854   **Dr. John Rae** is sent by the Hudson's Bay Company to explore the west coast of Boothia Peninsula up to Bellot Strait. He encounters Inuit at Pelly Bay who tell him about many dead men in the mouth of the Great Fish River south of King William Island. He returns to England with relics and stories of cannibalism.

1855-1856   **Chief Factor James Anderson** is dispatched by the Hudson's Bay Company to travel overland to the mouth of the Great Fish River to check out Rae's stories. He lacks an Inuit interpreter or suitable boats. On Montreal Island, he finds evidence of Franklin's expedition but no sign of bodies or records, and is unable to cross over to King William Island.

1857-1859 **Francis Leopold McClintock** sails in the *Fox* to King William Island. Bodies are at last discovered, a final record is retrieved from Victory Point and Simpson's Cairn is found to have been looted of whatever it contained.

1860-1869 **Charles Francis Hall**, an American, lives for nine years among the Inuit before finally reaching King William Island and spending four days searching for relics of the lost expedition. Of more importance are the stories he hears from his Inuit hosts, including stories of survivors.

1879 **Lieutenant Frederick Schwatka**, of the United States Army, searches King William Island and Adelaide Peninsula. He interviews the Inuit, discovers a complete skeleton at Victory Point and names Starvation Cove.

1903-1905 **Roald Amundsen**, aboard the *Gjoa*, is the first to successfully sail through the Northwest Passage.

1981, 1982 **Owen Beattie**, a physical anthropologist with the University of Alberta, and **James Savelle** search King William Island. They recover some bones and discover the first evidence of lead poisoning.

1984, 1986 **Owen Beattie** exhumes three bodies from the lost expedition buried on Beechey Island. He finds further evidence of lead poisoning.

1992, 1993, 1994 **Barry Ranford**, a photographer and Franklin scholar, finds bones and relics on King William Island.

1993, 1994 **Anne Keenleyside**, an archaeologist, and **Margaret Bertulli**, a physical anthropologist, recover bones from King William Island. They identify cut marks on the bones which they believe supports the stories of cannibalism.

Source Notes

Prologue: The Vanishing Ships

Prelude to Disaster

1. Pierre Berton, *The Arctic Grail: The Quest for the Northwest Passage and the North Pole, 1818-1909*, p. 31.
2. Samuel M. Schmucker, *Arctic Explorations and Discoveries During the Nineteenth Century*, p. 43.

Victory Point Revisited

1. Ibid., 160.
2. David C. Woodman, *Unravelling the Franklin Mystery: Inuit Testimony*, p. 15.

The *Fury* Vanishes

1. S.M. Schmucker, *Arctic Explorations*, p. 132.
2. Ibid., 136.
3. D.C. Woodman, *Unravelling*, p. 17.
4. P. Berton, *The Arctic Grail*, p. 88.
5. D.C. Woodman, *Unravelling*, p. 77.
6. Noel Wright, *Quest For Franklin*, p. 228.
7. Ibid., 229.

Never To Return

1. P. Berton, *The Arctic Grail*, p. 114.
2. Ibid., 141.

A Second 1824

1. William Gibson, "Sir John Franklin's Last Voyage," *The Beaver* (June 1937), p. 48.
2. Ibid., 46.
3. Paul Fenimore Cooper, *Island of the Lost*, p. 145.
4. P. Berton, *The Arctic Grail*, p. 146.

The Ghost and Lady Franklin

1. S.M. Schmucker, *Arctic Explorations*, p. 211.
2. P.F. Cooper, *Island of the Lost*, p. 148.
3. Roderic Owen, *The Fate of Franklin*, p. 288.

The Deception of James Clark Ross

1. Ibid., 261.
2. Ibid., 258.
3. Ibid., 247.
4. Ibid., 258.
5. Ibid., 267.
6. S.M. Schmucker, *Arctic Explorations*, p. 283.
7. Ibid., 284.
8. R. Owen, *The Fate of Franklin*, p. 271.
9. P. Berton, *The Arctic Grail*, p. 164.
10. Ibid.
11. R. Owen, *The Fate of Franklin*, p. 270.
12. S.M. Schmucker, Arctic Explorations, p. 285.
13. P. Berton, The Arctic Grail, p. 166.
14. R. Owen, The Fate of Franklin, p. 276.
15. Ibid., 268.
16. S.M. Schmucker, *Arctic Explorations*, p. 325.

The Turning of Captain Forsyth

1. Ibid., 331.
2. R. Owen, *The Fate of Franklin*, p. 276.
3. Ibid., 289.
4. Ibid.
5. S.M. Schmucker, *Arctic Explorations*, p. 321.
6. R. Owen, *The Fate of Franklin*, p. 297.
7. P. Berton, *The Arctic Grail*, p. 192.
8. R. Owen, *The Fate of Franklin*, p. 289.
9. S.M. Schmucker, *Arctic Explorations*, p. 353.
10. R. Owen, *The Fate of Franklin*, p. 310.

The Deception of John Ross

1. S.M. Schmucker, *Arctic Explorations*, p. 323.
2. P. Berton, *The Arctic Grail*, p. 31.
3. N. Wright, *Quest For Franklin*, p. 182.
4. Leslie H. Neatby, *The Search For Franklin*, p. 129.

The Dead of Beechey Island

1. Owen Beattie, and John Geiger, *Frozen in Time: Unlocking the Secrets of the Lost Franklin Expedition*, p. 23.
2. Ibid., 52.
3. Ibid., 102.
4. Ibid., 106.
5. Ibid., 122.
6. Ibid., 117.
7. Ibid., 139.
8. Ibid., 140.
9. Ibid., 142.
10. Ibid., 118.
11. Ibid., 153.

The Cashmere Gloves

1. R. Owen, *The Fate of Franklin*, p. 302.

Penny Versus Austin

1. Ibid., 312.
2. L.H. Neatby, *The Search For Franklin*, p. 138.
3. Ibid.
4. P. Berton, *The Arctic Grail*, p. 190.
5. N. Wright, *Quest For Franklin*, p. 142.

The Canadian and the French Lieutenant

1. R. Owen, *The Fate of Franklin*, p. 314.
2. S.M. Schmucker, *Arctic Explorations*, p. 468.
3. L.H. Neatby, *The Search For Franklin*, p. 153.
4. R. Owen, *The Fate of Franklin*, p. 327.
5. Ibid., 320.
6. Ibid.

Captain Collins and the *Enterprise*

1. P. Berton, *The Arctic Grail*, p. 298.
2. Ibid., 299.
3. Ibid.
4. N. Wright, *Quest For Franklin*, p. 200.
5. Ibid., 203.
6. Ibid., 204.

A Study in Contrasts

1. R. Owen, *The Fate of Franklin*, p. 333.

How to Lose a Flotilla

1. L.H. Neatby, *The Search For Franklin*, p. 214.
2. R. Owen, *The Fate of Franklin*, p. 340.
3. Ibid., 352.
4. Ibid.
5. L.H. Neatby, *The Search For Franklin*, p. 218.
6. R. Owen, *The Fate of Franklin*, p. 352.

The Ghost Ship

1. Ibid., 373.

John Rae

1. Peter C. Newman, *Company of Adventurers*, p. 305.
2. P. Berton, *The Arctic Grail*, p. 162.
3. P.C. Newman, *Company of Adventurers*, p. 411.
4. Ibid., 414.

Cannibalism and Other Relics of the Lost

1. R. Owen, *The Fate of Franklin*, p. 355.
2. Ibid., 350.
3. P. Berton, *The Arctic Grail*, p. 266.
4. W. Gibson, "Franklin's Last Voyage", p. 56.
5. R. Owen, *The Fate of Franklin*, p. 355.
6. P.C. Newman, *Company of Adventurers*, p. 394.
7. R. Owen, *The Fate of Franklin*, p. 365.
8. Ibid., 366.

Lady Franklin's Decision

1. L.H. Neatby, *The Search For Franklin*, p. 249.
2. R. Owen, *The Fate of Franklin*, p. 376.
3. Ibid.

The Voyage of the *Fox*

1. Ibid., 377.
2. Sir Francis Leopold McClintock, *The Voyage of the 'Fox' in the Arctic Seas: A Narrative of the Discovery of the Fate of Sir John Franklin and his Companions*, p. 208.
3. L.H. Neatby, *The Search For Franklin*, p. 258.
4. Sir F.L. McClintock, *Voyage of the 'Fox'*, p. 11.
5. Ibid., 251.

The Other Shoe Drops

1. Ibid., 226.
2. Ibid., 227.
3. Ibid.
4. Ibid.
5. Ibid., 238.
6. Ibid., 237.
7. Ibid., 239.
8. O. Beattie, and J. Geiger, *Frozen in Time*, p. 35.
9. Ibid., 36.
10. Sir F.L. McClintock, *Voyage of the 'Fox'*, p. 251.

Whodunit?

1. Ibid.
2. Ibid., 253.
3. Ibid., 254.
4. Ibid.
5. R. Owen, *The Fate of Franklin*, p. 359.
6. Ibid., 360.
7. P.C. Newman, *Company of Adventurers*, p. 417.
8. R. Owen, *The Fate of Franklin*, p. 356.
9. Ibid., 359.
10. Ibid.
11. L.H. Neatby, *The Search For Franklin*, p. 246.
12. P.C. Newman, *Company of Adventurers*, p. 418.
13. Ibid.
14. P. Berton, *The Arctic Grail*, p. 267.
15. Ibid., 268.
16. L.H. Neatby, *The Search For Franklin*, p. 245.
17. P.C. Newman, *Company of Adventurers*, p. 422.
18. Ibid., 424.

Two Bodies and a Note

1. Sir F.L. McClintock, *Voyage of the 'Fox'*, p. 255.
2. D.C. Woodman, *Unravelling*, p. 87.

3. P. Berton, *The Arctic Grail*, p. 331.
4. Sir F.L. McClintock, *Voyage of the 'Fox'*, p. 264.
5. Ibid., 265.
6. O. Beattie, and J. Geiger, *Frozen in Time*, 39.
7. Sir F.L. McClintock, *Voyage of the 'Fox'*, p. 264.

A Trail of Bones

1. W. Gibson, "Franklin's Last Voyage", p. 63.
2. Ibid., 24.

The Victory Point Record Explained

1. D.C. Woodman, *Unravelling*, p. 94.
2. Ibid., 104.
3. Ibid., 18.
4. P. Berton, *The Arctic Grail*, p. 331.

The Final March

The Second Winter at Beechey Island

1. D.C. Woodman, *Unravelling*, p. 70.
2. Sir F.L. McClintock, *Voyage of the 'Fox'*, p. 257.
3. R. Owen, *The Fate of Franklin*, p. 306.

The Passage From Beechey Island

1. Ibid., 390.
2. Stephen Leacock, *Adventurers of the Far North*, p. 125.
3. N. Wright, *Quest For Franklin*, p. 210.
4. P. Berton, *The Arctic Grail*, p. 250.
5. P.C. Newman, *Company of Adventurers*, p. 413.
6. L.H. Neatby, *The Search For Franklin*, p. 157.
7. R. Owen, *The Fate of Franklin*, p. 345.

Mock Suns and Other Northern Lights

1. Ibid., 227.
2. John Robert Colombo, *Mysterious Canada: Strange Sights, Extraordinary Events, and Peculiar Places*, p. 396.
3. Barry Lopez, *Arctic Dreams*, p. 213.
4. P.C. Newman, *Company of Adventurers*, p. 132.
5. P. Berton, *The Arctic Grail*, 175.
6. Charles Francis Hall, *Life with the Equimaux: A Narrative of Arctic Experience in Search of Survivors of Sir John Franklin's Expedition*, p. 68.
7. Ibid., 66.
8. R. Owen, *The Fate of Franklin*, p. 134.
9. George Francis Lyon, *A Brief Narrative of an Unsuccessful Attempt to Reach Repulse Bay Through Sir Thomas Rowe's "Welcome", in His Majesty's Ship Griper, in the Year MDCCCXXIV*, p. 119.
10. R. Owen, *The Fate of Franklin*, p. 225.
11. Sir F.L. McClintock, *Voyage of the 'Fox'*, p. 66.
12. Paul Nanton, *Arctic Breakthrough: Franklin's Expeditions 1819-1847*, p. 66.
13. Sir F.L. McClintock, *Voyage of the 'Fox'*, p. 68.
14. C.F. Hall, *Life with the Equimaux*, p. 200.
15. Ibid., 209.
16. Ibid., 212.

Inuit Tales and the Angikuni Connection

1. R. Owen, *The Fate of Franklin*, p. 407.
2. Ibid., 417.
3. P. Berton, *The Arctic Grail*, p. 371.
4. R. Owen, *The Fate of Franklin*, p. 412.
5. W. Gibson, "Franklin's Last Voyage", p. 60.
6. D.C. Woodman, *Unravelling*, p. 6.
7. Ibid., 125.
8. P. Berton, *The Arctic Grail*, p. 378.
9. D.C. Woodman, *Unravelling*, p. 130.
10. Ibid., 126.
11. Ibid.

12. Ibid.
13. Ibid., 128.
14. Ibid., 127.
15. Ibid., 134.
16. Ibid., 131.
17. R. Owen, *The Fate of Franklin*, p. 412.
18. D.C. Woodman, *Unravelling*, p. 131.
19. Ibid., 306.
20. Ibid., 309.
21. Ibid., 316.
22. R. Owen, *The Fate of Franklin*, p. 412.
23. D.C. Woodman, *Unravelling*, p. 310.
24. Ibid., 317.
25. Ibid., 318.
26. J.R. Colombo, *Mysterious Canada*, p. 389.
27. Ibid.

The Tunnit

1. Robert McGee, *Ancient Canada*, pp. 62, 63.
2. Farley Mowat, *Westviking: The Ancient Norse in Greenland & North America*, p. 454.
3. Ibid., 457.
4. Ibid.
5. J.R. Colombo, *Mysterious Canada*, p. 393.
6. Peter Freuchen, *Book of the Eskimos*, p. 231.
7. P.F. Cooper, *Island of the Lost*, pp. 12, 13.
8. Ibid., p. 13.
9. R. Owen, *The Fate of Franklin*, p. 417.
10. Ibid., 418.
11. Ibid., 421.
12. Jeff MacInnis (with Wade Rowland), *Polar Passage: The Historic First Sail Through the Northwest Passage*, p. 91.
13. D.C. Woodman, *Unravelling*, p. 91.
14. Sir F.L. McClintock, *Voyage of the 'Fox'*, p. 227.
15. R. Owen, *The Fate of Franklin*, p. 419.
16. W.G. McKenzie, "A Further Clue in the Franklin Mystery," *The Beaver* (Spring 1969), p. 28.

17. Ibid.
18. L.A. Learmouth, "A Divergent Opinion," *The Beaver* (Spring 1969), p. 33.
19. N. Wright, *Quest For Franklin*, p. 239.
20. L.A. Learmouth, "A Divergent Opinion", p. 33.
21. B. Lopez, *Arctic Dreams*, p. 164.
22. Ibid., 165.
23. R. McGee, *Ancient Canada*, p. 63.
24. O. Beattie, and J. Geiger, *Frozen in Time*, p. 139.
25. Ibid., 153.

The Last Resource

1. P.C. Newman, *Company of Adventurers*, p. 394.
2. P. Berton, *The Arctic Grail*, p. 268.
3. P.C. Newman, *Company of Adventurers*, p. 394.
4. O. Beattie, and J. Geiger, *Frozen in Time*, p. 61.
5. P.C. Newman, *Company of Adventurers*, p. 421.
6. O. Beattie, and J. Geiger, *Frozen in Time*, p. 59.
7. Barry Ranford, "Bones of Contention," *Equinox* (Spring 1994), p. 86.
8. O. Beattie, and J. Geiger, *Frozen in Time*, p. 61.
9. R. Owen, *The Fate of Franklin*, p. 419.
10. Ibid.
11. B. Ranford, "Bones of Contention", 86.
12. R. Owen, *The Fate of Franklin*, p. 418.
13. D.C. Woodman, *Unravelling*, p. 113.
14. R. Owen, *The Fate of Franklin*, p. 438.

Of a Sickness

1. D.C. Woodman, *Unravelling*, p. 338.
2. B. Ranford, "Bones of Contention", p. 87.
3. D.C. Woodman, *Unravelling*, p. 338.
4. O. Beattie, and J. Geiger, *Frozen in Time*, p. 161.
5. B. Ranford, "Bones of Contention", p. 85.
6. O. Beattie, and J. Geiger, *Frozen in Time*, p. 161.
7. Ibid., 35.

The Shaman Light

1. D.C. Woodman, *Unravelling*, p. 56.
2. P. Berton, *The Arctic Grail*, p. 268.
3. P.C. Newman, *Company of Adventurers*, p. 419.
4. D.C. Woodman, *Unravelling*, p. 58.
5. Ibid.
6. N. Wright, *Quest For Franklin*, p. 154.
7. Ibid., 155.
8. D.C. Woodman, *Unravelling*, p. 64.
9. B. Lopez, *Arctic Dreams*, p. 217.
10. Ibid., 266.

Rehearsal for Murder

1. P. Berton, *The Arctic Grail*, p. 137.
2. P.C. Newman, *Company of Adventurers*, p. 401.
3. P. Berton, *The Arctic Grail*, p. 133.
4. Ibid., 131.
5. Vilhjalmur Stephansson, *Unsolved Mysteries of the Arctic*, p. 162.
6. Ibid., 179.
7. Ibid., 186.
8. Ibid., 166.
9. P. Berton, *The Arctic Grail*, p. 136.
10. V. Stephansson, *Unsolved Mysteries*, p. 179.
11. P. Berton, *The Arctic Grail*, p. 137.
12. V. Stephansson, *Unsolved Mysteries*, p. 183.
13. Ibid., 184.
14. Ibid., 183.
15. Ibid., 188.
16. Ibid., 162.

Epilogue: Proof

1. D.C. Woodman, *Unravelling*, p. 292.
2. P. Nanton, *Arctic Breakthrough*, p. 228.

BIBLIOGRAPHY

Beattie, Owen, and Geiger, John. *Frozen in Time: Unlocking the Secrets of the Lost Franklin Expedition.* Vancouver/Toronto: Douglas & McIntyre, 1992.

Berton, Pierre. *The Arctic Grail: The Quest for the Northwest Passage and the North Pole, 1818-1909.* Markham, Ontario: Penguin Books Canada, 1989.

Colombo, John Robert. *Mysterious Canada: Strange Sights, Extraordinary Events, and Peculiar Places.* Toronto: Doubleday Canada, 1989.

Cooper, Paul Fenimore. *Island of the Lost.* New York: Putnam, 1961.

Freuchen, Peter. *Book of the Eskimos.* Cleveland: World Pub. Co., 1961.

Gibson, William. "Sir John Franklin's Last Voyage." *The Beaver,* Outfit 268, No. 1, June 1937.

Hall, Charles Francis. *Life with the Esquimaux: A Narrative of Arctic Experience in Search of Survivors of Sir John Franklin's Expedition.* Reprinted, Rutland, Vt: C.E. Tuttle Co., 1970.

Leacock, Stephen. *Adventurers of the Far North.* Chronicles of Canada Series, Vol. 20. Toronto: Glasgow, Brook & Company, 1914.

Learmouth, L. A. "A Divergent Opinion." *The Beaver,* Outfit 299, Spring 1969.

Lopez, Barry. *Arctic Dreams.* Toronto: Bantam, 1987.

Lyon, George Francis. *A Brief Narrative of an Unsuccessful Attempt to Reach Repulse Bay, Through Sir Thomas Rowe's "Welcome", in His Majesty's Ship Griper, in the Year MDCCCXXIV.* Reprinted, Toronto: Coles Pub. Co., 1971.

MacInnis, Jeff, (with Rowland, Wade). *Polar Passage: The Historic First Sail Through the Northwest Passage.* Toronto: Random House of Canada Ltd., 1989.

MacInnis, Joe. *The Breadalbane Adventure.* Montreal: Optimum Publishing International, 1982.

McClintock, Francis Leopold, Sir. *The Voyage of the 'Fox' in the Arctic Seas: A Narrative of the Discovery of the Fate of Sir John Franklin and His Companions.* Reprinted, Edmonton: Hurtig, 1972.

McGhee, Robert. *Ancient Canada.* Ottawa: Canadian Museum of Civilization, 1989.

McKenzie, W. G. "A Further Clue in the Franklin Mystery." *The Beaver,* Outfit 299, Spring 1969.

McMillan, Alan D. *Native Peoples and Cultures of Canada.* Vancouver/Toronto: Douglas & McIntyre, 1988.

Mowat, Farley. *Westviking: The Ancient Norse in Greenland & North America.* Toronto: McClelland & Stewart, 1973.

Nanton, Paul. *Arctic Breakthrough: Franklin's Expeditions 1819-1847.* Toronto: Clarke, Irwin, 1970.

Neatby, Leslie H. *The Search For Franklin.* New York: Walker, 1970.

Newman, Peter C. *Company of Adventurers.* Markham, Ontario: Penguin Books, 1986.

Owen, Roderic. *The Fate of Franklin.* London: Hutchinson, 1978.

Ranford, Barry. "Bones of Contention." *Equinox,* No. 74, Spring 1994.

Schell, Jonathon. *The Fate of the Earth.* New York: Avon Books, 1985.

Schmucker, Samuel M. *Arctic Explorations and Discoveries During the Nineteenth Century.* New York: Auburn, Miller, Orton & Co., 1857.

Stefansson, Vilhjalmur. *Unsolved Mysteries of the Arctic.* New York: Macmillan, 1939.

Woodman, David C. *Unravelling the Franklin Mystery: Inuit Testimony.* Montreal: McGill- Queen's University Press, 1991.

Wright, Noel. *Quest For Franklin.* London: Heinemann, 1959.